TOM JONES
JUST HELP YOURSELF

Iponymous Edition
First Published in 2012
By Iponymous publishing Limited
Swansea United Kingdom SA6 6BP

A CIP record for this book
Is available from the British Library

Cover photograph © Andrew Davies
www.andrewdaviesphotography.com

Design and typesetting: GMID Design|Brand
www.gmid.co.uk

(EBook) ISBN 978-1-908773-43-2
(Physical Book) ISBN 978-1-908773-44-9

www.iponymous.com

For Evan and Eva, and for Gareth.

TOM JONES
JUST HELP YOURSELF

VERNON HOPKINS

1

JUST HELP YOURSELF

Naked, in almost every sense of the word, I was thrust into daylight and into life, kicking and screaming, which was a precursor of how I was to make my way in life. Mind you, the timing could have been better. The skies above war ravaged Britain were heavy with German bombers, hundreds of them, dropping their deadly payloads on cities and towns all over the country.

Weighing in at ten and a half pounds, my birth must have been a rather painful experience for my mother, and coming into the world with bombs dropping everywhere, my life expectancy must have given her pause for thought too. My parents had spent most of that year under the kitchen table, listening to the terrifying drone of German bombers criss-crossing the skies overhead.

My first cries rang out in the tiny bedroom of 16 Gwilym Street, Rhydyfelin, a small village two miles down the road from Pontypridd. The terrace house was close to the banks of the River Taff, and its gurgling black water was probably the first sound from the outside world to reach my ears. The filthy coal-black river had once been teeming with trout, but those days were long gone. The Rhondda Valleys were teeming with coal mines and coal-tips. The Welsh rain filtering through the huge pyramids of slag and colouring the green-green grass a charcoal black.

My parents, Evan and Eva Hopkins, along with my five-year old brother, lived in what was known locally as 'the apartments', Number 16, a two bedroomed house owned by Mr and Mrs Evans, a kindly old couple. The downstairs had a front room, middle room and back kitchen. My family lived in the tiny middle room along the dark passage, and shared an even tinier back bedroom. I shared a single sized bed with my brother Norman, and my parents were in the three-quarter sized bed where I was born.

Aged three, I attended Hawthorn Infants School, and my initial recollection of my first day was trying to escape the playground and run after my mother. I got my head stuck in the school railings, this was every bit as traumatic as seeing my mother waving goodbye and brushing a tear from her eye. A year or so later, with the War finally coming to an end, my young life almost ended too. I almost departed this earth with a bladder full of pee soaking my Sunday-best trousers.

Every Sunday morning, Norman and I would attend Sunday school at Bethlehem Chapel, half a mile from home. My mother would give us both a penny each for the collection plate. My brother, who was aged around nine or ten, always had other ideas as to where those two pennies would end up. Inevitably it would be two lovely ice-cream cornets on our way back home. Our Sunday school teacher would always warn us that if we ever got up to any mischief the wrath of God would punish us. Before buying our ice-cream Norman would sometimes decide to knock on somebody's door and run away. We called it Rat-tat-ginger, and I pestered him to let me have a go. Banging on the knocker, in my excitement, I ran down the garden path and out into the main road.

I can clearly remember Norman screaming out behind me – Stop! Stop!

Thank God I listened. I stood there in the middle of the road. Glancing to my right, a large double-decker bus was bearing down on me. To my left was a lorry hurtling towards me. I shut my eyes and felt the slipstream from both vehicles, as they rushed past on either side. Eyes shut tight, I heard an almighty terrible crash and peed myself. The lorry laden with rationed butter had skidded into a telegraph pole, ripping it from its foundations. It was a hot summer's day and the slabs of butter had spilled onto the road. Telephone cables were draped over the wrecked lorry, its bonnet embedded in the telegraph pole.

I remember running for home, as fast as my legs would carry me, with Norman in hot pursuit. Needless to say my parents were not best pleased and contacted the police. I got a fierce telling off about the accident, but my parents were just relieved that I'd come to no harm.

If I hadn't stopped that day, in all likelihood I wouldn't have survived, and the events that unfold in these memoirs wouldn't have come to pass. There wouldn't have been a Tommy Scott (later Tom Jones) and The Senators. No fascinating stories to tell, no anecdotes, and probably no knighthood. In fact no Tom Jones at all, if truth be told.

But I'll get to that…

What follows are my recollections of my years as a professional musician with Tom Jones. It is a candid view of the music industry and the ruthless people who inhabit it. My journey begins in the South Wales Valleys, buying my first guitar, forming a band and bringing in a singer who would eventually become one of the greatest superstars in the world. Success came slowly for Tom Jones and the Senators (originally Tommy Scott and the Senators) until we were spotted by a ruthless manager, Gordon Mills, and catapulted into the London music scene of the sixties.

The group got caught up in the world of Fleet Street gossip, groupies, sex and drugs. Although we all started out as a tight-knit bunch of mates from Ponty, it quickly became clear that Tom had his own agenda. Tom was the star, driven by a streak of callousness that led him to neglect the other members of the group, his young wife, and everyone who stood in the way of his success.

The band struggled with Tom for eight life-changing years in pursuit of recognition and stardom. We all of us left the green Valleys for the stark concrete and rat-infested slums of Ladbroke Grove. We starved together but survived together, and through sheer persistence and hard work we broke through.

'It's Not Unusual' changed our miserable existence, but sadly it revealed a darker side to Tom Jones. There have been many biographies written about his life and times, but no-one was closer to Tom during those formative years than me. Inseparable in many ways, for so long, in the end we couldn't have been further apart.

Some of the comments in these pages will no doubt alienate me to Tom Jones' legions of fans, but I make no apologies. Sometimes the truth, in all its stark clarity, casts an unflattering spotlight on the actions and behaviours of people we think we know. But generally we are blinded by the glare of stardom and we see what we are meant to see, what is manufactured for public consumption. I got to stand behind the curtain with Tom, this is my story.

2

BIRTH OF THE SENATORS

My parents were married in 1935, at St. Mary's Church, Glyntaff, Pontypridd. My father was a qualified piano tuner and repairer, my mother in service as a housemaid. During the War he was seconded to work on the local trading estate. Being deft of hand, he was put to work on the line, assembling engine parts for fighter planes. Mercifully, he wasn't designated for the front line, much to my mother's relief and his great disappointment.

Two years after the War ended, we left Gwilym Street and moved to a brand new council house in the same village, 2 Glyndwr Avenue. My mother had recently given birth to my sister, June, and in 1948 my other sister Heather was born. My father continued with his trade, repairing the actions (inside workings) of pianos in an outhouse attached to the property.

The three-bedroom house was vast by comparison to the cramped apartment we had recently vacated. These days number 2 is owned by my nephew and his wife, Lee and Mel Hopkins. Number 2 Glyndwr Avenue was important in bringing The Senators together as a band, particularly the tiny front room. Perhaps one day in the future, a commemorative plaque may find itself onto an outside wall. After all it's where it all began for Tom Jones and The Senators.

As a four or five-year old music was something that came out of the wireless or gramophone. I didn't have the faintest idea about what made those magical sounds. My parents took me to see a revue show in Pontypridd's Town Hall. The orchestra in the pit struck up and the curtain opened. I wasn't remotely interested in what was happening on stage. I was transfixed by the magical sounds emanating from the strange objects being handled by the men in black suits. It was a revelation, I was hooked. With no television in those days, I had never seen a gathering of musicians before. I remember feeling overwhelmed by it all and absolutely fascinated.

After that experience, I took complete charge of the family's wind-up gramophone. My father had a collection of 78 rpm records and I would play them for hours. I didn't care, nor was I even aware of, what kind of music was on the records; all that mattered was that it was the same kind of sounds that had emanated from the orchestra in the Town Hall. A good few years later I would learn to differentiate between the bands. My father's collection was a mix of bands from the Twenties, Thirties and Forties, and a range of sole singers: Stan Kenton's 'Peanut Vendor', Jimmy Lunceford's 'White Heat', Glenn Miller's 'In the Mood', drummer Gene Krupa's astonishing drum solos, the list of riches was endless. I must have almost worn out the gramophone needle with overuse listening to Judy Garland, Vera Lynn, Al Jolson, Edmundo Ross and a load of other records.

My father, being an accomplished pianist, was overjoyed that we now had enough room for a piano. Apart from a kazoo, it was the first instrument I ever had a crack at. I played the two-fingered bass line to 'Mule Train' while my father knocked out the melody.

Leaving Hawthorn Senior School, aged fifteen, I started work as an apprenticed compositor at The Pontypridd Observer, a weekly newspaper. Years later, when I formed The Senators, I would coax the editor, John Lewis, into giving the band valuable publicity in his newspaper. He duly obliged and we got numerous favourable mentions right up until we left for London in 1964. My first real interest in music came about when I was seventeen. My father paid eight pounds for a second-hand acoustic Spanish guitar. The guitar belonged to a former school friend, John Lawrence, but he had lost interest in playing it. After mastering the basics, and suffering sore fingertips, I just knew this was for me. I would never, to this day, lose my interest in playing one of the greatest musical instruments ever invented.

Like most other teenagers of that time I thought Rock 'n' Roll was king, and Elvis Presley was the king of Rock 'n' Roll. But 1959 was a very black year for me. Buddy Holly, The Big Bopper and Richie Valens were killed in a plane crash, and Eddie Cochran died in a car crash. Their tragic deaths were mourned the world over, but closer to home it was a tragic time for our family also. My mother Eva died from cancer on December 5th that same year aged forty-seven.

My mother's passing left a chasm in all our lives. But something happened in the New Year that would eventually help me to come to terms with the heart-breaking loss. I had been tinkering with the idea of forming a band for some time, and my father had been aware of it. In February 1960, he was tuning a piano for a local family and noticed that their sixteen year old son, Jeff Maher, was very adept at playing the guitar. My father mentioned that I was keen on forming a band. Jeff contacted another sixteen year old guitarist, Keith Davies, and before very long both of them came knocking at my door.

I opened the door of number 2 Glyndwr to two boys carrying guitars, and with the same stars in their eyes as mine. It was the birth of The Senators. By an amazing coincidence, the three of us all owned blonde Hofner guitars. Jeff's model was a 'President', Keith's a 'Club' and mine was called a 'Senator'. We spent days trying to think of a name for the band and eventually settled on 'The Senators'.

It wasn't very long before The Senators developed into a five-piece band, adding a drummer, Colin Price, and a good looking singer, Tommy Pitman, who had just completed his National Service in the Navy. The fashion for bands at that time was to have a lead singer with the rest of the band singing backing harmonies, emulating the likes of Cliff Richard and The Shadows, Buddy Holly and The Crickets, Bill Fury and Tornadoes, Gene Vincent and The Bluecaps etc...Our singer sounded like Elvis, so there was a good slice of The King in our repertoire

My father allowed the band to rehearse in the front room, or parlour as it was quaintly referred to back then. You could just about swing a cat in it, but the five of us managed to squeeze in there, along with our amplifiers, guitars and snare drum. We all had our day jobs and would practice every Wednesday night. Sometimes halfway through a pounding rock number, the electricity would fail, creating a dead stillness, followed by the chink of a shilling coin being dropped into the electricity meter courtesy of my father. The music would resume but not before my father bellowed out, 'Right you lot, that's another shilling you owe me when you become famous, boys!'

We derived a great deal of satisfaction experimenting with popular music. It was a great learning curve, and we improved our technique, starting to become more established in and around Ponty. I was keeping busy between the band and working as a compositor for the local newspaper. John Lewis and his charming sub-editor wife Margaret were a happy-looking couple, always smiling and welcoming. But beneath their charming personalities, the stress of running a newspaper was becoming apparent in the dark shadows forming beneath their eyes. They were very generous in giving the band free publicity and keeping up with our progress. The staff photographer supplied some great shots of us in action. On one occasion we were given a banner headline announcing that The Senators were appearing on a television show called Discs a GoGo. The programme was fronted by the famous Canadian disc-jockey, Kent Walton.

The band appeared alongside Screaming Lord Sutch and Monty Sunshine's Jazz Band. Madcap Sutch was enjoying a number of freaky-sounding hit records themed on vampires and Count Dracula. He came on after our performance, appearing out of a coffin, swathed in dry ice. The lid opened on cue, with his hand appearing, then his black top-hat, followed by a chalk-white face with theatrical blood dripping from his mouth. Rising from the coffin, wrapped in a flowing black cape, he leapt out and proceeded to frighten the living daylights out of his young audience, and the millions watching at home.

The television appearance did the band a world of good, and we got a lot of respect up and down the valleys back home.

Television is a great vehicle for getting a toehold on that ladder to fame. But we all quickly realised that having one isolated appearance wasn't going to be enough. It certainly encouraged us to stick at it and press on with the dream.

1961 saw us continuing to play the dance halls, and we started to become increasingly popular. We even scored with the business acumen, after all it's not just show, its business as well. We started hiring out our own halls and putting on dances. We profited from the entrance fees, cloakroom tickets, light refreshments and such. We thought we were the bee's knees, entrepreneurs!

John Lewis, the editor of The Pontypridd Observer, bless him, continued publicising the band. My job at the newspaper sometimes entailed having to operate the keyboard on the linotype, churning out columns of typeface matter for the presses. There was one article of news copy that caught my attention. It was information about a band from Liverpool that was being tipped to hit the big time. When I reached the part that spelled out their name, I almost fell out my chair laughing. It was the most ridiculous name for a band I had ever heard – Beatles. 'They must be joking', I thought at the time, but as history testifies, they were certainly no joke!

Those several years working at The Observer left me with many happy memories and naturally a few sad ones too. One memory that's stayed with me, and illustrates just how much working conditions have changed for the better, concerns an ex-miner employed as a lackey on a measly wage. Bill Enoch was forced to quit mining after almost a lifetime underground. Poor Bill had contracted emphysema; his air sacs were grossly enlarged, causing severe breathlessness. All those years of breathing coal dust had cut short his career at the coal face. He hadn't yet reached retirement age so he was very grateful to The Observer for employing him.

Bill was a typical miner, short, stocky and his arms and face were scarred purple with coal dust tattoos. One of his 'easier' jobs at The Observer was manhandling the heavy reels of blank newsprint paper, getting them ready for attaching to the huge letterpress machines. Other times, he would pack bundles of newspapers and carry them out to the vans ready for distribution. As you may imagine, these duties left him wheezing and literally choking for breath. As a young apprentice, it was distressing to see this proud, likeable old man doing such heavy work. But the saddest sight of all, and no way should he have been doing it, was witnessing him collecting old columns of typeface for recycling. The recycle foundry was situated in a claustrophobic windowless room. The temperature there must have been well over a hundred degrees, and it was impossible to be in there for any length of time. Bill's job was to fill the foundry with used type, made up of tin, antimony and lead. When it became molten he'd open a valve and pour it into moulds. Once the metal had cooled, Bill would hurl the mould to the floor and the ingots would be released.

The recycled metal resembled bars of gold. The fumes from the dross floating on the molten metal were choking and irritated the eyes. I found it incredible that a man with emphysema was made to work in such a suffocating environment. From the mines to this, it was tragic, poor man.

Pontypridd is the gateway to the Rhondda Valleys and there

was always plenty of news around to fill The Observer's pages, it kept us printers very busy. Ponty is a market town surrounded by a number of collieries and mountains. Its greatest claim to fame is that it was the birthplace of Evan James and James James, father and son composers of the Welsh National Anthem, no less. It's also the birthplace of a notable singer, Sir Tom Jones, but more about him later.

As for The Senators and our dreams of stardom, we were going from strength to strength. We had plenty of gigs lined up throughout the Valleys and we invested the money we earned in buying better gear. We all had day jobs so upgrading our equipment was affordable. Compared with today's amplification, the volume of decibels our equipment produced was very low. The legendary American guitarist Duane Eddy, whose hits included Shazam, Peter Gunn and Dance with the Guitar Man, used one of the most powerful amplifiers available at that time. All 30 watts of it, and that was when he was performing on stage! Our amplifiers were pitiful in comparison. Amplification in venues today amounts to thousands of watts of power. The average household stereo set produces more volume than we were producing as a whole band back then. The drum kits back then were also pretty basic and generally consisted of a small diameter bass drum, modest high-hat cymbal and one mediocre crash cymbal and snare drum. Modern kits have so much equipment that the drummer is almost lost behind it all, and on top of that the kit is usually miked with all the instruments going through the mixer creating a perfectly balanced sound. The Senators used to reckon we were pretty loud back in the day!

Back then the most prestigious venue to perform in was Ponty's Regent ballroom. The first time we played there we were incredibly nervous and apprehensive. It was a cavernous hall with a wide and high stage, with bunches of flowers skirting along its edge. A big dance band was resident most weekends, about fifteen musicians in all, with trumpets, trombones, piano, saxophone, the lot. Mr Freeman, the owner of The Regent, had seen our write-ups in The Observer and wanted to experiment with how a rock band would be received. Up until that point ballroom dancing was all that had ever been held there. He gave us a midweek booking, crossed his fingers, and hoped for the best. I remember the first night we stood there behind the plush curtains, tensely awaiting Mr Freeman to announce us.

'Welcome to the Regent Ballroom everyone. For the first time ever on stage, a pop group for your entertainment. Pontypridd's very own Senators!'

We heard cheering and clapping filtering through the heavy curtains, and then they swished open. There we stood, in front of a sea of faces. We kicked off with an Elvis number, Tommy Pitman singing and gyrating just like The King. It was a thrilling unforgettable experience and we seriously thought we were going places. We were playing the fabulous Regent Ballroom, for Christ's sake. That was something else, man!

Mr Freeman was also on a high. The rotund middle-aged grey haired businessman thought all his Christmas had rolled up at once. With such a phenomenal turn out on the night he knew he was on a winner, and began booking a host of other groups for the venue. During the years that followed, the venue was visited by Brian Poole and the Tremeloes, Freddie and the

Dreamers, along with many famous bands from the era. The Senators were there first and had initiated it all.

The Senators were in high demand. During those heady Disc a GoGo and Regent Ballroom days we were the first rock band playing the valleys, we were unique in that sense. Then other bands began sprouting up. Cardiff had their fair quota of impressive bands doing the rounds in their own territory, but never venturing north of the City.

The Valleys Teddy Boy culture was very popular at the time, and none were more aggressive than Ponty's gangs. They hated the Cardiff Teds and vice versa, there was little love lost between both factions. Cardiff City bands like The Raiders, starring a then unknown singer-guitarist Dave Edmunds, The Heartbeats, The Afro-Cuban Combo, all stayed well clear of the valleys if they didn't want their equipment and possibly their heads kicked all out of recognition.

There was one incredibly violent confrontation between the Cardiff and Ponty Teds at the town's railway station. Ponty Station has the longest platform in Wales, and one Saturday night in 1960 around one hundred Cardiff Teds pitched up, with knuckle-dusters, bicycle chains, coshes. Some were even armed with old fashioned cut-throat razors. Their intention was clear; they wanted to sort out the Ponty boys, once and for all.

As you can imagine all hell broke loose. The Ponty Teds had got wind of the invasion and were out in force to meet them. With only a few Bobbies on the beat, the warring gangs were uncontrollable. The fighting lasted for around two hours with both sides beating the hell out of each other and the railway station. Police reinforcements finally arrived forcing the Cardiff gang back onto the train, outclassed by Ponty's 'elite' Teds.

I say 'elite' with my tongue planted firmly in my cheek. There was nothing elite about the Teds who prowled around the streets of Pontypridd in feral packs of six or seven. Their sideburns, drape velvet collared suits, lace ties and drainpipe trousers marked them out for trouble, and boy did they go looking for it!

I am and always will be proud of my home town. Many of my ancestors lived and were buried or cremated in Glyntaff Cemetery. My parents married in the church there, St Mary's. The crematorium was the first to be built in the United Kingdom and Dr William Price carried out the first legal cremation there in 1800. Ponty also boasts it's stunningly beautiful War Memorial Park, with tennis courts, swimming pools, cricket ground, golf course, and bowling green. The town also boasts a vibrant annual music festival, Ponty in the Park, which attracts the cream of British bands and solo singers.

As a very young child the Park held only one attraction for me and other kids: the open air junior swimming pool. My parents would take me there often, relaxed in the knowledge that I couldn't go wandering off. As I grew in height, so did my yearning to test the water in the nearby senior pool. It was a whopping seven foot six inches at its deepest end, resplendent with a three-tier diving board. Diving from that top plank was a pretty scary proposition. I must admit the closest I ever came was holding my nose and jumping, happy days.

Up until my 10th birthday I was a rather skinny child, not undernourished I have to point out, but far from robust. My condition was put down to the endless attacks of tonsillitis I suffered, and of course the deprivation through war rationing during the first five years of my life. Anyway, out came the offending tonsils, along with the adenoids for good measure and all was well. I remember my mother telling me after that I practically sprang up like a bean stalk. I entered my teens sturdy, bright eyed and no longer a slave to religious beliefs. I had put the Chapel, fire and brimstone behind me and had my sights set on rock n roll.

My hometown was my world, cradled by protective mountains, with coalmines in every direction. Back then unemployment was very low and rock n roll was just breaking through. Jiving was all the craze and dance halls were springing up all over town: The Ranch, The Jive Club to name but a few. Even established dance halls like The Coronation and St Patrick's opened their doors to the rock n roll fever sweeping the land.

It wasn't all sunshine and light, there was a fair underbelly of violence pervading the town back then too. I abhorred every aspect of it. The Ted battle at the railway station wasn't an isolated incident. Mini versions of it were quite common in Ponty's dance halls, pubs and streets. After working hard all week I looked forward to the weekend, with a couple of pints on Friday and Saturday nights before heading for one of the dance halls. The intention was always to score with a pretty girl. But it was all undermined by one simple fact. Whenever you were lined up on the edge of the dance floor, you had one eye on the girls and the other trying to see through the back of your head. Predictably a gang of Teds would saunter into the hall and eventually cause havoc, giving everyone a hard time. They were always looking for a reason to start a fight. I picked up my fair share of black eyes and bruises. But my father had taught me how to defend myself from an early age, and being six foot tall and twelve stone I was as fit as a fiddle. I didn't come off so bad, people who picked on me once seldom did again.

During the years leading up to me forming the Senators I didn't know of anyone else in Ponty that played guitar. I was always on the lookout for someone perhaps who could teach me some new chords and so on. It was around 1958 when I heard through the grapevine that a young singer, who also played guitar, was regularly performing at The Wheatsheaf, a local pub located near the foot of the Graig hill. The community living on the Graig have their own natural border. To enter the Graig from the southern end of the town centre you have to travel under the railway station platform. The tight-knit community that lived there looked out for each other, especially when the mines were going strong. For me as a teenager to venture onto Graig territory wasn't advisable, unless it was completely unavoidable. The young bucks who lived there, especially the Teds, didn't take kindly to young strangers wandering around their turf. But that didn't deter me; I wanted to know more about this singer, Tommy Woodward, and what I might pick up from his guitar playing.

I thought that visiting the Wheatsheaf on my own would cause a lot less aggravation than if I went along with a couple of friends. It was a really warm summer's evening and the pub's door was wide open. I could hear music filtering through the open windows upstairs. I entered and made my way through the crowded bar and up a flight of stairs. As I entered the room the music stopped. I had arrived just in time for the interval. The room covered most of the first floor, rows of foldable wooden chairs, about twenty in all, were lined up facing the far end. A sunburst acoustic 'Hawk' guitar was leaning against an empty chair. The place was pretty full, with a clutch of Teddy Boys in the mix. I ordered a pint, took a seat, and quietly waited.

Today, if The Wheatsheaf were still standing, it would probably have been an evening of Karaoke. But back then there were no backing tracks to sing along to, you either accompanied yourself on the battered honky-tonk piano or just sang your heart out to a foot-tap or hand-clap. But Tommy Woodward on the other hand was a very rare sight, he had a guitar.

I clearly remember a rather tubby, ruddy faced kid performing a couple of Frankie Laine numbers in the second half. He was attired in full Teddy boy gear, his moon face sweating and lashings of Brylcreem greasing his hair. He sounded so much like Frankie Laine that I was very impressed. A couple of other singers got up and sang well, but I was impatiently waiting for Tommy Woodward (later Sir Tom Jones) to sling that guitar over his shoulder. I really wanted to see what he could do with it.

Eventually his name was announced. I didn't have a clue what he looked like until he loped past my chair and picked up his guitar. Tommy was about 5' 10" or 11", with tight jeans and an open-necked shirt; he was not at all what I had imagined. He had a shock of black curly hair with a Teddy boy quiff and a large broken nose and crooked teeth. He had a good physique and an intimidating presence.

I can't remember which song he started with. I may have been too engrossed with his guitar playing. At that time it hadn't crossed my mind to form a band. I was still trying to get the hang of my guitar. I recognised that Tommy had a powerful voice and was getting a good response from the crowd. But I didn't hang around too long. I could see that he only knew two or three chords and I wasn't any more advanced than him, to be quite honest. Once he had finished his short spot, ending with a rock n roll number, he headed for the bar downstairs. I followed him out heading for home. I was a little bemused to see Tommy blocking my way at the bottom of the stairs. There were three or four girls cosying up to him. I couldn't see what the attraction was, what with the broken nose and all. I made my excuses squeezing past and left the pub. I remember thinking at the time it must have been his tremendously rich macho voice that was the attraction for pulling the girls, it certainly wasn't his looks at that time.

A few years later when I had decided on forming a band my interest in singers became more acute. I took myself along to a couple of workingmen's clubs where Tommy Woodward was appearing. I had the idea of him joining The Senators. It was a different ball game than when he performed at the Wheatsheaf. There he had the Graig neighbourhood encouraging him. But the clubs were filled with hardened miners and some of them were fine tenors and baritones. Tommy would lope on stage, the epitome of a Teddy boy, wearing a powder-blue drape jacket with velvet collar, drainpipe trousers, lace tie and crepe-soled beetle crushers. He would stand there centre stage and belt out a selection of Frankie Laine songs: I Believe, Ghost Riders in the Sky, Lucky 'Ole Sun and then some rock n roll numbers. The bulk of his set was mainly Jerry Lee Lewis hits, and he didn't move an inch, concentrating mainly on his guitar chords. The entire image he portrayed, especially with the broken nose, was pretty dire. He needed working on badly. You're nobody until you're somebody, and Tommy Woodward was certainly that. Back then some were very critical of him. Not to his face mind you. But once out of earshot they said he shouted and that his singing was all over the place, 'Why can't he sing those songs straight, like every other singer around here,' was the usual complaint. In reality the 'singing all over the place' was Tommy's interpretation of a song. When I tried to explain that he was giving some cool phrasing, people just scratched their heads in bewilderment, 'Phrasing? What the bloody hell's that? A right bloody noise if you ask me!' If his audiences had only known then just how famous he would later become.

The few times I watched him perform in those clubs I had the feeling that he didn't particularly want to be there. But he was making a few quid from each gig and he had a wife and young child to support. Tommy had got married when he was just sixteen, to his childhood sweetheart, Linda Trenchard. I didn't think he had much drive in him, back then, to become a star. He was just drifting along, drinking, singing and eyeing up the local talent, with the occasional rumble along the way with his Teddy boy buddies.

I mentioned to him once or twice that I was forming a band, but I didn't get any feedback. I think he realised that joining a band meant sharing the fees and that would have affected his earning power. But as The Senators became more established, especially after appearing on television, Tommy would always enquire about how the band was getting along. I got the impression that he would have liked to be part of the action. But by then we had recruited the other Tommy, Tommy Pitman, as our singer. But something happened that would change all our lives.

Around the spring of 1962 The Senators had a regular Friday night booking at the local YMCA, situated at the top end of town near the Old Bridge. The red-brick three storey building first opened its doors in 1910 and celebrated its anniversary on the 9th August 2010. I used to love playing there. The windowless concert room was deep within the building, and it held about two hundred people, who liked nothing better than rocking their socks off every Friday night. There was a roomy stage with red velvet curtains and the acoustics were fantastic. Our fee, shared between the five of us, wasn't so great. The YMCA relied on donations and had little money to spare. We weren't that bothered as it was such a pleasure to play there. The girls used to throng around the front of the stage and make a real fuss over us, who wouldn't enjoy that?

Tommy Pitman, our singer, like the rest of us was a huge Elvis fan. He used to emulate the King with his leg shaking and pelvis swinging. The rest of the band would join in with some harmony on certain numbers. We used to give Tommy a break by playing The Shadows entire song book of instrumentals, along with The Ventures and some Duane Eddy hits.

Then some uninvited gremlins interrupted the band's easy going rhythm and we struck a few bum notes. The bum note was Tommy Pitman's continuing absences. It started with him not attending rehearsals and then occasionally not turning up at gigs. Eventually we found out that Tommy's penchant for playing cards for money was becoming more profitable than sharing the eight pounds fee we got at the YMCA. In a nutshell he had become disenchanted with playing in the band. This kind of thing happens in every band sooner or later. We were disappointed because he was a good singer and a hell of a nice guy.

That fateful Friday the YMCA was packed to bursting point. Tommy hadn't shown up again, we had lost out to a game of cards. Facing up to another night without our singer we got through the first set. We were looking forward to our half hour break but dreading the second set, our only option was to play a number of repeats and hope nobody would notice.

Tommy Woodward's regular haunt on a Friday night was the White Hart Hotel, the other side of town, near the Graig. It was a safe bet he would be propping up the bar with his buddies. I told the band my intentions, and with a window of about twenty minutes before we were due back on stage I raced the half mile through Taff Street. The White Hart was situated on 'The Tumble', the most vibrant part on entering town from Cardiff. All roads lead through it and onto the Graig, the Rhondda Valleys and back through town to the YMCA. It's an open area surrounded by five pubs and the railway station. The pubs were The Clarence, The Greyhound, The Half Moon, The Criterion and the one I was dashing for, The White Hart. It's hardly surprising the area was called 'The Tumble', what with all the boozing that went on there!

23

I charged into The White Hart and Tommy was there, as anticipated, and propping up the bar along with the other Teds. He was dressed in his trademark powder-blue drape suit with all the necessary Ted requisites. He looked deep in thought supping his pint, whilst his friends were in animated conversation. Maybe he was dwelling on the fact that he was absolutely in a rut as far as his singing was concerned. The Liverpool sound had recently caught on, it was all the rage, bands had never been more fashionable, we were turning down bookings we were so busy. Poor Tommy was a soloist, strumming his guitar, singing his heart out in social clubs to indifferent audiences who didn't know or care about phrasing and thought Tommy's singing was all over the shop. The Senators by contrast were on the up, appearing on television and building a loyal following. Tommy's future in the music business looked bleak.

I tapped him on the shoulder and he came out of his trance, 'Hey, Tommy,' I said breathlessly. 'Pitman hasn't turned up at the YMCA. How about joining us for the second half? We're due back on stage in about ten minutes. There's a couple of quid in it for you if you're interested.'

He was visibly taken aback; perhaps a little stunned that The Senators wanted him right then and there to sing with them. The bar was silent with anticipation while Tommy gathered his thoughts. Coughing nervously into his hand he replied in his rich gravelly voice, 'Yeah, Vern, okay. I'll do it for a couple of quid.'

He quickly gulped down his pint and was heading for the exit when a thought struck him, 'Hold on, the YM doesn't serve booze.'

'I know, its run by the Young Christian Association, they're not allowed to serve booze,' I said.

'Oh, I don't know then,' he tutt-tutted, shaking his head. 'It's Friday night, I'm out for a good drink Vern. You know, out with the boys like.'

I wasn't going to leave it at that, especially after belting all the way across town, 'Look,' I said, 'what if I buy you some light ales and smuggle them in. Will that be okay?'

He didn't hesitate, 'you're on,' he chuckled. 'Get them in and let's piss off!'

We were out of the pub and tearing back to the YM in no time. It was such a mad dash back that I was surprised Tommy had the breath left to sing a note. The band was waiting for us nervously behind the curtain. I dumped the light ales backstage, and we were just in the nick of time for the second set. Tommy was twitching a bit, having never sung with us before.

'What are we going to kick off with?' he asked, 'Christ we've never even practised together.'

I didn't have the heart to tell him that it was only recently The Senators had acquired two new members: guitarist Mike Roberts and drummer Alva Turner. Our previous members had decided to form their own band, The Strollers. It has to be said that Mike and Alva were a vast improvement on the two that left. But Tommy didn't know that at the time, and to be quite honest we were all of us twitching a bit. Especially as regards unfamiliarity and how these new changes would go down with our audience at the YMCA.

Tommy seemed less tense when I suggested we stick to classic rock n roll and twelve bar blues, like Linda Lou, Lawdy

Miss Clawdy and Fats Domino. I thought with, no fancy stuff, and if we stuck to songs with three or four chords we'd do okay.

With only a few seconds before the curtains would open, I asked Tommy what he'd like to kick off with. Without hesitation, he quickly replied, 'Great Balls of Fire.'

'What key?' we all chorused, adrenaline pumping through our young bodies.

'It's in C,' sniffed Tommy, legs wide apart, his hand holding the microphone in a steely grip.

Next moment, the curtains opened and we were off!

The YMCA members seemed stunned by the spectacle. All two hundred of them stared open-mouthed at Tommy the Ponty Ted, his face contorted as he belted out the aggressive music and lyrics. Those youngsters had never seen anything like it. Tommy Woodward standing stock still with an intimidating stance, chest out and legs positioned as though he were about to pounce off the stage into the crowd.

There was no applause after the first number, nor the second or third. He was just too much for those kids to take in. What with his huge voice, huge presence and scary persona they didn't know how to react. We ploughed through song after song. Then something magical happened to Tommy. Having no guitar to deal with, and concentrating only on the chords, he began to command the stage, moving from one end to the other and giving some rhythm to his body.

The audience latched onto it and soon they were all dancing. Tommy took a break halfway through the set and polished off the light ales. We carried on with some instrumentals. When he came back a little glassy-eyed, there was no holding him back. He was like a man possessed. The band was streaming along cranking out the rhythm and Tommy was steaming sweat and leaping all over the stage. We finished the night to huge applause and it was a huge sense of relief all around, we had cracked it!

I gave Tommy his couple of quid and thanked him for standing in. He was off like the clappers, hurrying back to The White Hart before last orders were called.

As we packed away our equipment I had to say what was on my mind. I told the band that I wanted Tommy to be part of the line-up. There was no doubt in my mind that he would jump at the chance, especially after the way we had jelled on stage that evening. A couple of the boys weren't in agreement, they argued that Tommy's image was crass, he was always fighting and some accused him of being a petty thief. They wanted to give Tommy Pitman another chance. The band was dead unsure about broken-nosed Tommy Woodward. But I was pretty persuasive and stuck to my guns. Who would have guessed that four bottles of light ale would play such a pivotal role in the ascent of Tommy John Woodward to Sir Tom Jones, superstar!

There was now a bit of a crisis within the band. I lay awake that night wondering how I could convince some of the other members about letting Tommy join. Although Tommy Woodward was a bit of a rough diamond, I recognised instantly that his singing far outshone the other Tommy. We simply couldn't rely on Tommy Pitman anymore, he was a great friend, but he would only turn up for gigs when he wasn't embroiled in a massive card game down at his local pub.

I kept at it, but my pleas fell on deaf ears. I simply couldn't get everyone to agree with letting him join. I finally decided that the best way forward was to hold a meeting at my home. On the fateful night we all trooped into the little front parlour, where we used to practise our set. I instantly recognised my mistake, just imagine six tense young musicians, testosterone oozing from every pore, crammed into a tiny room, jockeying for position. In retrospect it would have been better to hold the meeting down the local pub. You could have cut the atmosphere with a knife. I had visions of tempers, tantrums and turmoil erupting before the end of the evening.

Tommy Pitman could handle himself. He was especially fit after recently finishing his national service. Tommy Woodward had a bit of a reputation for nutting people. He didn't get his broken nose by accident. I wondered how I would stop the pair of them going for each other's throats if things got out of hand. One of them was going to be disappointed whatever the outcome of the meeting. I persuaded my sisters, June and Heather, to provide some tea and sandwiches to help calm things down.

Nothing was mentioned to Tommy Woodward regarding his rough edges. The meeting was mainly concentrated on whether we should reinstate Pitman. I had already given my view about that, and spoke up for why I thought Tommy Woodward should join The Senators. But by the end of the evening we were still at stalemate with two votes for Pitman and two for Woodward. Someone then suggested that we have two singers in the band. But I instantly rejected that as a non-starter. Tommy Woodward hadn't come to the meeting to be told that, and who could blame him. It was imperative that a decision was made that evening or The Senators were in danger of splitting up. No one would budge, so I took a deep breath and said, 'Look boys. I'm the one who set up this band, so I think it's only fair that I make the final decision, either that or we're going to be here till the cows come home!'

I was chancing my arm a bit but, thank God, nobody challenged me on it. I turned to Tommy Pitman, I'm sure he knew what was coming, especially as my eyes filled up a bit.

'Tom,' I said, 'I know you still want to be part of the band. Otherwise you wouldn't have bothered coming here tonight. But I don't think you feel the intensity anymore. The spark isn't there for you. Otherwise we wouldn't be playing second fiddle to a game of cards.'

He shrugged his shoulders and lowered his head. He didn't deny it. I held out my hand and he shook it, 'Yeah Vern, you're right,' he said. He turned to Tommy Woodward and shook his hand.

'Looks like you're in Tommy.'

The room was deathly silent. It was an awful moment and I felt sick to my stomach. I'll never know how I managed to go through with it. But there it was we were now on a new track. That's how Tom Jones came to join The Senators.

3

THE LADDER TO STARDOM

The ladder to stardom is a slippery climb at the best of times. Tom had joined The Senators and we all felt that we'd taken our first steps on that journey. None of us were under any illusions about how difficult a climb we were embarking upon. Along the way there would be tears of joy and heartache, laughter and sorrow, and love and anger.

Having Tom on board was a massive step forward. As 1962 progressed the band went from strength to strength. I used to spend every Saturday afternoon at Cliff Terrace, where Tom, wife Linda and young son Mark, lodged with Linda's mother Vi Trenchard. The family lived in the basement area and the ground floor room above was where Tom and I would listen to the latest music hitting the record shops.

Tom had a great selection of records, mainly of his hero Jerry Lee Lewis, and other rock n roll legends like Chuck Berry. But sometimes he would radically change tack and play more sophisticated artistes and music. Brook Benton, Ray Charles, Chuck Jackson, real quality singers. In all honesty he introduced me to a whole world of music that I had no idea existed. It was a pleasure to listen to them on Tom's two and a half watt Dansette portable record player.

Tom would often ask me to pop a hundred yards up the road with him to visit his mother, she lived a couple of streets away. Freda would always welcome me with a cup of tea and a biscuit.

She was always enquiring about how the band was getting on.

'Tom never tells me anything,' she would scold, 'I have to drag the information out of him.'

'We're getting there Mrs Woodward,' was my usual refrain, 'we'll be in the charts one day, just you wait and see,' I would say. I remember being fascinated by all the huge brass plates decorating the walls, along with the Shire horse brasses on wide leather belts. There were brass ornaments everywhere. On the sideboard, the mantelpiece, nest of tables, wherever you looked there was a brass figure or music box. Everything was highly polished, it was a bit of an Aladdin's Cave. Where on earth Freda found the time to keep it all dust free and sparkling I'll never know. She must have been keeping Brasso in business.

At that time Tom was working at Treforest Trading Estate, on the paper mill where they made huge rolls for dispatch all over the United Kingdom. The band would usually roll up at 7pm to pick him up for a gig. On the pavement outside 3 Cliff Terrace was a metal grille that protected the kitchen window. Tom would be finishing his dinner after work and one of the boys would stamp on the grille, shouting for him to hurry up. Inevitably he would appear about fifteen minutes later, wiping shaving cream off his neck with a towel, and chewing on a piece of bread.

The neighbours must have cursed us like hell, rattling on that grille, it used to set off all the dogs in the area, barking and howling. Tom used to get into the back of the van and immediately fall asleep. While the rest of us were generally too high-wired by the impending gig, Tom just used to lay there, out for the count. We always had a hell of a job waking him up when we arrived at the venue.

After Tom had joined The Senators we had drawn up a fresh list of material, and with a little coaxing we made further changes. We persuaded Tom to drop his Teddy boy image, and he decided on wearing a black leather outfit, Gene Vincent style. It gave him a sexier appearance and was less intimidating for our audiences. I also changed his surname to Scott, Woodward just wasn't very rock n roll. One sunny afternoon we were having a few beers in the Upper Boat Inn. Tom wasn't very keen on the names we were trying to come up with. I nipped out of the pub and into one of those now redundant red telephone kiosks close by.

I went through list after list of names. It being Wales, a good three quarters of the phone book comprised of Jones', so I discarded that early on! I finally came up with a tight name, Scott, which I thought would ring with The Senators. Tom immediately took to it and we had some new business cards printed: THE SENATORS, with twisting Tommy Scott.

We still had our residency at the YMCA, and were booked into dances up and down the valleys. One of our regular venues was Newbridge Memorial Hall, 'the Memo', in the Rhymney Valley. If any one of us had fallen off that stage it would have been curtains. It was that high. But it was also high on our list of great venues to play; they used to love us there. It was a large venue with plenty of space to move around. Our lead guitarist Mike Roberts was a happy go lucky character, and worked for BBC Wales Television in Cardiff. He was involved in camera work and always looked on the bright side of any situation. If the band were feeling down for whatever reason,

Mike would be the positive one, 'C'mon, it's only a blip, get over it,' he would say. I liked him immeasurably, he was great for the band's morale. Not only that. Mike could play a mean guitar solo, with the guitar behind his head, not even looking. Not that he had any option, we would always goad him into doing this during a gig, the audience used to love it.

Mike had a sexy middle-class girlfriend at the time, Carol. Tom tried it on a couple of times but nothing ever came of it. In fact we all had girlfriends except our drummer, Alva Turner. He was small in stature, with large protruding ears, and cruelly christened Dumbo, after the cartoon elephant. I think he secretly took to it, after all the elephant is the largest land mammal, and Alva only weighed in at about eight stone soaking wet.

Alva's power lay in his arms; he would beat the hell out of his drum kit. He was a perfectionist as a musician and in his personal life as well. Always neat and tidy, always taking care of his drum-kit, polishing it after every gig and carefully stashing it away afterwards. His father, Horace Turner, was another perfectionist and would eventually become our 'manager'. Horace found us work in social clubs and up market hotels like The Angel, in Cardiff. He was married to Pearl, a tiny lady with a sweet soft voice you had to strain to hear. Horace worked hard for us, refusing to take any commission, other than a small remuneration for petrol expenses when he oversaw gigs some distance away from his home in Treharris. Sadly the whole family are no longer with us.

Keith Davies had been with The Senators from the beginning, he was a rhythm and lead guitarist and a huge fan of The

Shadows. Keith could cover their instrumentals to perfection. He had only just left grammar school when the band was formed. Tall and lean, he was softly spoken, and inclined to be a bit morose at times. But you had a job to stop him chuckling when something tickled his fancy. After all these years, and all the water under the bridge, we still keep in touch. He calls in to see me in Pontardulais, and vice-versa, when I'm over his way in Rhydyfelin. Keith married his girlfriend, Tegwyn, a pretty brunette. I've known their children, David and Debbie, since they were born, and now they are proud grandparents. How time flies.

As for Tom (everyone called him Tommy back in those days) he was going through the throes of puberty when he was struck down with tuberculosis. He had to stay in his bedroom for close on two years. Unfortunately he lost out on much of his schooling and although he was tutored at home, his spelling was atrocious. Later, when we found ourselves living in London, Tom would ask one of us to help compose letters to Linda, who was back in Wales. He could read pretty well, but his spelling was a nightmare for him. He might not have been the sharpest when it came to academia, but streetwise he certainly was. Having married at the tender age of sixteen, and with a wife and child to support, he was old in the head for his years. There were no flies on Tom. He had a good grasp on how to get the most out of things, especially the girls.

Although married, he couldn't keep his eyes or his hands off them. He was rampant, sex mad and an expert at getting laid. The band learned a lot from him, especially how to go about chatting them up. Tom was an extrovert alright, nothing like his father Tom Senior. He was a quiet unassuming character, who was always sitting in the background whenever I called around to Tom's parents' house in Laura Street.

Sheila, Tom's elder sister, his mother, Tom and I, would be gassing away ten to the dozen and Mr Woodward Senior would be taking everything in, but not uttering a single word. The only time I ever heard him speak was if we passed each other in the street. He was always smartly dressed in a beige suit and brown trilby hat. 'Nice now, innit,' he would always say, and off he'd pass, usually on the way to the Wood Road Social Club. He was a miner, and a shrewd one too, I think much of that streetwise shrewdness was passed onto his only son.

Tom had told me about when he told his father that Linda was pregnant. The old man had hit the roof. After he had calmed down he shoved a wad of pound notes into his hand and told him, 'Get your arse down to Cardiff Docks and join the bloody merchant navy.' Needless to say the idea of scrubbing decks at dawn was not an attractive proposition for Tom, and he chose marriage as the better option.

Today, Tom Jones lives in the rarefied atmosphere of super stardom. After almost a life time partaking of the finer things in life and travelling the world, he's delved into the encyclopaedia of life in a way that would have seemed impossible back then. Tom was always very single-minded, that is to say that in his thinking everything was, 'It is or it isn't': a very black and white approach with no shades of grey. Tom's shrewdness rarely took any prisoners; right from the start self-preservation was paramount. When the authors of his biography, Stafford Hildred and David Gritten, asked Tom what his most precious possession was he replied, 'My health, because although I love my mother, I love my sister, I love my wife, I love my son and daughter-in-law and grandchildren, they are all very important to me but if I don't have me I don't have them. The most important thing is my well-being.'

You might argue that there's an innate egotism in that remark, but it's that thinking that illustrates Tom's driven self-preservation. Tom was always out for Tom and inevitably left in his slipstream a trail of callous and ruthless decisions that adversely affected those around him. Looking back on our time together with the band, he was seemingly unconscious of the physical, emotional and financial sacrifices we all made.

Back then Tom was always quite laid back, even though he had a bit of a reputation for being a lout, always in trouble and fighting. But with the band he was dedicated, always turning up for rehearsals and gigs. Before joining The Senators he was always hanging around the Teds from the Graig. Roy Nichols was probably the closest to him, along with Dai Perry, who Tom eventually employed as his minder. Tom sacked him after he punched someone in South America and the authorities didn't take too kindly to the assault. After having such a glamorous job travelling the world, he returned to Pontypridd a broken man. Ushered onto the first flight out of South America, and quickly forgotten by his famous school friend. He lived out the rest of his short life alone in a poky little flat in Treforest. His body was found on the mountainside where he and Tom used to play as school kids. Georgie Toms, Johnny Cleaves, and Alan Barratt, who also passed away at a young age, were all Tom's buddies from that time. They were all part of a formidable gang off the Graig that looked out for each other whenever trouble came their way.

Those close ties with his pals had begun unravelling quite early on, due to his commitment to the band. We had an abundance of work thanks to Horace Turner. He came up with the idea of forming a concert party around Tommy Scott and the Senators. We had dropped the twisting Tommy bit. The party consisted of Tom, the Senators, comedian Bryn Phillips and a sweet young female singer. Also around that time our guitarist Keith Davies decided to leave the band. He and Tegwen had decided to tie the knot and wanted to settle down and have kids. Although he didn't cut ties with the band altogether, always popping up to where we were playing and helping with the equipment.

We auditioned a few guitarists and settled on a diminutive, good-looking young fella, Dave Cooper, or Dai as he was known. His parents ran the Thorn Hotel in Abercynon, which eventually became our rehearsal studio. Much later, by a quirk of fate another Welsh band used it for the same purposes, The Stereophonics. The residents around 2 Glyndwr Avenue, our former rehearsal space, were chuffed to pieces; they almost threw us a street party. They had peace for the first time in years.

Once we had the concert party up and running we were a force to be reckoned with, our bookings went through the roof. The first act on was The Senators minus Tom. We used to warm up the audience with the Coasters Yackety Yack, and a few instrumentals. Then Tom would join us on stage and belt out thirty minutes of power ballads, pop songs and finish with some rock n roll. This was always well received by the audience, with Tom really giving it some welly and leaping about the stage. Then it was the turn of the comedian Bryn Phillips or 'Bryn the Fish' as he was called around Abercynon. Bryn had a fish round in Abercynon, delivering fresh cod, haddock and other sea creatures from door to door. His transport was a distinctive green Morris van, with sliding side-doors and double back doors from which he would trade his smelly fish.

In the future, long after we had departed for London, Bryn would achieve fame with The Comedians, an extremely popular 70s TV show, starring the likes of Bernard Manning, Frank Carson, Mike Read and other well-known comics of the era. When he was performing with us he used to arrive on stage dressed as a Hawaiian dancer, with nothing on but a bra, raffia skirt, and long black wig. To say that Bryn was a little on the large side would be an understatement. He loved his beer and his stomach reflected his taste for it. He used to sing along to a tape recorder playing popular Hawaiian tunes, with his great big belly flopping all over the place. It was some sight to behold. Bryn always inevitably had a slight pong of fish about him, even though he'd scrub himself pink in the bath before every gig. He came to the rescue of the band on more than one occasion, when our van broke down. Once he picked us up in his van straight after work. By the time we got to the club we were stinking to high heaven of haddock. That evening neither Tom nor the rest of the band had a cat's chance of scoring with any girls. Bryn the Fish smelt even worse than us and nobody would go near him. Even the club's cat beat it out the back door!

A little prank we used to set up for the interval was to get little Dai, our guitarist, to crawl inside the bass drum case back in the dressing room. Then we'd roll him out to the side of the stage, pretty well unnoticed, Dai must have felt like a hamster in a rotating wheel. When the audience was settled down after going for a pee and getting their drinks in, Dai would burst out dressed in a Gorilla suit, thumping his chest, roaring and growling. There wasn't a woman in the clubs that stayed in their seats. Dai used to chase them around the room, screaming hysterically, and right out the room and into the car park. Drinks would be spilt, chairs knocked over, it was chaos. The whole concert party would be doubled up with laughter, even though we'd seen the same routine a million times. It was hilarious and we always looked forward to it as the highlight of the night. Poor old Dai would return to the dressing room and climb out of the Gorilla suit, bathed in sweat and exhausted. 'Was that okay boys?' he used to gasp, 'Quick fetch me a pint I'm burning up.'

One memorable night we played a club in Ystrad Mynach, about five miles from Ponty. After the show Tom and I got chatting to a couple of girls we recognised as hairdressers. They had a shop situated on The Tumble, back in Ponty. Ignoring the pleas from the rest of the band to hurry up, they got fed up and left without us. Tom just smiled and said we'd find our own way home.

We were so busy necking with the girls that we didn't notice that the club had been locked up. The car park was deserted, we were stranded. It was a chilly night and overcast but we had no option other than to walk the five miles back to Ponty. We had only travelled about a mile along the long winding country roads when it began pouring with rain. The only cover I could make out in the pitch darkness was some kind of shed on stilts. I could just about see it illuminated by a distant lamp post, in an allotment beside the road. The four of us made a dash for it, taking shelter under the shed. Lying low in the dark, waiting for the rain to subside, one thing led to another and we got down to some serious hank-panky, it certainly kept us warm!

Afterwards, what with the effects of the beer Tom and I had consumed and the shorts the girls had been knocking back, we all fell asleep, with the rain battering the shed above.

We were abruptly awoken at the crack of dawn by a bloody great cockerel crowing in the allotment. The rain had finally stopped and the sun was up. Rubbing the sleep from our eyes, we heard a soft coo-cooing from above and the pattering of tiny feet. I could just about make out movement through the inch wide gaps in the wooden planked floor above and the sound of fluttering wings.

We had taken shelter under a bloody pigeon cot.

The girls had a right fright and started screaming, we were all of us covered in pigeon shit. They must have been bombing us through the gaps in the floor throughout the entire night. The stuff was in our hair, splattered all over our clothes and faces, we stank of ammonia. Bryn and his ponging fish couldn't hold a candle to the terrible stench.

I could remember being aware of a strange bitter smell when we took cover the previous evening, but what with the beers, and having other things on our mind at the time, we all ignored it.

We crawled out from under the shed. The girls were weeping,

beating the shit out their clothes and trying to shake it from their hair. Me and Tom caught sight of each other, covered head to toe in pigeon shit, and couldn't help but see the funny side, and we were falling about laughing.

The girls were not amused, hitting us with handbags, and kicking us in the shins with their pointed high heels. They called us everything under the sun, but we couldn't help ourselves. The cockerel was still crowing its head off and passing motorists were slowing down and craning their necks to catch a look at the show.

Eventually the girls calmed down and we began the long trek back to Ponty. We tried to hitch a ride, but drivers would slow down, take one look at us covered in bird shit and speed off. The most embarrassing part of the long trek home was passing the many chapels and churches along the way. It was a Sunday morning and the Sabbath was in full swing. The rather prudish congregations arriving at their places of worship stopped to stare open mouthed. The girls both looked like they'd been dragged through a hedge backwards and they were limping along, high heels clutched in one hand and handbags in the other.

The sun was blazing overhead and the four of us stank to high heaven. There was no Sunday morning bus service in those days and Tom was becoming a bit agitated. There were white pigeon stains all over his creased jeans. He was in a bit of a state, not only visually but mentally as well. He would have some explaining to do when he got home. What could he say? 'Sorry love, I got delayed. I've been sleeping with a few birds alright. You know the feathered...'Linda would have gone

41

ballistic. Setting the cat amongst the pigeons would have been putting it mildly.

For the life of me, I can't remember what excuse Tommy made when he got home. But it must have been a cracking one, that's for sure, because he rocked up to the next gig smiling.

Another time the band was playing at a club near Merthyr Tydfil, without the rest of the concert party. Fochriw Workingmen's Club was always packed on a Saturday, all the clubs always were back then. It was heaving and with the summer temperature soaring it was suffocating inside. We came off stage after the first set soaking wet with sweat; it was as if we'd been swimming. Tom, after prancing and gyrating all over the stage, was in a right state, the sweat was running off him and forming a pool around his feet.

During the interval the entertainment secretary appeared, carrying a large freshly killed chicken on a silver platter. It was a prize ready for cooking by the lucky person with the winning raffle ticket. It was placed beside a box of chocolates and a bottle of whiskey at the foot of the stage. The intention was to raffle them at the end of the evening.

We went on for the second half, belting out a load of rock n roll numbers, and before long we were dripping like taps again. The audience were well worked up too and were dancing on the floor, on the tables and even on the bar, it was crazy. What with the heat and the beer, always a combustible mix, suddenly it all went off like a rocket.

To be quite honest it wasn't unusual back then to witness many a punch up from the safety of the stage. A great many of our audiences, up and down the valleys, comprised mostly of miners and they worked hard and played hard. The band used to have fun rating the venues, sometimes it was entertaining to see the fists flying and heads butting, they used to knock seven shades of shit out of each other. It was like a cabaret spot, the highlight of the evening you might say. The band was never that bothered, as long as we weren't involved.

Unfortunately on this occasion it was no ordinary punch up. It just went on and on, tables and chairs and pint glasses flying all over the place. It was a battleground, totally out of control. Every man in the place was involved in the melee, including the entertainment secretary and the rest of the bloody committee.

We had to stop playing when they started fighting at the foot of the stage. We had to use our microphone stands to keep them from spilling onto the stage, it was like Rorke's Drift. The curtains were suddenly drawn and we started packing up our equipment like our lives depended on it, which they probably did. We were unable to hear each other as we carried the equipment back to the van, it was bedlam. They were still fighting as we drove off, we were lucky to get out in one piece.

We were cursing not finishing the night and getting paid. We headed back to Ponty in silence. We were all of us pissed off about losing out on our wages for the evening. I was up front and Tom and a couple of the boys were in back. Suddenly a loud gravelly voice boomed out of the darkness, 'I'm 'aving chicken tomorrow boys!'

That was way back in 1963. You can imagine my surprise when I opened my morning newspaper in early 2010. I almost choked on my bacon and eggs. The headline read: Village lifts ban on Tom Jones!

The article went on to declare that the village of Fochriw in South Wales had decided to end the banning of superstar Tom Jones from entering the village. Almost forty five years previously Jones was the chief suspect in stealing a fresh chicken that was meant to be raffled on behalf of the Fochriw Workingmen's Club. The chicken went missing during a brawl in the club and was never seen again. But the finger of suspicion pointed at Tom Jones.

Now that the singer is about to enter his seventh decade, the villagers have decided to lift the ban, and not take the incident any further. The villagers went onto to report that there was no danger of a citizen's arrest being made and Tom was welcome back at the club, and perhaps he might like to perform a couple of songs!

The report brought me tears of laughter and vivid memories of that barnstorming night.

Tom's hands were forever wandering somewhere they shouldn't have been, and not only in connection with girls he used to chat up. Nicking things had been part of his rebellious nature, right from his youth.

I remember being at home in Glyndwr Avenue one sunny morning in 1963, it was sometime over the weekend. Suddenly a car horn blared impatiently outside. I remember thinking, 'who the bloody hell's that idiot.' The horn kept blaring causing the net curtains to twitch in every window up and down the street. Finally I went to the front door to see what all the fuss was about.

I got the shock of my life. There was Tom, beckoning me from the driver's seat. He was driving a spanking new red Ford

Corsair, his face was a picture of happiness. I ran down the garden path and opened the passenger door. 'What the hell are you doing Tom,' I said, 'You haven't passed your bloody test, you can't drive to save your life.'

'Oh shut up Vern and hop in, we're off to Barry Island,' he said.

It was Tony Thorn's car, Tom's brother-in-law; he'd only bought it the week before. I remember saying, 'what the hell is he thinking, letting you of all people take it out for a spin?'

'He doesn't know I'm taking it for as spin does he, he's in bed sleeping one off. Come on Vern, get in, we're wasting time. I'll have to have it back outside the house in a couple of hours.'

I thought well on your head be it, he was a damn sight madder than I thought, and I hopped in.

Tony Thorne was married to Linda's younger sister, Rosalind. He had struck lucky with the football pools and won £3000. This was a considerable amount of money back then. The first thing he'd splashed out on was the red Corsair. It was his pride and joy. The day he bought it he rocked up to one of our band rehearsals to show it off, he was so excited he took us all out for a spin in it. I've never been so scared in my life; he was tearing along the winding country roads, taking the scenic route to Cardiff. Tony pushed the car flat out racing down the valley high on the side of the mountain with cliff-edge-drops hundreds of feet whizzing below us. What Tony hadn't realised was that the newly produced Corsair was prone to losing control, due to having a very light rear end. Tom and the rest of us were clinging on for dear life, as the back end slewed across the road, it was white knuckle stuff.

By the time we reached Cardiff my stomach was in my mouth. I was close to throwing up. Then the finale. On approaching Cardiff Castle, the road bends sharply, Tony was still driving manically, foot to the floor. Taking the corner, the back end spun out of control and we crashed smack into the Castle wall. We were all badly shaken up, but thankfully there were no injuries. Tony had to take the car to the panel beaters to get the dents beat out.

Now I was sitting in the very same car with Tom at the wheel, driving down to Barry Island. Tom was uninsured, unlicensed, inexperienced and travelling in a vehicle without the owner's consent. I was also now aware that the car had a dangerous fault and was in dire need of modification.

Was I scared? You bet. Did I let on to Tom? No way, I was too proud.

Fortunately Tom took the direct route to Cardiff and then onto Barry. To his credit he didn't behave like his maniac brother-in-law and it was all plain sailing. Tom took it slow and was focused intently on keeping on the right side of the road; he was no doubt worried about damaging it or worse writing the car off.

With our hearts in our mouths we arrived at Barry seafront all in one piece. You might recollect Barry seafront from the popular BBC comedy Gavin and Stacy. Its Greek pillars back then fronted a penny arcade and numerous fish and chip cafes. Barry catered for the hordes of Valley folk who used to make a beeline for the beach at the first sign of hot weather. From an age almost too young to remember, my parents would take us kids there on the Sunday school outing and we'd be enthralled by the funfair.

Leaving the Corsair parked on the front we treated ourselves to some ice-creams and made our way down to the sandy beach. It was a lovely sunny day and we fell to talking about the band and our chances of making the big time. Living so far away from London and the bright lights, we both realised our chances of being discovered were pretty remote. We could only dream and continue plugging away.

The sea was mirror calm that day and we both found ourselves collecting pebble stones and skipping them across the water and out to sea. I clearly remember saying to Tom, 'I'm desperate to get away from Ponty and the valleys, we're working off the radar, we need to get recognition farther afield, it's the only way,' I sighed, 'besides making it with the band. I've been nowhere, done nothing. I feel suffocated.'

Tom agreed. We were packing them into the clubs and dance halls, but we didn't have a clue about how to take the next step. Today, we would have made a cracking demo and sent it off to record companies. But back then there were no small recording studios, no home recording facilities to produce anything of quality. We believed we had everything talent wise, but no one to guide us in the right direction. Horace Turner was a loveable character, straight as a die, but like us he didn't have a clue about stepping up the ladder. He was great at finding us work up and down the valleys, but we longed to spread our wings.

Being there together on the beach, with the expanse of the ocean in front of us we both realised we'd have to stretch out across that void if we were to make anything of ourselves. Walking back up the beach each deep in our own thoughts, we climbed back into the Corsair. Tom crunched the gears into first and we were off back to Ponty. Tom was worried about getting the car back before his brother-in-law missed it, and he gave it some stick on the journey home. There were a few hair-raising moments along the way, but we got back safely and Tom dropped me off at number 2 and raced off for Treforest, a mile away.

I was to learn the following day that, about two hundred yards from his destination, Tom was flagged down by a police officer. He was immediately arrested. He was informed that Tony Thorne had reported the vehicle stolen from outside his home that morning. Tom was in deep trouble, with no drivers licence, uninsured and without L plates. I had tried to warn him of the risks.

Tom went to court and was fined, he was spitting feathers about it, and he thought Tony, being his brother-in-law and all, would have been able to get him off. But the wheels of justice are merciless. After the court case I heard from one of the band that Tom wasn't very happy with me. He'd been moaning to the boys that he expected me to pay half the fine, as I was in the car with him, well prior to him getting pulled over.

I thought this was rather cheeky and told him so, he only had himself to blame and had reaped what he'd sown. He gave me a right black look, but as I pointed out, he was earning good money with the band and could afford the fine, and it wasn't like I hadn't tried to talk him out of taking the car in the first place.

Tom's escapade with the car rubbed off on me and I took an interest in wanting to own a car of my own. Later that same year my brother Norman sold me his 1947 brown Morris 11.

At thirty quid you couldn't go wrong, he fondly called it 'Old Bess'. But I must admit I didn't notice any tears of nostalgia when he handed me the keys. He seemed glad to be shot of it. I subsequently learned that 'Old Bess' was an apt nickname and it should have been put out to pasture years before.

But it was my first car and I thought I was the bee's knees, especially sitting behind the steering wheel, stationary outside 2 Glyndwr Avenue. I had to be stationary as I hadn't passed my test and didn't even have a provisional licence. I couldn't even afford a tax disc or insurance. But it was mine and one day after I had saved enough cash I would obtain all those things.

It stood there for months on end, gathering cobwebs on the wing mirrors.

Being young and foolish I was tempted to do what Tom did and drive it without all the necessary paperwork. I started tentatively at first, driving it about a hundred yards up the road and back again. It was addictive and I did it more and more often, getting a greater buzz each time. Pretty soon I was driving Old Bess all over the place, without a care in the world.

I began picking the band up, while our new volunteer roadie, Chris Ellis, drove the van with all our equipment to the gigs. What a blast, now the band was travelling in luxury.

On one particular evening the band were booked to appear at Wattstown Workingmen's Club in the Rhondda. It was a filthy winter's night and the rain was lashing down. We were all crammed in like sardines. Poor Old Bess was struggling up the steep Rhondda hills, engine labouring, wipers squealing, the car was really struggling with the weight of the band. The wipers were barely operating and my nose was pressed against the misted windscreen. My passengers were all deadly silent, bracing themselves for us tumbling over the edge of the mountain road and into the abyss below.

We all breathed a huge sigh of relief when the blurred sign for Wattstown appeared out of the driving rain. The car was travelling at around 20mph and backfiring badly every few hundred yards. A single headlight on full beam cut through the darkness ahead of us, blocking our way. Through the dazzle of the full beam we could just about make out the ominous profile of a police officer. He was stood next to his motorbike and flagging us to stop.

My heart leapt into my mouth, 'Oh shit,' I groaned, 'they're going to throw the book at me. I think you're going to have to find another bass player for the gig. I'll be in nick in no time.'

I pulled up in front of the police officer and buried my head in the steering wheel. The first thing he would probably notice was the distinct lack of a tax disc, and that would inevitably lead onto everything else. I was well and truly done for. The officer tapped on the window. I wound it down and a blast of wind and rain came rushing in.

'Excuse me sir,' said the officer in a muffled voice, 'would you mind stepping out of the vehicle. I need your details. Are you aware that both your sidelights are not operating?'

I was about to get out of the car when the officer lifted his goggles up over his crash helmet.

'You bastard,' I screamed in shock.

The boys were startled and little Dai, our guitarist piped up, 'Vernon button it, you're going to get life talking to the law like that.'

Then I started laughing hysterically, the band must have

50

thought I'd gone into shock.

Tom leaned across the seat and shouted in my ear, 'Calm down Vern, it's not the end of the bloody world man!'

I calmed down and said, 'it's okay boys, this is my brother Norman. He's had me good and proper.' I introduced Norman to the band, and there was relief all around.

Norman had joined the police force and was on duty that evening. What's more he was aware that we would be on his patch in Wattstown for our gig. He had been waiting patiently in the rain for Old Bess to come chugging along. He had taken me aside and warned me on more than one occasion that I was taking a risk with no licence and insurance. This was his way of teaching me a lesson. He had decided to show me the consequences of my actions.

After everyone had stopped splitting their sides with laughter, Norman got on his motorbike, gave us a little wave and sped off into the stormy night. We went onto the club and played a great gig.

After the gig we decided to head for Cardiff. You would have thought I'd learned my lesson earlier. But since I'd been driving it was becoming a bit of a regular thing to do on a Saturday post-gig. We liked to head for Cardiff for a curry and finish the evening at the Haven Club. That evening the black singing star, Danny Williams was appearing at The Haven. At that time he was riding high in the charts with Moon River.

On the way to Cardiff, travelling down the A40, the road slopes down from the mountains and into the flat suburbs on the outskirts of the City. This was always my opportunity to let Old Bess of the leash and get some real speed up. The long slope was perfect for pushing the car to its maximum. That evening we broke our past records and managed to get the car just over 50mph. The whole car was shuddering violently and the band was egging me on to see if we could go any faster.

Halfway down the incline we sped past two stationary vehicles on our left. The first vehicle was obstructing a decent view of the other, which turned out to be a police patrol car. Two officers leapt into the patrol car and gave chase. I remember thinking just my luck, twice in the same evening, although this time I wouldn't be lucky enough to run into my brother. To make matters worse, Dai our guitarist had been putting pint after pint away back at the club and was absolutely legless. He was leaning half out the window, with his finger pointing at them and firing imaginary bullets, he must have thought he was on a stagecoach being chased by Apache Indians, for all I knew!

At the bottom of the incline were a set of traffic lights, luckily they were on green and I took a sharp left almost on two wheels. A hundred yards ahead was another set of lights, and they turned red as we careened through them. Old Bess was now overheating badly. I knew I had to stop soon or the car would blow a gasket. I turned down a quite side street and coasted to park in front of a couple of cars. I turned the engine and the lights off, and we all of us ducked down. The flashing light from the patrol car washed over us, and it sped past its siren peeling out enough to wake up the entire neighbourhood.

It was a very narrow escape, and we all gave Dai a right rollicking for his John Wayne impression.

We finally made it to the curry house and had the works.

Then it was onto The Haven Club. It was a fairly small venue, and when we rolled up Danny Williams was just about to go on stage. We all stood near the bar, Tom was using the bar to prop himself up, like Dai he'd sunk a good few pints and was glassy eyed.

Danny Williams was a diminutive slight Jamaican, with a lovely silky voice. He began rolling off his hit songs and was getting a fantastic response from the audience. Then he began to sing Moon River and the room fell completely silent, this was by far his biggest hit to date.

Then it happened. I was standing beside Tom. He put his pint to his lips, took a sip, cleared his throat and began singing along with Moon River. Danny was singing through the house system but Tom was singing even louder, leaning back against the bar, belting it out. Here we go I thought there may be trouble ahead.

Halfway through the number Danny finally conceded defeat and left it to Tom to finish off the song. I think in part the decision had been made for him. The audience had all turned in their seats and were staring intently at Tom propped up against the bar. As Tom finished the song the audience were astounded and began applauding. It was very naughty of him to have intruded on Danny's performance, but the star took it very well and said, 'Man, I know you Welsh folk can sing. But that was something else. They must be putting something in the water down here!'

It was a memorable evening. At the time I thought it quite surreal, it was like something you only see happening in movies. But it did demonstrate just how badly Tom craved attention; he was hungry for recognition, we all were. But boy did Tom get buckets of attention that night! The audience were trying to drag him up on stage for an encore.

When we finally left the club, we made our way back home to the valley. After the earlier incidents I drove very slowly and kept an eye out for any patrol cars. I remember feeling utterly deflated as we reached the outskirts of Cardiff. A lone police constable flagged us down with his torch. It had been a long evening; I was exhausted and felt resigned to my fate.

'Here's prison looking at ya,' quipped Dai, probably getting his own back after the rollicking we had all given him earlier about his 'shooting Apaches' episode.

I would down the window expecting the worse and wishing I'd listened to my brother and gone straight home after playing our gig.

'Good morning sir,' said the constable, peering into the car and shining his torch in our eyes, 'Out rather late aren't we?'

'Yes Officer,' we chorused sheepishly.

'Been anywhere interesting lads?'

'Not really,' I gulped, 'we've been for a curry, after going to the pictures,' I lied.

'Oh yes and what film was that then?'

Before I could think of an answer Dai slurred, 'Shnowight an the Sheven Dwarfs ofhiffer!'

'Very funny, 'snapped the constable, 'I suppose you're wondering why I flagged you down.'

'Here we go,' I cringed, 'after the evening's freakish events and near misses with the Police I assumed they'd throw the book at me.'

'Get out of the vehicle son; you have some explaining to do.'

That's putting it mildly I thought. The constable grabbed my arm in a vice like grip and pulled me to the front of Old Bess, 'I have to caution you,' he said pointing at the headlights, 'you're side lights aren't functioning. Get them fixed, now clear off.'

I never drove old Bess again; I'd definitely learnt my lesson. As for my brother Norman, he sure put the fear of God into me that night. But how could I not forgive him, it was Norman that got the band one of our first big breaks. He wrote a letter to the TV station that broadcast Discs-a-GoGo recommending they check out an exciting new band from Pontypridd.

4

THE GREEN FLY

Women defined Tom, even at that stage of our careers. Linda was his wife, but she didn't crave fame like he did, neither did she have his energy. He was a party animal and he was always on the lookout for new conquests, in that respect he was insatiable, even then.

All the Senators had girlfriends. I was going steady with Jean Evans, who also lived in Rhydyfelin. She and Tom's wife Linda wore identical hairstyles, very short and platinum blonde, in the style of the Hollywood actress Kim Novak. They were just about the only girls in town daring enough to sport such a vivid style, they certainly made heads turn. Jean was also very friendly with Tegwen, our guitarist's girlfriend. We all had some great laughs together. But rock n roll got in the way of courtship, especially when the band headed for London in search of fame.

At that time the band had secured a residency at Bedwas Workingmen's Club, near Caerphilly. The venue was more commonly referred to as The Green Fly. A curious title and one I never got around to solving, nobody seemed to know the origins of the name. We played there every Tuesday and Thursday in the packed concert room. Our fee for each night was £11 shared five ways. It was at The Green Fly that three individuals became involved in our lives, and they were to prove a decisive factor in Tom and the Senators taking the next step.

Along with our guitarist Keith Davies I was a hairs-breadth

away from not making that particular gig. I had recently bought a 125cc Ariel Leader motorbike, a phut-phutter in canary yellow. I was a provisional driver with L plates. One gloriously sunny morning, having the day off from work, I called in on Keith, who lived just down the road. We both decided a day trip to Bristol Zoo was on the cards. I whipped off the L plates, as it was illegal back then to take a passenger if you were a provisional driver, it likely still is I imagine.

There weren't any problems getting there, but getting back in time to fulfill our role at The Green Fly was another matter entirely.

Somewhere between Bristol and Newport the bike got really noisy, and with every mile it just kept getting louder and louder: we phut-phutted on at a slower pace to try and keep the rattle down. Then the exhaust pipe began bouncing up and down, the bolt holding it to the chassis worked itself loose and fell off. The pipe dropped scrapping along the road and throwing out a trail of sparks.

I pulled over and Keith had a stab at reattaching the damn thing with a piece of string. Each time we got going again the string snapped. Time was against us, the gig was looming and we were miles away from Caerphilly. After our third attempt at fixing it failed, Keith yanked off the exhaust and slung it over his shoulder. We kept our eyes peeled for a garage that might be able to fix it. The bike began backfiring badly, the noise was like rapid machine gun fire, it was deafening.

By the time we came across a garage that was open, we realised we simply didn't have the time to get it fixed and make The Green Fly in time for the gig. There would have been hell to pay from Tom and the band if we missed it, not to mention the entertainment secretary, who might have cancelled our residency. We made a decision and decided to push on. It was a miracle we weren't pulled over by the law. But we finally made it to the club with minutes to spare. Tom and the band were on pins, the place was heaving and they'd been wondering where the hell we'd got to. When they caught sight of the pair of us they fell about laughing. Not out of relief mind you, it was our appearance.

Keith and I had been wearing goggles riding the bike. We were filthy soot black from head to toe, and when we removed the goggles it was the only bit of clean skin on our person. We both looked like head lights. We were both desperate for a pee and a freshen-up, but there was no time, and we were bundled on stage. God knows what the audience must have made of us. By the time we finished the first set my bladder was fit to burst.

As for the Ariel Leader, I came off it one icy morning close near the Old Bridge in Ponty, sliding across the road and into the path of an oncoming lorry. What is it with me and lorries? It was a close call and I got rid of it.

Chris Ellis came to the gig at the Green Fly that night. Chris was a TV engineer by trade. He had heard about Tom and the Senators, and how popular they were becoming. He had decided to come along to form his own opinion. Dark haired and slightly built, Chris was a chain smoker and as wired as the TVs he repaired. He stood at the back of the concert room mesmerised by the band. Little did we know then how important he would become to Tom and the band, and that he and I would become friends for life.

Chris started coming along regularly to the Fly and befriended the band. When one of our amplifiers played up, he was always on hand to fix it. With his engineer's knowledge he would soon get rid of the buzz and everything would be working perfectly.

Our amplifiers weren't the only thing that used to play up. Occasionally so did our van. When the inevitable happened and it was out of service for a few days Chris came to the rescue. He offered to drive us to gigs in his works van. He formed a really close bond with the band, and from that day on became our roadie, continuing to work on TVs during the day and with us at night.

Unassuming to anyone who didn't really know him he was a bit of a character: wiry, alert and as courageous as a Jack Russell. Chris could smell a rat a mile away. Many years later, long after Tom and I had acrimoniously parted company, Chris remained Tom's personal road manager. He took care of all manner of business on behalf of the star; he was incredibly loyal and as close to Tom as his own shadow.

During that spell at the Fly Tom was involved in a very serious incident. Although he was completely absorbed with the Senators and dreams of stardom, he still found some time to hang out with his Graig friends when the opportunity arose. One evening a bunch of them drove over to the Fly to see the band. They offered Tom a lift back home. Tom, Johnny Cleaves, Roy Nickolls (Nicko) and Dai Shephard all got into Johnny Cleaves' black Austin A70 and left the club after our set, they took turns driving back home to Ponty.

I was shocked to hear the following day that they'd been involved in a crash with another vehicle. Whilst rounding a bend on Nantgarw Hill there had been a nasty collision. All four passengers were ambulanced to the local Miners Hospital, near Nantgarw Colliery.

Roy Nickolls had broken his jaw, Dai Shephard had been sliced from ear to ear and needed 36 stiches, and Johnny Cleaves' ear was hanging off by a thread of gristle. Tom miraculously had escaped with just a nasty bump on his forehead. He was seated in the back, nearest the pavement and furthest away from the impact. Roy Nickolls was later transferred to Chepstow hospital where they specialised in facial injuries. Johnny Cleaves' head injuries were very serious, he walked around like a zombie for months afterwards and his speech was impaired, but eventually he made a full recovery. Tom had concussion, and his head pounded if he sang a note, so we cancelled a number of bookings. Singing demands a lot of straining to reach the top notes, and increases the blood pressure in the head. Knowing Tom he was always going for gold, hitting the top of his register, it was just too risky.

Some months later after Nicko had fully recovered from the accident he visited us at the Green Fly. Nicko's favorite song was FBI by The Shadows, as soon as he walked in the club we broke into a loud rock rendition of it, much to his amusement.

We started earning good money and there was some discussion about quitting our day jobs and going full time with the band. After a lot of thought I decided to continue with the day job and gig at night, the rest of the band arrived at the same decision, with the exception of Tom. He packed in the day job and signed on the dole instead. He told me that from then on, his only job was going to be singing, and so it has remained to this day.

We all felt a real sense of momentum with the band; things were moving in the right direction. We were looking for that final piece of the jig-saw to fall into place. That night at the Green Fly, there were two student-type characters that stood out like sore thumbs from the rest of our usual crowd. Ray Godfrey and John Glastonbury approached us with the offer of management.

The dark haired Ray Godfrey was of medium build and height, and the better looking of the two. John Glastonbury was smaller framed with lighter hair, thin lips. He was a bit sly of eye and hard of voice. They were both a few years older than the band and dressed fairly conservatively. Ray came from Ystrad Mynach and I believe John was from somewhere near Caerphilly, you could never be sure of anything he said, so he could have come from anywhere really. John was a bit of a slippery character and to be quite honest none of us trusted him an inch, but we like Ray a lot.

We told them we'd need some time to think about it, but the general consensus was, what did we have to lose? We never agreed to anything there and then, but they returned the following week and convinced us they could get us a record deal with one of the major labels. It wasn't before very long that we all signed a contract with them. They met us at the Thorn Hotel in Abercynon, where we rehearsed, and we put pen to paper.

We were young and naïve and like lambs to the slaughter. Looking back it was like every cliché you've seen in every movie, right down to the dialogue, 'Sign here kid and we'll make you a star.' About the only props missing were the big fat cigars, as they handed us their pens to sign the contract. As I recall the two stand-out clauses were: they would share 10% of all we earned and they would take another 10% for any venues they arranged for us to play. To be completely honest none of us took much notice of the small print, there was so much of it, and it was full of words like 'perpetuity'. We would certainly come to regret it all many years later, in London's famous 'Old Bailey' Law Courts, but more of that later.

They were certainly a couple of oddballs. The radio comedy The Goon Show was very popular at the time, and both of them were huge fans. They'd both of them ape the show and indulge in silly humour which didn't always come off. They didn't really click with the band; they were two squares in a circle of musicians. It transpired that they had no contacts in show business or any real knowledge of the music scene. They just saw an opportunity to exploit our talent.

The band nicknamed the pair of them Myron and Byron. I got on quite well with Byron (Ray Godfrey) he was quietly spoken and always respectful to the band. Myron (John Glastonbury) on the other hand was sly of eye and full of mouth. He was arrogant, brash and condescending. Overly fond of giving orders, he rubbed up the band the wrong way and created a lot of friction.

Alva Turner, our drummer, disliked him so intensely he wanted out. Alva agreed to stay until we found another drummer, but he could hardly stand to be in the same room with Myron. Invariably there were always fireworks when the pair clashed.

Good drummers were a scare commodity back then. There were only two other bands in the Rhondda, The Strollers from Ponty, which were formed by the ex-Senators Jeff and Brian, and The Bystanders, Owen Money's band, based in Merthyr, neither particularly wanted to give up their drummer. Then we heard on the grapevine about a talented kid, Chris Slade Rees. Chris had just left Pontypridd Grammar School and was working as a shop assistant in Clark's shoe shop in Taff Street.

Tom and I called into Clark's one afternoon and sure enough there was young Chris down on one knee, fitting a shoe on a customer. He was fair-haired, about five foot ten inches tall and slim and good looking. If he could play as good as he looked, we had found our new drummer. We arranged to call in at his home in Treforest later that evening. His mother answered the door and led us into the front parlour. Chris was already waiting for us, all set up at his drum kit. Tom asked him about his experience and if he had played with any bands. Chris screwed up his nose and scratched his head awkwardly, 'I've never been in a band Tom.' Tom looked at me and was preparing to leave.

Our hopes vanished, 'Oh dear,' I sighed, 'well we're here now, you might as well have a bash on the drums. Why not try a drum solo?'

'I've never tried a drum solo,' he mumbled.

'Well can you play anything we might know? Something from the charts maybe?' I said.

'I know the intro to Walk, Don't Run by The Ventures,' he finally volunteered.

'Well go on then,' said an exasperated Tom, 'give it a bloody crack.'

Clearly nervous, poor Chris warmed up with a roll around

the kit before steaming into the intro. The windows vibrated as did almost everything else in the room. The volume was awesome, especially considering how lightweight Chris was in stature. He beat the hell out of those drums.

I winked at Tom and he nodded back. The intro Chris played wasn't particularly difficult for an average drummer. It was the way he had tackled it that put smiles on both our faces. Tight, aggressive, enthusiastic and stylish: we had found our new drummer.

Chris Slade not only performed all over the world with Tom Jones and The Senators, or The Squires as we later were called. Chris went on to join a number of super bands: Manfred Mann's Earthband, Uriah Heep, Led Zeppelin, ACDC, Asia and other big names. When we played The Flamingo Las Vegas in 1968, Elvis Presley came along to watch us and he was so knocked out by Chris's great drumming he tried to recruit him for his comeback tour. It was a chance in a million, Chris was really keen, but our manager at that time was Gordon Mills and he said no. It still haunts Chris to this day, especially after how badly he was treated by both Gordon and Tom.

With Chris on board the band was back on track. Myron and Byron had big plans for the band. They got us a great gig playing Porthcawl's famous Pavilion. We were supporting Billy J.Kramer and the Dakotas. Billy and the Liverpool based band were riding high at the time and regularly making the hit parade with big sellers like Trains, Boats and Planes and Little Children.

Playing the Pavilion was a big deal for us; it was our best venue to date. We arrived early for our set up and sound check.

The Dakotas' roadies were busy checking out their amps, tuning the guitars, and even giving them a polish. It was a different world, pampered wasn't the word; we could hardly believe it, being so used to lugging our own kit around.

Billy was on a roll at the time, and even though it was a large venue they had to start turning people away at the doors; it was packed to the rafters. We were on first as the warm up and we went down a storm. The place was electric and the crowd went wild when Tom and the rest of us started leaping about the stage. Talk about raising the roof it was pandemonium; we were used to getting a good reception from our audiences but nothing like this.

Billy and the Dakotas were watching us from the wings, and they didn't look entirely happy with the reception we were getting from the audience. Tom couldn't help but notice this and winked at me, we were all hell bent on showing them how a Welsh band could perform, we really went up a couple of gears that night.

The band got so carried away that we over ran our half hour spot. Even when we finally finished, the audience wouldn't let us get off stage. They kept on demanding more. Finally it was Billy's turn and the place went wild as soon as The Dakotas took to the stage. In all honesty compared with Tom's voice Kramer's was pretty timid, and I thought their act was a bit static. But still the girls in the audience were screaming and fainting as soon as he opened his mouth. However after a few numbers their excitement seemed to fizzle out and you could practically feel the crowd begin to deflate.

There were no dynamics in their set to speak of, and once

they'd exhausted their laid back hit singles, they ran out of steam. The Dakotas started to struggle to keep the audience's attention. The set finished on a low key and Billy and his band disappeared back to the wings. Quite suddenly the audience began chanting for us to come back on.

We had only been booked to play the one set. Kramer was booked to finish off the show. But the audience just kept on chanting for us and refused to leave the venue. The Pavilions manager took us aside and asked if we would go back on stage. It didn't take us very long to reach a decision and we belted out another half hour of high powered music. We converted a lot of Dakota fans to Senator Fans that night!

Later during the early 70s Billy J. Kramer recorded a song I had written. It was entitled 'Walking' and was a brooding Tony Joe White style back beat number. It told the story of an escaped convict with only one thing on his mind, to reach his girlfriend before the bloodhounds picked up his scent. It even had the sound effects of chains dragging with his every step. Billy cut a great disc and I'll always be thankful to him.

After the success of the Pavilion gig Myron and Byron put together a portfolio of the band and they wanted to include a demo of four tracks. They thought this would be a great way of trying their luck with the major record companies. We recorded the songs on a portable eight track studio in the changing room toilet at Ponty YMCA. The band still had a residency there so it was easy to arrange and the acoustics were ideal, having a natural echo effect.

Myron and Byron took the reel-to-reel tape up to London, promising us this was it, the big time. Unfortunately nothing came of it and they returned tails between legs. That was the last we heard about the recording until 2008.

You can imagine my surprise when I read the following headline in the newspaper 'OUR TOM SINGING IN THE LOO UP FOR GRABS'. The article went on to report that a rare recording made by Tom Jones in the toilets of Pontypridd YMCA was expected to fetch thousands of pounds at auction. The four songs were recorded by 'Jones the Voice' two years before he became famous and were recorded by a soundman at the former TWW TV Company.

The soundman wished to remain anonymous and placed the tape in a Rock and Pop memorabilia sale at London's Christies. It was the earliest known recording of Jones and the band to have survived. A spokesman from Christies said, 'these recordings have genuine historical significance as they mark the birth of the Tom Jones phenomenon.'

I obviously remember recording the tracks. But it was so long ago I can't remember which songs we put down. It was probably a couple of ballads and rock n roll numbers. It would be interesting to hear them again, but unless the mysterious soundman comes forward there's little chance of it happening.

At the time Chris Ellis was driving us all around in a cream Morris J Van. Chris had gone to town and carpeted the floor and the walls. He'd even put in a couple of sofas for us to stretch out on. Whenever we had the opportunity, we did a lot more than stretch out in them, and there were a lot of opportunities. We christened the van the passion wagon. We grew very fond of that van and its facilities. Soundproofed by the carpet inlay there were seldom any squeals or groans filtering from it to attract unwarranted attention. Needless to say the springs and suspension took a bit a battering.

We all went into mourning when the van skidded into a wall on an icy road one night. It was a write off. Myron and Byron forked out some cash on a replacement. But it was a clapped out yellow Thames Van. It was much smaller than the Morris and with none of the legroom for amorous encounters. The Senators were a lot less passionate about it, particularly Tom.

After getting a poor response from the major labels in London, Myron and Byron changed tack and decided on an independent record producer. Nis name was Joe Meek.

Joe had a bit of a reputation as a raging homosexual with a violent temper. He was pretty far out there and the general consensus at the time was that he was mentally unstable. But he was a gifted record producer and way ahead of his time. He was famous for composing the legendary instrumental 'Telstar'. The Tornados' had a massive hit with it, topping the charts in both the UK and the US.

The Telstar recording had a unique sound. Joe had experimented with combining a number of Copycat Echo Chambers and compressed the sound, giving it a searing atmospheric bite. He also had a number of other artistes on his books. The fair haired John Leyton topped the charts with 'Johnny Remember Me', and Joe Meek's live-in-lover, Heinz, had recently had a hit with 'Just like Eddie', a tribute to the great Eddie Cochran.

We were all pretty excited about working with him. When the recording was finally booked and agreed we all piled into the van for the trip up to London. It was a ten hour journey back then; there was no M4 Motorway back in 1963. With Chris Ellis at the wheel we made it as far as Shepherds Bush. Chris pulled over and refused to go any further, 'I'm bloody shattered and it'll be a maze from here on. I'll be lost within two hundred yards. Let's unload the gear and get the Underground from here to Holloway Road.' We unloaded the van and carted everything across London, changing underground trains a few times to get to our destination in North London.

Joe Meek's flat and studio were above a leather shop, selling handbags and hold-alls. The building was a typical Victorian three-story terrace, number 304 Holloway Road. There was a separate entrance at the side of the shop with a steep set of stairs leading up to Joe's flat. It was a bit awkward for me to climb as I was on crutches at the time. I was in plaster having broken my ankle a few weeks earlier. I'd been on a coach trip to Barry Island to see Dave Edmunds and the Raiders perform. The venue was heaving and a fight broke out. The next thing I knew I was flung down the stairs and somersaulted to the bottom breaking my ankle. I'd been playing gigs up and down the valleys, leg in plaster, ever since. My arms were aching like hell after crutching it across London. But I didn't have to carry any of the gear, much to the boy's chagrin, so I was ready to play and looking forward to it.

Joe introduced himself; he was black-suited, with the complexion of a corpse. We set up in his front room under his steely shadowed gaze. There was a massive white mantle-piece and a cavernous fireplace. Joe told Chris Slade to set up his drum kit there and explained that he got a better sound that way. The opposite wall had a huge glass pane fitted into it and gave a view of the bedroom.

We all of us stopped dead in our tracks midway through setting up. There lying stark naked spread out on the double bed was Heinz. He was calmly observing us and gave us a little wink when he noticed our amazement. None of us knew where to look; it was a bit uncomfortable to say the least.

Both Meek and Heinz exchanged smiles. I got the impression that they'd deliberately set the embarrassing scene up, on the off chance that one of us might be that way inclined, and could be persuaded to join in the fun in the bedroom after the session. The whole thing left us feeling a little edgy.

Joe sensed our discomfort and nipped into the bedroom and closed the curtains. Thankfully that was the last we saw of Heinz. It was all a bit risky back then. In 1963 Homosexuality was still illegal and utterly frowned upon by the general public. God only knows what people must have made of Heinz, mincing along the Holloway Road with his dyed peroxide blonde hair. He had no inhibitions whatsoever.

I plugged my Epiphone Bass into the amplifier and Mike Roberts and Dave Cooper followed suit. Chris was positioned in the fireplace as requested by Meek. Tom was ready with the microphone; we were all just waiting for the sound check. Joe was next door in the control room with the door ajar. We could see him fiddling around with switches and knobs and spools of tape. He was surrounded by echo chambers, control desks, amplifiers, speakers and all manner of strange looking gadgets. He looked like the Dr Who of music producers ensconced in his own private tardis. He was in a whirl, wild-eyed and sweating profusely, a real genius at work.

There was no intercom between the control room and the front room. Joe shouted instructions through the door. We were just about ready to lay down the first track when he bounced in and snatched my guitar lead out of the amp and plugged it into a direct line to the control room. Un-amped I was unable to hear myself play. Off he went back to the control room leaving me totally baffled. When I protested that I couldn't hear myself play, he shouted back, 'Don't worry I can!'

How I managed I'll never know. He explained that the bass sounded better going through a direct line. It was all part of the special Joe Meek sound.

The session produced a number of songs. One in particular Meek had written about himself, 'Lonely Joe.' Another was written by the songwriter who had penned the Dusty Springfield hit, 'I Only Want to be with you.' We also laid down a couple of Jerry Lee Lewis numbers including the hit, 'Great Balls Of Fire.' We finished off the session with a song called 'Chills and Fever.' It was agreed that we all return in a few weeks to finish off the sessions, and the plan was to have several complete tracks in all.

Joe decided we needed some publicity photos taken. We all tramped out to some nearby parkland. It was rather awkward for me, what with my leg in plaster. I had to stand behind some tree stumps, foliage and other stuff in the various photos to hide my broken ankle. When we got back to the studio we began packing away our equipment. Joe had been all over Tom like a rash from the onset. With the band out of the room, shifting the equipment downstairs, he made his move, 'You sound great Tom, but I haven't seen you perform, how about a little demonstration?'

'I can't do that now, come and see us at a gig. We'll play a pub nearby if you set it up,' replied Tom.

Tom told me later, on the long journey back to Wales, that, 'the bugger was giving me the come on. I couldn't believe it. He couldn't stop admiring my jeans, he kept telling me they fitted me like a glove.'

We'd all realised something was amiss when the bass drum came bouncing down the stairs and rolled across the pavement and into the road, closely followed by a clearly livid Tom Jones.

'You've get a nice set in there haven't you, and the bloody bastard stroked my crotch, he just made a lunge for my balls Vern!' said Tom.

We were all in stitches but Tom was fuming he didn't like it one bit.

A few weeks later we rocked up again for the second session. Tom had come to terms with Meek's nature at that stage and just wanted the session completed as quickly as possible, all business. We were midway through a song when Joe shouted through the door. He wanted Tom to sing a certain passage differently. Tom just rolled his eyes. Off we went again and Tom sang it just as before. Joe burst into the room clearly agitated and insisting Tom sing it differently.

Tom being Tom he stubbornly repeated his version on the next take.

Joe Meek stormed into the studio waving a gun around his eyes blazing. He levelled the gun at Tom and pulled the trigger. There was an almighty bang and Tom's face turned a deathly white. Meek let out a manic laugh and stood toe to toe with

Tom, their noses practically touching, 'Now will you sing it the way I want?' he hissed through gritted teeth.

Only then did he inform us that the gun was a harmless starting pistol. On the next take Joe got his way.

Joe Meek was a law unto himself. He was probably getting his own back after his advances were spurned by Tom. We had hoped that this was the final session but he insisted we come back for a final recording. On that occasion we made the long journey back up to London as arranged. The door to the studio was answered by his landlady, 'Sorry boys, Joe must have forgot you were coming. He's down in Gloucester attending a family wedding. I'll tell him you called.'

Mrs Violet Shenton must have innocently thought we were living somewhere in London.

'Just called in Mrs Shenton,' I wearily replied, 'we've been on the road for the last ten hours up from Wales. How about putting the kettle on?' She duly obliged and put a smile back on our faces.

Later Joe Meek contacted Myron and Byron. He told them he'd made a deal with Decca and they would be releasing one of the songs within the next few months. The months dragged by, it was an eternity. Eventually he stopped taking calls when our managers kept pestering him for a release date. He left it to one of his cronies to tell Myron and Byron that he was constantly out of the office.

Fair play to Myron and Byron, they weren't going to let matters rest there. They decided enough was enough and charged up to the studio in London to confront him, arriving at 10am with black bags under their eyes after travelling through the night. They banged on his door and were met with a resounding silence. Refusing to give up they kept hammering away at the door. Eventually Joe appeared looking dishevelled and gave them a murderous scowl, demanding to know what all the commotion was about.

He started screaming and ranting and literally began pulling his hair out. Obviously there was to be no release date with Decca. He screamed that he was sick to death of Tom and The Senators and he was twenty pounds out of pocket after paying for the publicity photos. Myron and Byron informed him that they had been in contact with Dick Rowe, the boss at Decca, and he'd informed them he'd never heard of The Senators or any proposed release date. What a hammer blow.

Joe Meek went berserk. He ran up the stairs wailing threats and reappeared waving our contract around. He ripped it to shreds, spraying it around like confetti, and slammed the door in our managers' faces.

When Myron and Byron recounted the events back to the band in Ponty we were livid. What a complete waste of time and energy. Tom was so angry he insisted on going back to London to confront Meek. He insisted that he was going to nut Joe and give him a good going over. Tom persuaded Chris Ellis to drive him to Meek's studio in his little Mini.

They both managed to burst their way into Meek's studio and confront him. Tom went for him and Joe ran around his desk wailing, to escape Tom's clutches he climbed up onto the big mantelpiece out of harm's way. Tom later told me, 'He thought I was gonna kill him Vern. He was hysterical, crying 'Don't touch me, leave me alone'. It was pitiful so we left him to it.'

Tom and Chris had searched through Meek's studio before leaving looking for the tapes, but came back empty handed. That was something we would all later regret.

I must give some credit to Myron and Byron. Up until this point they'd both given the band the best of their limited capabilities. It was a massive task trying to get a record contract for an unknown band, especially with so much competition in swinging London. Getting Joe Meek to even take an interest in us was remarkable in itself, even though it proved to be a dead end. He was after all riding high in the business at the time. Looking back we must have seemed like a right bunch of country bumpkins to him, completely out of sync with contemporary music trends, and not at all sophisticated by London standards.

The whole episode was certainly a body blow, a real set back. Myron and Byron were really disenchanted with the whole music business and who could blame them. Still, the Senators were not going to be defeated. We were five fingers on the same hand. No way were we going to call it a day and disappear back into the relative obscurity of the mountains of Wales. We bounced back and decided on recording a few more demos which Myron and Byron took with them to London. If that door won't open you got to keep on knocking.

5

THE TOP HAT CLUB

Myron and Byron discovered that the top disc jockey of the time, Jimmy Savile, often stayed in a bed and breakfast hotel in Paddington. He needed to be close to Central London for his work at the BBC studios. They hatched a plan to get the demos to him in the hopes that he would be able to pull a few strings and get us the right exposure.

They'd both been gone a few weeks trying to pin Savile down and we hadn't heard a dicky-bird back from them. They might have been gadding around Soho for all we knew. We were getting impatient and it was decided that Tom should go up to London with Chris Ellis in the Mini and find out what was going on.

They tracked our wayward managers down to the same bed and breakfast hotel that Jimmy Savile frequented. Unfortunately they didn't have enough money for a room so Tom and Chris kipped in the Mini overnight. It must have been quite a squeeze. They awoke at dawn hungry and as stiff as floorboards. They kept their energy up by pilfering two bottles of milk from a nearby door step.

Tom informed us on his return to Wales that Myron and Byron might just as well have been Pinky and Perky for all the good they'd accomplished. They'd both been swanning around London and hadn't even spoken to Jimmy Savile. Later Tom got agitated and decided to give Myron and Byron a rocket to hurry things along, he was getting tired of kipping in Chris's Mini. He rocked up to their hotel door one morning at 8am and kept banging on it trying to get an answer. Quite suddenly Jimmy Savile popped his head out of another room along the long corridor complaining about the racket. Tom was speechless but quickly regained his composure and had a chat with Jimmy, explaining about the band and asking his advice.

Later that same evening Tom had a massive row with our errant managers, and who can blame him. Tom and Chris stormed off and went for a few pints to calm down. Feeling a little courageous and full of Dutch courage they snuck back into the hotel and knocked on Jimmy's door. Savile welcomed them both into his room and Tom poured his heart out and explained he'd lost all faith in our managers. Jimmy Savile sympathized and told Tom to call back the next morning with the demo tapes. Savile 'fixed it' handing the tapes over to Decca and into the hands of their top record producer, Peter Sullivan.

Savile later wrote in his autobiography 'As It Happens' that one group represented themselves at his hotel door, 'earnest and solemn of face, they were down from Wales and things weren't going right for them at all. Several discussions we had all at odd hours of the day and night. They would tell me their progress and I would suggest a course of action. It started things going right for them and the caterpillar that was Tommy Scott and The Senators crystallized into the world-beating winged wonder that was Tom Jones.'

Not long after, Peter Sullivan made the long journey down to Wales to see us in action. We obviously wanted to make a good impression and arranged for a coachload of our fans to come along to the gig and support us. Most audiences in Wales were used to seeing us on a regular basis; we had become part of the furniture. We paid for a coach out of our own pockets and it picked up a bunch of kids from outside the YMCA in Ponty and transported them over to the gig in Newport. Sure enough when Peter Sullivan turned up the kids were raring to go. They put on a great show, hollering and screaming throughout our set. Sullivan seemed very impressed with the fan worship.

Afterwards the London based producer found himself locked out of the Cardiff hotel we had booked him into. He'd enjoyed the gig a little too much and misjudged his journey time from Newport to Cardiff, arriving too late to check in. He ended up spending the night sleeping in his posh car and wasn't best pleased.

We felt like we were back on track and, even though that was the last we heard of Peter Sullivan for a little while, he eventually became Tom Jones' recording producer.

It was the spring of 1964 when things really seismically shifted. Gordon Mills entered our lives and nothing would ever be the same again. Gordon was born in Madras, India in 1935. Although his father had been born in the valleys he joined the army as a young man and was posted to India. Whilst there he met and married an Anglo-Indian girl who was a lot younger than him. When the Second World War broke out the family moved back to Wales and settled in Tonypandy.

Gordon was an only child and left school at fifteen. He tried his hand at a number of jobs before being called up for National Service. He was very popular with his fellow soldiers and used to entertain them with his harmonica playing. Gordon had won a few competitions and used to play in a band with a school friend, Johnny Bennett.

When he was released from the army he got a job as a bus conductor in the valleys. Just like Tom and The Senators, who were to follow in his footsteps, he dreamed of stardom and travelled to London in search of it. Hohner, the famous harmonica manufacturers, staged a British championship at the Albert Hall. Gordon came second and this gave him the incentive to leave home for good and continue pursuing his dream in London.

Eventually he formed a group of his own, The Viscounts. They were a close harmony vocal group and got plenty of work. Gordon learnt a lot about show business during this period: the wheeling and dealing, the cut throat attitude of agents and managers, the general rat-race that is show business. He was a diligent student and much of it rubbed off on him as time went by.

Toward the end of the Fifties Gordon became very friendly with another artiste who was also aiming for the big time. The artiste's name was Gerry Dorsey, and despite perseverance he was getting nowhere. Later he would change his name to Englebert Humperdink at Gordon's instigation. They both had something in common. They were born to Anglo-Indian mothers. Gerry had a fine voice and Gordon was a whizz with the harmonica. Gordon and Gerry shared a flat in Bayswater. It was a real dump with hardly any furniture and all the cooking was done on a single gas ring. The trains kept them awake at nights rumbling by outside the window, close enough to touch. As time went by the pair of them became so skint that the rent arrears got out of hand and they were forced to do a moonlight flit.

It was around this time that Gordon met his future wife, Jo Waring. Jo was a stunningly beautiful white Rhodesian. She had come to London after touring Europe as a dancer, her elegant blonde demeanor attracted a lot of attention and she was 'discovered' by a top modelling agency.

When Gordon married Jo, Gerry was the best man and Gordon reciprocated later when Gerry married Pat Healy, a secretary who lived in Leicester. They were inseparable and very close friends. Gordon and Jo settled down to married life in a nice flat in Campden Hill Towers, near Notting Hill Gate. Gerry and Pat moved to less salubrious surroundings and took a dismal flat above Times Furnishing in King Street, Hammersmith. They were both still living there in June 1964 when The Senators made the move to London in search of the big time.

I remember visiting them later that year. Pat was a smoldering-eyed beauty of Italian descent. They were parents to two very young and striking children and living in abject poverty. They had a few sticks of furniture and the stuffing was bursting out of a couple of easy chairs. The thunder of traffic from the major artery, Hammersmith, was deafening and the stench of exhaust fumes overpowering.

Poor Gerry was stick thin with sunken and shadowed eyes. He looked completely stressed out trying to make ends meet and feed and clothe his family. Gordon was managing his old friend at this time and trying his best to get him a break in show business. I've always reckoned Gerry a great singer.

He had a three-octave range and a voice as smooth and crisp as brushed steel. I remember thinking that surely the world would recognize those qualities eventually. And as Englebert Humperdink they eventually did. Gerry worked hard for his success and he deserved every bit of it.

Gordon Mills and his wife, who was pregnant at the time, decided to pay a visit to his parents in Tonypandy. Gordon had hit pay-dirt earlier that year. He'd written a song for Johnny Kid and The Pirates, 'I'll Never Get Over You'. It went straight into the top ten and he received £3000 in royalties, which was a fortune back then. But he was aware that even that large amount wasn't going to guarantee him long term security. Gordon had been sniffing around London on the lookout for a band to manage that would make those royalties seem like peanuts. He knew which way the wind was blowing and was only too aware of Brian Epstein and his success with The Beatles. Gordon was hungry for a piece of the action and he had the financial clout to invest in a promising act that he could mold into real star quality.

During his stay in Tonypandy two of his old school friends, John Bennett and Gordon 'Gog' Jones, got talking to him about The Senators. We were packing them in everywhere we played and had quite a reputation throughout Wales. Gordon wasn't convinced, but his friends persuaded him to check us out. They told him we were different to most of the bands on the circuit and we had a fantastic singer to boot. A couple of days later Johnny Bennett picked up Tom, rhythm guitarist Dave Cooper and me and drove us all over to the Lewis Merthyr Club in Porth. Johnny had arranged for us to meet Gordon and his wife. We arrived early and sat near the stage. There was a comedian performing and he had the club members in fits of giggles. None of us had much of a clue who Gordon Mills was at the time and he obviously didn't have much of a clue about us either. It wasn't the most auspicious start to proceedings when he strolled in with Jo and 'Gog' Jones and on seeing us turned to Gog and said, 'Well they're a scruffy bunch of bastards, especially that one with the broken nose!'

At that stage he wasn't at all impressed. Still he didn't turn on his heel and leave, which was something I suppose. He sat with us and watched the comedian go through his routine. Jo was the only female in the club. It was a Sunday morning matinee performance and all the wives were at home preparing the archetypal Sunday Roast. At one point the comedian said something a bit risqué and Gordon admonished him in a flash, wagging a warning finger at him, and glaring daggers. I remember thinking at the time it was a bit uncalled for, Jo didn't seem bothered in the slightest. It was a bit of an early indication of what was to follow. Gordon was a classic control freak, and soon it would be our turn to fall under his control.

Later outside the club Johnny Bennett insisted that Gordon and Jo come along to the Top Hat Club in Cwmtillery that evening. We were due to play there with our concert party. Gordon was reluctant but Johnny finally persuaded him. He gave a little wave and hopped into his Ford Zephyr and zoomed off. I remember Tom looking wistfully after it and saying, 'I'll have myself one of those one day Vern.' I don't recall if he was talking about the car or Gordon's super model wife!

Gordon and Jo did come along to see us perform that

evening. The full concert party was in attendance, including our old friend Bryn 'The Fish' Phillips. The Top Hat Club was heaving and it was a members only night, with a strictly no visitors policy in force. Gordon and Jo were turned away on arrival but we managed to persuade the committee to let them in. I remember telling the entertainment secretary that, 'This important man has driven all the way from London to see us perform,' it did the trick. Unfortunately it was standing room only in the club and Gordon was not best pleased to find himself propping the bar up with Jo and Johnny.

Gordon was scowling at us as we took the stage so we thought we better soften him up a little. We opened up our spot with 'I'll Never Get over you.' Gordon's hit record with The Pirates. He seemed to appreciate that and his scowl actually disappeared. We ran through our set with songs like 'Spanish Harlem' and 'I Can't Stop loving you.' Jo seemed mesmerised by the show, especially with Tom leaping about the stage.

Tom stayed in the dressing room after our first spot. He was very quiet which was unusual. I knew he was twitching about Gordon's reaction. Linda tried to calm him down, but she was a bit tipsy at that point, and just seemed to make things worse. I tried to calm him along with our guitarist Mike Roberts, but Tom was a bag of nerves. It was finally decided that I go and speak with Gordon and get his feedback on the band.

Gordon was standing with Jo, Johnny Bennett and Gog Jones they were getting bustled by a scrum of club members yelling to get served. They all looked uncomfortable and a bit intimidated by all the pushing and shoving. Bryn Phillips was on stage telling jokes and singing a song or two. He had a fair old voice did Bryn, but it wasn't a patch on Tom's.

I managed to push my way through the scrum at the bar and order a pint. I turned to Gordon and asked, 'What did you make of us Gordon?' He nodded toward the stage his scowl was fixed firmly back in place. 'What do I reckon? I reckon that comedian has a better voice than your singer.'

This guy's a real joker I thought. I didn't remonstrate with him, I thought why bother, just leave it at that. It was another disappointment to overcome. I grabbed my pint and headed back to the dressing room to tell the band Gordon's opinion. Johnny Bennett grabbed me, all smiles, and congratulated me on our set. He asked me what Gordon had made of it and was gobsmacked when I told him. Johnny turned to Jo and relayed Gordon's words, 'Nonsense,' she said, 'that's just Gordon's warped sense of humour. Tom is a fantastic singer and you guys are a great band,' she laughed, ' do you really think Gordon would still be crammed in amongst these rowdy beer bellies if he didn't think you had talent? He'd be on his way back to London.'

I headed back to the dressing room to relay the conflicting signals. Our former guitarist Keith Davies was returning from the bar with a tray of drinks for the band. 'Great news innit Vern,' he chuckled.

'What do you mean Keith?' I said.

'That Gordon Mills bloke just told me at the bar he wants to take the band on. He wants you all to relocate to London.'

I was a bit taken aback, but happy never the less, 'Come on, we better go and tell Tom and the rest of the band,' I said.

Tom was too nervous to communicate with Gordon directly

about the proposal. As with many of the big decisions that were to follow he left matters in the hands of the rest of the band to decide. I was elected band leader at that time and everyone was happy to go along with my judgment. After much discussion we all agreed that it was too good an opportunity to miss, after all what did we have to lose? Quite a lot it would prove, but that all came later.

The night ended on a real high note with Gordon promising us the world if we stuck by him. He headed back to London with Jo. I remember Jo telling me much later that he pulled the car over somewhere along the way and with the engine ticking over he turned to her and said, 'I'm really excited by that singer, I have to do something with this band, this is just what I've been waiting for, this could be really big.'

In hindsight I've always wondered why Gordon was so offhand with me about Tom's voice at that initial meeting. I think it's fair to believe that he was playing down his interest in Tom, and planting seeds of discontent even then, it was all part of his divide and rule strategy, as we were to learn the hard way.

Gordon was back in London and making plans: he was eager for Tom and the band to be under his wing. But we found ourselves in a bit of a pickle. We were already contracted to Myron and Byron and they were in no mood to relinquish their control to Mills. The band poured over the initial agreement and by our reckoning there were only a few months left before the original agreement elapsed. Tom was proving a bit of headache, he was caught in two minds, unsure if it was the best course to sign with Gordon. We hardly knew the man at that stage and for all of Myron and Byron's failings; it was a case of better the devil you know, so to speak.

Tom admitted he respected my judgment concerning the best moves for the band. But on this occasion he was clearly apprehensive. Well we all were it was a big leap into the unknown. London seemed so very far away and to make a permanent move there was a monumental decision. Tom had Linda and his son Mark to think about.

I said, 'Look Tom we're at a crossroads here. We can either hang about dithering on which path to take or we can follow our instincts. We may not get another chance like this. Gordon Mills has got a decent track record in the business. Myron and Byron have had their opportunity and we're no farther forward than we were before. I say it's time to move on and give it a shot.'

Tom recognized the opportunity and finally came around to our way of thinking. The band was all on-board taking that leap into the unknown. The next thing to be done was to face the music with Myron and Byron. A meeting was arranged at the Thorn Hotel in Abercynon. As you might imagine they tried everything to change our minds, finally falling back to their default position, and pointing out we were still under contract. But our minds were made up and we asked them to call Gordon and sort out the particulars with him.

Gordon travelled down from London for a meeting with Myron and Byron. It was decided to hold the meeting in a workingmen's club in the area. That way Gordon could sort out the log jam with the contract and watch the band in action again. Gordon did his best to smooth things over, he said, 'Look, I'm not trying to steal Tom and the band from you. I'm aware that you've spent a lot of time and money getting them to this stage. I'll make a deal with you. I'll have a separate contract drawn up and I'm willing to give you both five percent of the band.'

I'm sure that Myron and Byron recognized which way the wind was blowing and with only a few months left of the original agreement they both jumped at the offer. I'm certainly no contract lawyer but I remember thinking at the time, what about dates? Five percent from when to when exactly? I obviously didn't say anything at the meeting but I did mention it to Gordon later. He just smiled at me and told me to worry about the music and leave the business to him.

Gordon was always determined to prove a point and would argue his case as long as needs be. He had a habit of wearing you down until you threw up your hands in resignation. Quietly spoken, he rarely raised his voice, but there was an unmistakable steely determination ever present. He was constantly biting his nails when the pressure was on. They were always bitten down to the very quick; he seemed to live on his nerves.

In his eagerness to get Tom and the band under contract Gordon had made a pretty fundamental error. But as far as he was concerned five percent of nothing is nothing. I don't believe he ever had any real intention of giving Myron and Byron a piece of the action. It was just a ruse to get rid of them. But Gordon was on a high and it was infectious. He had convinced us to go home and pack our bags, we were off to London. Gordon's words were ringing in our ears, 'We're heading for the top!'

Unfortunately our guitarist Mike Roberts decided to quit the band. As soon as the practicalities hit home, and he realised he'd have to forsake his job as a TV cameraman and move to London, he wanted out. But Dave Cooper quit his job and I waved a fond farewell to The Observer. As a parting gift the paper ran a big spread about the band and our move to London. We played a farewell gig in The White Hart the night before we left Wales and the beer flowed until the taps ran dry.

We were stuck with one major problem before we could complete the move: the search for a new lead guitarist willing to up sticks and make the move with us. We organized auditions at The Thorn Hotel and finally settled on a twenty one year old Cardiffian, Mickey Gee. He was a red-hot guitarist and lived for the music he wrestled out of it, the boy could play. When he was eighteen he had travelled to New York and hitched a ride along the famous route 66 all the way to Nashville. He was on a mission to meet his guitar hero: the legendary Chet Atkins.

Mickey found out where Chet lived and knocked at his door only to be told that Chet was away on tour. He was clearly crestfallen and explained how far he had travelled to meet his hero. He was presented with one of Chet's guitar strings which he treasured like it was spun from gold.

Mickey could play finger-picking style just like the cream of Nashville. Later, after parting with Tom Jones on the worst possible terms, he went to work with Dave Edmunds, Shaking Stevens and the legendary Bruce Springsteen. Sadly Mickey passed away in January 2009, he was aged just sixty-four. I attended the funeral in Cardiff and there was a phenomenal turn out. There were over three hundred musicians there and we all paid our profound respects to one of the best musicians to ever grace a stage.

I went home that day remembering all the highs and lows I'd shared with Mickey. Chris Ellis happened to call me from Sweden. He'd settled there some years previous with his Swedish wife Eva. We fell to reminiscing about Mickey and the old days and both ended up in floods of tears. Mickey was the first of The Senators to die, it was a very sad day.

Tom had finally come around to the idea of us all departing for London and was a bag of nerves at the prospect. Tom took me aside and said perhaps he should have some singing lessons before we departed. I told him not to be so soft his voice was in phenomenal form. But he was adamant and mentioned my next door neighbor Brenda Warlow. Brenda was an opera singer and voice coach and I told Tom I would have a word with her. In all honesty if Tom had decided to go down the opera route he might well have made it, it was well within his reach. Brenda was a lovely lady in her forties, and had the elegant bearing of a trained opera singer; we all used to call her the 'Valleys' Maria Callas'.

After setting up the meeting on Tom's behalf, I took him along to meet Brenda. I introduced them both and went back next door to let them get on with it. Pretty soon I could hear Tom's muffled voice tackling the musical scales. After a while everything went very quiet and about forty minutes later a dishevelled Tom fell into my house, his face flushed.

'Get the kettle on Vern,' stammered Tom,' I could really do with a cup of tea, I'm gasping mon.'

I asked him how he had got on with Brenda and he rolled his eyes, 'get on, well I got on great until she got on top of me.'

I did a double take and thought, surely not, my mind was going off in all manner of directions. 'She told me if I wanted to be an opera singer I would have to forget about singing pop music. It's a completely different technique apparently'. I nodded and asked him if he was sticking with Rock n Roll for the time being, 'well yes, but she showed me how to breathe properly, you know to get the best out of my voice like'. Tom told me that Brenda had him lying flat out on the carpet and suddenly straddled his chest, 'This is great exercise for breathing', she had told him and suddenly started bouncing up and down, 'I thought I was gonna pass out Vern, she never let up, bouncing away like a mad thing, I almost passed out I swear.' Thankfully the kettle boiled displacing the image of Brenda bouncing up and down on top of Tom and I served him a well deserved nice cup of tea. Tom looked in shock and tea always helps in those situations. Brenda's son Wayne went on to become a renowned classical pianist in Europe.

6

BASEMENT BLUES

Chris Slade's mother would always fuss over him as though he were made of china. She was always making him wear a scarf and jumper when the weather turned nippy. You can imagine how upset she was when our seventeen year old drummer kissed her goodbye on his way to London. She tearfully followed his suitcase into the back of the yellow Thames Van. If she had only known the trials and tribulations that lay ahead she would probably have laid herself out in front of the van to stop him leaving. I wouldn't have blamed her in the slightest; we were all of us in for a very rude awakening.

Our final call was to see my grandmother Hannah Mills, who was staying with my Aunt Lilly, just down the road in Rhydyfelin. Having lost my mother in 1959 and having to break the awful news to my grandmother, we were very close. She was a great comfort to me and the family helping us to come to terms with the tragedy. I'll always remember that beautiful sunny day in late June with my grandmother waving us off as we drove away with a sharp blast on the horn. We were finally off to London and our excitement was palpable.

We arrived at Gordon's flat in Notting Hill. He was living on the third floor of Campden Hill Towers. Jo welcomed us in and gave us tea with biscuits. Gordon got out a map and gave us directions to a rather grotty hotel nearby. He explained we'd only have to spend a couple of nights there as he was sorting us out accommodation at 6 Clydesdale Road in Ladbroke Grove. After spending two nights at the flea bitten doss house we couldn't wait to move to Clydesdale Road, it was a real pit, the boys were scratching like crazy.

Gordon picked us up from the flea-pit in his Ford Zephyr convertible, it was a mighty impressive car. We made the short trip from Notting Hill down to the Grove. Halfway down the incline the wide leafy road was fronted with large affluent houses and they gradually gave way to less salubrious surroundings. At that time the Grove was a notorious ghetto. It was an eclectic mix of West Indians, Greeks, Portuguese and all manner of other settlers. It was a real melting pot. It had a well-earned reputation for drugs, prostitution and all manner of crimes. We had truly left the green green grass of home well and truly behind.

I took a quick look around the car and the band were looking shell-shocked, their mouths were practically in their laps. The streets were bustling with hookers and pimps and drug pushers, it was a real carnival.

Gordon pulled over at Clydesdale Road, a fifty yard row of four story terraced buildings. I'd describe them as run down but that would be an understatement, they looked like they were held up by string and a good wind would have flattened the entire terrace.

Gordon jumped out of the car all smiles and led us down to a basement flat. It looked pretty grim from the outside. Gordon said, 'This is all I could find available at the moment lads. But don't worry you'll soon be out of here. I've got big plans for Tom and The Senators. This is just a little blip on the road to stardom.'

Gordon turned the key on the door and had to give it some shoulder to force it open with a loud creak. We filed into the gloomy passageway and our senses were assaulted by a variety of vile smells. Dry rot, mice droppings and the deathly pong of something long dead, which turned out to be a rotten mouse. The ancient wallpaper was sweating damp and alive with a vibrant fungus. The cheap ragged carpet was so stained that the original pattern had long been forgotten. I looked up to the heavens for inspiration and noticed the ceiling was bowing so much from damp it was practically touching my nose.

Our new manager led the way further into the dismal abode and we followed like zombies in utter disbelief. There was a poky room with two single beds and a window with minimal daylight, the view being a set of stairs leading to the street above. There was another slightly larger room and this consisted of three single beds. The window had a glimmer of light fronting onto another building within arm's reach.

Tom piped up, 'Gordon this flat is like the Black Hole of Calcutta!' And rightly so, it was an apt description. The name stuck and we all of us referred to it as that from then on.

Gordon made his excuses and beat a hasty exit. Left to our own devices we got into a debate about who was sleeping where. It wasn't much of a debate considering that both rooms were equally as bad. I settled for the back room and the bed nearest the door. Tom wanted the bed in the corner opposite me and Dai grabbed the bed under the window. Chris and Mickey were left with the front room, after removing the dead mouse.

That was our welcome to London. Bothered, bewildered, but definitely not bewitched. We had a big discussion about leaping back in the van and heading back to Wales. But cool heads prevailed and we decided to slum it for a little while and see what materialized. After all Gordon had assured us that this was just a blip and he had big plans for the band.

The first time we ventured out of the flat we went looking for a café. Apart from the tea and biscuits provided by Jo we hadn't eaten since breakfast. The weather was hot and sultry and the air was richly permeated with a heady sweet scent. We'd later recognise that smell as top grade marijuana, the area was awash with it and supplied the whole of greater London. Whenever we passed an open doorway the repetitive heavy beat of reggae music filtered out.

We headed for Portobello market and stumbled upon a tiny Greek café. Its basic British menu was scrawled across the front window. We dived in and were welcomed by 'Pete the Greek', a cheerful handsome Cypriot in his early thirties. The food was reasonably priced and we dug into egg and chips, Pete filled us in on our whereabouts and gave us the lay of the land.

'Never ever venture down All Saints Road,' he warned us, 'it's a no go area for the likes of you boys. The police don't even venture there. If you get into trouble there you're on your own, so stay away.'

He couldn't understand why any manager would let a band live down The Grove and advised us to get the equipment out of the van as soon as possible, if it had not been stolen already.

With our bellies full we headed back to the flat. We drew a lot of stares, being the only white faces on the street. We quickly emptied the van and stashed our equipment in the passageway of the flat. We spent the next few days cleaning up the flat and trying to rid ourselves of the mice infestation. After a few weeks our money dried up and we were all flat broke. Gordon sat down with the band and told us because we were under contract he would pay the band one pound a day to be shared between the five of us. We were speechless, that was only twenty pence each a day, and we had to find food, toiletries and our laundry out of that. He pointed out that he was also paying the rent on the flat and he asked us to be patient, our big break would come soon.

We tried to budget for one main meal a day, one pint of beer at night and ten woodbines shared between the five of us. With our daily allowance and rent Gordon was spending around twenty pounds a week. After the first six weeks our morale was at rock bottom and we were no nearer to getting a record deal than when we first arrived.

We wanted to start lining up some gigs in and around London to pay our way. We were missing being on stage and were itching to get back in front of a live audience. But Gordon was adamant that this wasn't part of his plan for getting us a record deal. He said he didn't want to over expose us just yet and we needed to be patient. In retrospect the reason Gordon wouldn't let us play live gigs was probably because he was paranoid that we would be discovered by someone with a bit more clout in the music business, and then we wouldn't need him. After all he had already done something similar in persuading us to leave Myron and Byron.

Pete the Greek had become a great friend and had been busy introducing us to all the locals. We had quickly become accepted into the Ladbroke Grove community. I remember one warm night in late September; a jolly West Indian had befriended the band and he invited us along to an illegal basement club, around the corner from the flat. Being relatively new to London we were unaware we were breaking the law by attending. The place was very dark inside and the walls throbbed to the sound of Bob Marley and the Wailers. The by now familiar scent of marijuana permeated the room. We filtered our way through the bustling crowd of dancers and made for a small bar at the back of the room. We were each served with a bottle of fruit juice. The air was so stale and humid in the club that I took a long thirsty swig. It almost blew my head clean off. The drink was about two-thirds imported Jamaican Rum. The illicit drink was disguised as simple fruit juice to avoid any excise duty. We soon got a taste for it and it was much cheaper than any legitimate pub could offer. Once again we were the only white boys there, but we were becoming used to that by now. It wasn't very long before we were on the dance floor and mixing it with the best of them.

An hour later all hell broke loose.

We were so much under the influence of the one hundred percent proof rum that we weren't initially aware that the place was teeming with police officers. They had charged down into the basement and were now charging back out with men and women in arm and head locks, shepherding everyone into the waiting Black Maria police vans parked just outside.

We just stood there goggle-eyed with the place in uproar, it was bedlam. A women standing beside me snatched something out of her handbag and pressed it into my hands. Then she disappeared into the darkness. I examined the small scrunched up envelope; I didn't have a clue what it was and innocently stuffed it into my pocket. The police left as quickly as they had come, they seemed to know exactly who they were looking for in the swoop and didn't even give us a second glance.

We didn't hang around to ask questions and decided to make a bolt back to the 'Calcutta' as fast as we could. We avoided those places like the plague after that.

The next morning, nursing an almighty hangover, the envelope fell out my jeans pocket as I was climbing into them. Inside were six blue tablets, I had no idea what they were. I later found out from Pete the Greek that they were Purple Hearts, which were amphetamines. I didn't know what the hell he was on about but decided to hang onto them in case they ever came in handy.

Autumn was now drawing in and we were still in limbo. Gordon would visit once a day and hand over one pound to share between us. But there was no good news to report whatsoever. Pete's Greek café was a godsend during that lean spell. It got us out of the flat for a while, and even though the limited menu consisted of either egg and chips or sausage sandwiches, the banter kept us in some spirits. Our weight was beginning to plummet though. Relying on just the one meal a day our clothes were hanging off us, and starting to wear a little thin to boot. Our shoes were pretty scruffy too, we contemplated saving up the food allowance and buying some shoe polish, but rumbling bellies put paid to that noble ambition.

We tackled Gordon again about letting us play some gigs to bring in a little money, but he wouldn't budge. It was his way, or no way. We were beginning to neglect ourselves, not cleanliness wise, we did wash and shower regularly, but our general appearance was a little shabby to say the least. We had nothing to feel good about. It was almost as if we had been abandoned and forgotten.

We tried to keep our spirits up and were forever winding each other up and playing practical jokes. The tatty shower unit in the flat was situated in close proximity to the kitchen, and the ancient gas stove took up most of the room. We tried not to use it as it was so unreliable, the gas would cut on and off at will. We were hanging around the flat one afternoon and Tom decided to take a shower. Off he went to the kitchen closing the door behind him. He seemed to be gone for an age. On the clock ticked and there was no sign of him. Suddenly there was a tremendous crash followed by a commotion and Tom crying out in pain. We all rushed into the kitchen to see what the fuss was about. There he was half hanging out of the cubicle naked as the day he was born. The shower was still going strong and flooding the kitchen floor.

'Help us up boys,' he groaned, 'I was having one off the wrist when I slipped on the soap. I was just about bloody getting there too!'

'That'll teach you Tom,' I chuckled, 'you can't leave it alone for five seconds. It'll be the death of you if you're not careful you mucky bugger.' Roaring with laughter, we turned and left him to it.

Tom has often mentioned that he should slow down on his sexual adventures, or they'd end up being the death of him. I'm sure that if he'd been a guest on 'Desert Island Discs' back then and been allowed one luxury item, it wouldn't have been a pair of boxing gloves: more likely a bumper edition of Playboy Magazine. Back then we were all forever warning him that he would go blind and grow hairs on his palms. But that didn't deter him in the slightest. He was forever making tents in his bed once the lights were out.

It wasn't any wonder that he was losing weight faster than the rest of the band. After three months of living on the breadline all of us had lost over two stone each, but Tom was looking like a scarecrow. We weren't getting enough of the right vitamins and minerals and great big boils were breaking out on our emaciated bodies. Tom was getting them really bad on his back. He kept having these massive eruptions and they certainly looked painful. I think he was more susceptible to them because he had quite oily skin. That went hand in hand with his dark looks. There was one funny incident where he decided to take matters of nutrition into his own hands.

It has been well documented in countless biographies that Tom was a bit of a teenage tear-away, with all manner of petty thieving and fighting and so on. But after joining the band, apart from borrowing the club's chicken and his brother-in-law's Corsair, he never put a foot wrong. He was friendly with every band member, easy going and laid back, and never lifted a finger in aggression during the eight years we were together. Well, apart from a petty altercation with our guitarist Keith Davies, but that was quickly forgotten. The band had become ever more loyal to each other during those wretched months in the 'Calcutta'.

It's fair to say that through shared adversity we had formed a very close bond. So it came as a bit of a surprise when Tom slipped into old habits. As you may imagine surviving on one light meal a day our young stomachs would be rumbling for food come nightfall. To relieve our hunger we would pool what was left from our daily pound and see if we could rustle up a snack. On this occasion we were pleased that we had just enough to buy two sausage rolls from Pete's café to share between the five of us. This early evening snack fetching was usually done on a rota, and that night it was Tom's turn.

Time went by and there was no sign of him, it was like the shower incident all over again. We were beginning to wonder where on earth he'd got too. Our stomachs were rumbling like cement mixers, but pretty soon they were rumbling with anxiety. It was a pretty rough area after all; surely Tom wouldn't have been mugged for less than a shilling?

Finally the front door creaked and in he strolled, deviously wiping away any evidence of a crumb from around his mouth.

'Took the scenic route Tom?' I asked.

'No boys, you're not going to believe this,' he said rather sheepishly, 'I'd just arrived outside the café and you know that bloody big drain. Well some bugger bumped into me and the lot fell down the drain.'

'Every penny,' we all groaned in unison.

'Every bloody penny, on my life,' he said.

'You lying bastard, you've got crumbs all down your shirt,' we all wailed.

Naturally we all sent him to Coventry for the rest of the week, and it was never his turn to go on the snack run again after that. Looking back I can see the funny side now, but we didn't half give him hell back then. Little did we realize it was a harbinger of what was to come.

The nights at the 'Calcutta' sometimes became unbearably long and depressing, so we would sometimes take a stroll up to The Gate, calling in on Gordon and Jo hoping for some good news. Our intention was to kill a little time and wander around the area for a bit before heading back down to the Grove.

We used to pass the same Indian restaurant on every excursion. We always wished we had some money to buy a couple of Barhjees and maybe more for a curry. One evening we were so arrested by the fine aroma wafting out of the restaurant that one of the band decided to go in and check it out. He returned and told us the toilet window was open and possibly big enough for us to scrape through and into the alley behind.

It was a big temptation, we all looked each other in the eyes and thought the hell with it, and if we got busted at least we'd get ourselves fed in the process. In we piled and found ourselves a table near the toilet. The waiter came to get us seated waving five menus for our inspection, we didn't waste any time studying and ordered five Vindaloos with Nan, Barhjees and all the trimmings. As you may imagine we were ravenous and devoured the meal in lightning quick time. So much so that Tom actually lifted his plate and licked it clean. It was the first square meal we had tasted for months.

Afterwards we all exchanged some guilty looks. The toilet window was high in the wall and the only way out was to stand on the toilet pan and try and wiggle through. It was a mad scramble to get through that window. It was incredibly narrow but luckily we were all stick thin after starving the previous months and we all managed to get out.

Performing that caper and getting away with it gave us great heart. We would never have imagined doing that back home in Wales. But it's surprising the lengths you will go to when the chips are down, or you really need to get some chips down you! Sadly to be completely honest it didn't stop there. A little while later we found ourselves with just enough money to buy a Chinese Special.

The singer Max Bygraves, who was big at the time, got in contact with Gordon and asked if the band would record a demo of a song he had written. Gordon promised our fee would be five pounds between us, but with the potential of more recording work with Max. We were beside ourselves, at last some movement and an opportunity to get back on stage and make some music, we were chuffed. It was agreed that Max would provide the vocal and we recorded the track at Regent Sound in Denmark Street in the heart of Soho. Tom was a bit miffed obviously as he couldn't be on the demo, but we softened the blow and gave him an equal one pound share in the recording. After all we were all in it together, at that stage at least.

We were on a high after the session and made our way back up to Notting Hill Gate. We all headed for the nice Chinese restaurant that we had walked past about a million times before and always fantasized about eating in. We each of us had about a pound in our pocket, it's hard to believe now, but back then that would have got us a half decent meal. We didn't have to do a runner, we were quids in. The waiter gave us a table near the open door, which was much appreciated as the place was packed and it was a very hot evening. There was a nice cool night breeze and we all spent some time pouring over the menu.

The waiters produced plate after plate, and we got stuck in. I remember thinking at the time that we had enough money to return the following evening for another blow out. When the bill arrived Tom went white, the color just drained right out of his face. He seemed really edgy and his foot was beating the floor like he was desperate for the toilet. I grabbed the bill and gave out a long whistle. I had no idea it would have cost so much, I groaned inwardly. The next moment Tom was out of his chair, and he flew for the door as if a wasp had stung him on the arse. Panicking, we all followed suit, like lemmings hurtling ourselves through the open door in pursuit of Tom. The waiters were fast on our tails screaming blue murder.

We were so sluggish after the feast that I was tiring and waddling about close to vomiting. One of the band grabbed me by the lapels and dragged me into a front garden behind a high hedge. I was surprised to see most of the band panting and hiding there also. The waiters and kitchen staff came screaming past waving kitchen knives and machetes. We were terrified. We didn't move from the garden for an age. Then finally they all trooped back cursing us as they passed.

Every time we went for a curry or Chinese after that we were always on tenterhooks, waiting for Tom to do a runner. Nine times out of ten he did, he seemed to have acquired a taste for the excitement of bolting. We got used to making a run for it and always travelled light in anticipation.

Windswept autumn leaves finally gave way to snow. The two miserable gas fires in the 'Calcutta' gave out as little warmth as the naked light bulbs hanging from the ceilings. We felt old beyond our years and were having serious discussions about Gordon and his plans for the band. At one stage we were so despondent that we decided on returning home to Wales, but we had no money for petrol and the clapped-out van stood idle outside gathering dust. The boys pushed me to go and get some petrol money from Gordon for a trip home. He must have realised that that would have been the last he'd see of us because he dug in his heels and refused point blank.

To be fair, unbeknown to us at the time, Gordon was like a man possessed. He had been trying everything in the book to get us a record deal. There finally came a high when he managed to get us a gig supporting the Rolling Stones at the One Hundred Club. It really gave us heart after all the hanging around, but it proved to be a false dawn and things dried up after the gig.

Bill Wyman, the Stones bassist, describes it better than I ever could: 'The eighteenth of July hundreds and hundreds of fans jammed the streets around the West End and there were police everywhere when we played the One Hundred Club. Inside the heat was fierce. Tom Jones and his band were our support. The temperature was so high that stewards were throwing buckets of water over us and the audience'. Bill describes it perfectly, from what I remember it was an inferno, it was that hot you felt as if you were melting. We played a forty-five minute set to an audience of six hundred, it was crazy, girls were fainting left right and centre and being carried out. After being so long off stage we were rocking, The Stones had to drag us off stage, we didn't want to leave.

Tom got some ribbing from the band later. Wearing white trousers and a white t-shirt he sweated so much that his trousers turned see-through and the buckets of water flying around didn't help matters any. The audience got a bit more than they bargained for that evening. Even Jagger looked shocked and that's saying something. We shared the same dressing room as the Stones, and we all fell about laughing when Mick Jagger pointed to Tom after we came off stage dripping wet, he said, 'Christ it must be hot out there look at him and he's only the compere,' I thought Tom was going to stick the head on him but he was too knackered after the set.

It was after that gig that Gordon re-named us 'Tom Jones and The Playboys'. The movie, 'Tom Jones' with Albert Finney had just won three Oscars; it was about the eighteenth century jack the lad who shagged his way through a bevy of beauties, how prescient! It was a very sharp move by Gordon, the name 'Tom Jones' was so established on the back of the film that everybody just associated it instantly with the band, it was a stroke of genius. It was a formula he was to use again for the other acts he'd signed: Englebert Humperdink, Gilbert O'Sullivan, Gordon had a knack of coining a name that would capture the public attention.

During that period Gordon was working full time on re-igniting Peter Sullivan's interest in the band. Peter Sullivan was a record producer with Decca. Peter had taken the time to come and see us perform in Wales when we were with Myron and Byron. He thought we had talent but needed some polishing. Gordon was trying to persuade him to release 'Chills and Fever', the song we had recorded with Joe Meek. Gordon was convinced it would be a massive hit.

The band recorded it again with Tom. We gave it a rhythm and blues feel, and Tom did a fantastic job with the vocal. Then Peter Sullivan ruined the cool arrangement by adding loads of brash sounding instruments, creating a totally over-produced single. It was released in late August and got nowhere in the charts.

There was bitter disappointment all round. Gordon was at the end of his tether. He was fast running out of money. He finally relented on the gig front and now wanted us back playing live as we all needed the money badly. The only caveat he insisted on was that there would be no gigs performed in London. He wanted all gigs in venues well outside the London area. I guess he was still paranoid that we might get poached away from him and he'd invested too much in the band to allow that to happen.

We started gigging regularly again with all the proceeds going directly to Gordon. But it wasn't enough and he pleaded for a bank loan to continue developing the band. He got a small amount that kept his head just above water. Eventually he sold his wristwatch for fifty pounds, which was a lot back then, and much later he sold his beloved Ford Zephyr.

7

THE SQUIRES

Gordon changed the name of the band again, this time to The Squires. We were going through so many name changes it was making our heads spin: The Senators, Tommy Woodward, Tommy Scott, Tom Jones, The Playboys and now The Squires. I remember asking Gordon if we were going to hang onto this name a little longer than the previous and just got a scowl in response. Apparently this change had been forced on him. There was already an American group using the name Playboys and they'd been upset to learn about us using the same name in the UK and had threatened Gordon with legal action.

Another of Gordon's acts, Englebert Humperdink, had secured an important booking at one of London's most famous nightclubs, the Astor Club. Englebert asked a favor of us, he wanted the band to support him. He could have used the house band but he wanted to impress an important person in show business who was coming along that evening to see him perform. Englebert confided in us his hopes that this person could get him out of the doldrums and off the breadline. Gordon's management had failed to open any real doors for Englebert and like us he was becoming a bit disillusioned.

The Astor Club was situated in Berkeley Square and the owner, Bertie Green, was friendly with some shady characters, including the legendary underworld figures Reg and Ronnie Kray. They both just happened to be in the audience that particular evening. Tom had decided to come along even though he wasn't needed for the gig. He was probably checking out the competition, after all he was vying with Englebert for Gordon's attention, them both being on the books. Also I don't think he particularly relished spending the evening alone at the 'Calcutta'.

The Astor was a massive club. We had set up our equipment during the afternoon so we were able to arrive about an hour before we were due on stage. An Italian waiter led us to our dressing room. It was back stage near the bustling kitchens. The dressing room was really no more than a broom cupboard with a black curtain for privacy. You may imagine our surprise when we saw another entertainer already there and snoozing away. The other entertainer was a bloody great big python snake.

Bertie Green had booked another supporting act that evening, a belly dancer come snake charmer. The snake was obviously waiting for his mistress to finish the belly dancing part of her set and then come get him for the finale. The snake was coiled up in a hold-all snoozing away. I prodded it with my finger but it didn't stir and this was a great relief to the rest of the band.

There was some heavenly scents emanating from the kitchen and we all remembered how hungry we were. We'd blown our one pound allowance from Gordon earlier. The dressing room was right next to the waiters' station. The food trolleys would be parked outside ready for delivery to the diners in the cabaret room. As soon as one waiter disappeared through the flexible rubber doors to serve the food, another fully laden food trolley would appear from the kitchen ready for the next waiter to collect. It was a regular assembly line of fine culinary production.

The aromas from under the silver tureens on the trolleys were making our mouths water. I lifted one of the tureens to see what they were serving and the boys gathered around too. Underneath the tureen was the largest and most succulent T-bone steak, it was still sizzling.

'Have a sniff of this then boys,' I practically drooled. Just as I was about to replace the lid a hand darted out and grabbed the steak. We all stared in amazement as Tom made a dash for the fire exit trying to make good his escape. Unfortunately for him the door was blocked from the outside and wouldn't open. So there he crouched devouring the steak like a rabid wolf. We all dragged him back into the dressing room, and then thought, what the hell. We shared the steak passing it around until we had devoured every last morsel, it tasted wonderful.

What with all the commotion we had awoken the snake and it slithered out of the hold-all. Suddenly a waiter appeared screaming half in English and half in Italian accusing us of stealing the steak. We vehemently denied it of course but the waiter was almost hysterical. He informed us that the steak had been for Mr. Kray and he was far from happy, the waiter sobbed, 'The bad man he will 'sleeta' my throat!' I pointed to the snake slithering across the floor, 'tell Mr. Kray the snake ate his steak and prepare him another one.'

The next day Gordon gave us a right dressing down, he was livid. Bertie Green had been onto him complaining about the missing steak. Of course we all continued to deny it. To be completely honest we didn't feel any remorse, after all we were there to do Englebert a favour, it wasn't like we were getting paid or anything. We just took our payment in kind. We tried to fob Gordon off with our story about the snake eating the steak, but he just wasn't buying it.

We had by now made so many friends in Ladbroke Grove that we felt comfortable leaving our equipment in the van. We had been accepted by the locals and we all used to look out for each other. Unfortunately one of the tires on the van had been punctured after the last gig and no-one had volunteered to repair it. We had all grown so apathetic that anything that required any effort, other than to do with music, we shied away from.

One afternoon it was drizzling with rain and we were all hanging around the flat, bored to tears. I was rummaging through the kitchen drawers and came across the envelope containing the Purple Hearts that the women had dumped on me during the police raid. I remembered what Pete the Greek had said about them perking you up. Sod it, I thought, we all of us need perking up living in this shit hole.

'What's that you've got there Vern?' yawned Tom as I popped one into my mouth.

'One of those pills that Pete the Greek said perks you up. It gives you the stamina to shag anything on two legs,' I said.

'I do that already thank you very much,' said Tom.

'Don't we all know it,' chorused the boys.

Thinking nothing more about it I slumped back onto my bed and stared at the ceiling before dozing off to sleep again. I remember opening my eyes a little while later with the determination that I shouldn't be wasting my time hanging about doing nothing. I was feeling restless and took to pacing the floor, wandering from room to room.

'Can't you keep still for five minutes?' moaned Tom, looking up from the magazine he was reading, 'I'm trying to bloody concentrate here.'

'It's about time someone sorted out the flat tire on the van,' I piped up enthusiastically, 'If Gordon comes up with a gig at short notice we'll be in a spot of bother. I'm going to change the wheel.'

'But its bloody raining,' everyone chorused.

Undeterred, off I went up into the drizzling rain. Out came the jack and the spare wheel. I was feeling as bright as a button despite getting soaked through to the skin. All our equipment was piled up in the back of the van and it was a miracle that the jack didn't collapse under all that excess weight. Job finished I was back in the flat and decided on giving the place a good clean from top to bottom. I was driving the band barmy. I can't remember quite how long this went on for but much later that day I crashed and became very depressed. It was an awful feeling and seemed to last for ages. I never took one again after that and flushed the rest down the toilet. But I did notice another pill was missing. Tom admitted to taking it but said, 'It did nothing for me. All I did was keep staring at the ceiling.'

The nights now began drawing in and the temperature in the flat was plummeting. We became ever more reliant on our two miserable little gas fires for warmth. It made a bit of a dent in our food allowance as we had to keep feeding shillings into the meter to keep the heat on. One evening there was a banging at the front door. I opened the door on two women of the night.

We soon recognized them as local prostitutes who worked the corner nearby. They both pleaded with us to let them come in and warm themselves, the poor girls looked frozen.

In exchange for some piping hot tea they offered us a few cigarettes. They stayed for a while chatting and then were off again to work their patch. The following night they hammered on the door again although this time there were four of them. Soon the kettle was whistling and there was tea and cigarettes all round. This routine continued whenever the weather turned bitterly cold. Over time we got to know all the girls that worked the area quite well. We listened to their stories about abuse and wife battering and all the terrible events that had befallen them: it was understandable that they had turned their backs on society.

We felt sorry for them and the marginalized lives they were forced to live. They were young lost souls, vulnerable to the local pimps and drug dealers who exploited them ruthlessly. Many of the girls had descended on London from as far afield as Glasgow, Belfast, Cardiff and the north of England. They were all putting as much distance between themselves and the traumas they had suffered as possible. London offered the attraction of relative obscurity, but with little or no money they were easy targets for the unscrupulous.

During their visits we always tried to persuade them to make a break, and turn their backs on prostitution. But they seemed to be too much under the influence of their pimps. One thing was certain; we never needed to worry about our van or equipment being stolen. The girls informed us that they had put the word around that we were to be left alone or else.

During our time together it hadn't entirely escaped my notice that Tom's priorities in life seemed concentrated on shagging, singing and sinking beer, quite possibly in that order. They were his three favourite subjects of conversation. I got the impression that if a doctor had informed him that he could no longer get an erection he would have headed straight for the nearest railway line or bridge.

Tom certainly liked to check that everything was in fine working order on a regular basis. One bitterly cold evening there was the usual knock at the door and we let the girls in for their regular visit. There was one girl who stood out from the rest; she was certainly no oil painting. She was a Glasgow Lass named Charlotte in her mid-twenties with short cropped ginger hair. Short and quite sturdy, she was your archetypal tough little Scot. Her accent was so broad we could barely understand a word she said.

At that time the band were forever coining nicknames for people to keep all our spirits up. Charlotte had unfortunately been saddled with the moniker 'Grotty Lottie', never in her presence of course. That particular evening Tom sat her down on his bed for a heartfelt conversation about getting out of the life and getting a regular job. It's fair to say that she was a bit of an ugly duckling, and the other girls informed us that due to her appearance she wasn't getting much business. She was the most vulnerable and needed to get out of her self-destructive situation.

Tom was chatting to her for hours suggesting possible jobs and things she might consider. They were still talking long after the other girls had left and we had all gone to bed. When I awoke the next morning Tom was still in bed fast asleep. When he finally roused himself he had a lecherous grin on his face.

'No Tom, you didn't, say you didn't.'

'Sorry Vern I had to,' he replied.

'You must be joking you dirty sod,' I said.

'Well a standing cock has no conscience boys.'

Many years later, long after the band had gone their separate ways, I was watching Tom Jones at the London Palladium on television. The show was hosted by Jimmy Tarbuck. When Tom had finished his set and left the stage, Jimmy quipped, 'By the way Tom, Grotty Lottie is waiting for you outside the dressing room. She's gone and lost the other autograph you gave her.' I almost fell out of my chair; you could have knocked me down with a feather. No doubt Tom had proudly recounted some of his conquests from his time at the 'Calcutta'.

Every now and again we would get a little homesick for the green grass of home. Being totally skint we obviously couldn't afford the petrol money for the van and Gordon kept refusing to help in case we didn't come back. Our only option was to hitch a lift on one of the many lorries travelling down to Wales on the old A40. The M4 hadn't been built at that stage.

We used to leave the flat together and then split up as there was more chance of getting a lift that way. Today hitching a lift is a far more fraught experience. What with yob culture and all manner of stabbings and muggings it's a different world. But back in 1964 it was the 'done thing'. People were far more willing to give a lift to strangers back then, especially if the weather was bad. We all hitchhiked home a number of times that year. Sometimes I would get a lift as far as High Wycombe and have to walk the ten miles to the next busy spot to catch another ride. Other times one of us might get lucky and catch a lift from Shepherds Bush all the way down to Cardiff. I got really lucky on one occasion. I managed to flag down a lorry on the A40 near Reading. Climbing up into the cabin I was met with a lilting Welsh accent, 'Get in butt, where are you heading?'

'South Wales,' I replied.

'Well you're in luck that's where I'm heading, whereabouts exactly?'

'Pontypridd,' I told him hoping he'd be able to drop me off somewhere nearby.

'Ponty, I'm heading there myself.'

It was the beginning of a wonderful friendship between John Jones and the band that would continue for many years. Our 'King of the Road' was a real blessing. John was a giant of a man in his thirties with fair hair and a wicked sense of humour. He had a regular run from Pontypridd to different parts of London. From that moment onwards he used to go out of his way to pick us up and drop us off on route to Wales or back to London. He knew we were going hungry at the time trying to catch our big break in London. Out used to come his sandwich tin crammed full of sandwiches and fresh fruit, 'Here we go boys, get stuck into that lot. I had a big breakfast this morning and I'm full to bursting. It's a long haul back to Ponty and Mam's cooking.' Tragically John died at a relatively early age from the same disease that took my mother.

Chris Ellis, our roadie from back home in Wales, was another godsend at that time. He would pay us a visit in London every now and again and come laden with tins of beans, corned beef, soup and preservatives. He knew the dire straits we were in but thankfully kept it to himself. Our local paper back home, The Observer was forever informing its readers about our successful transition to London and how we were on the cusp of great things. They would have had a field day reporting that Tom and The Senators were living like tramps in a doss house in Ladbroke Grove and wasting away through lack of food. Chris Slade's mother would have hit the roof if she had got wind of the situation we were in. He was still only seventeen and she would have been up like a rocket to London to drag him back home.

On some occasions Chris would pick up Tom's wife Linda and drive her up for a visit in his white Mini. Tom and Linda would spend the weekend at Gordon's flat in Notting Hill. There was no way she could have stayed in the 'Calcutta'. Having a familiar face around like Chris Ellis lifted our spirits no end. He would fill us in on all the gossip from back home, as he heated up tins of beans on the dodgy gas cooker. Chris was a real diamond, from our first meeting back in the Green Fly, and all his driving us around the clubs, and even up to Joe Meek's studio for that first recording, he was a great friend to us all. I don't know what we would have done without his support. Tom has even more to thank him for. Chris did a superb job as his personal road manager, long after we had all parted company acrimoniously. Unfortunately he was paid a pittance by the multi-millionaire superstar, but he never complained and performed his highly responsible job with complete professionalism.

The situation had become quite desperate for Gordon and

the band during that time. Gordon was in deep trouble with the bank and it felt like everything was falling apart. One morning one member of the band was missing. Tom had risen early and was paying a visit to Gordon's flat. Having all the worries of a wife and child to support he was in a bad place psychologically. Linda was having a rough time of it back home in Ponty having to scrape and struggle to make ends meet. She wanted her husband back home and told Tom that.

Tom had a heart to heart conversation with Gordon. He wanted the manager to slip him a few extra pounds a week to send home to Linda and explained how she was getting restless about how things were going. Tom told us all later that Gordon also unburdened himself at the meeting. He informed the young singer that he was fast running out of money. Jo's modelling career was on hold because she had recently given birth to a baby girl, Tracey. They had been relying on songwriting royalties but they were slow in coming through. His overdraft was rising daily and he was on the verge of selling his car.

'I'm sorry Tom. I can only just about manage to feed you and the boys. You'll have to tell Linda to go out and find a job.'

That cut Tom like a dagger to the heart, he was really upset. Back then housewives never went out to work, they stayed home, washing the laundry, keeping the house tidy and looking after the kids. It was a different culture, I know it's hard to imagine now but that's how things were back then: particularly in the traditional mining communities of South Wales. Tom must have thought it was the end of the line. After all those hard months of struggling it had now come to this. He was on the edge, staring into an abyss of humiliation and defeat.

'I understand Gordon,' he was a broken man. He left Gordon's flat and headed for Notting Hill Tube Station a few hundred yards away. He bought a ticket and stood on the platform waiting for the next train.

We were all at Pete the Greek's café ordering our usual egg and chips. I finished first and was desperate for a pee so I left the band there and headed back to the 'Calcutta'. I found our troubled singer sitting on the edge of the bed with his head in his hands. I noticed that he was trembling and wondered what the hell had happened.

'You okay Tom?' I asked but he was completely silent so I asked him again. He raised his head and his eyes were red and tearful.

'I nearly topped myself Vern,' he said.

'What,' I asked shocked.

'At Notting Hill Tube I watched the train coming in and got ready to jump in front of it.'

'Why, for Christ's sake?' I shouted.

He then told me all about the meeting with Gordon. He recounted how Gordon was in 'the shit' and could barely afford to keep the band going. By his reckoning that was it, we'd had it, the dream was all but over.

I told him it was not worth topping yourself over. We were all in this together. Okay, things were pretty desperate but we had come this far together. I felt sure Gordon would come up with an answer. I explained to Tom that Gordon was just as desperate as the rest of us for the band to be a success.

'He's not going to throw himself under a train, neither are

the boys and neither are you,' I told him.

I reminded him about our great send off at the White Hart. I wasn't ready to go back home with my tail between my legs. Not while there was still an outside chance that things might work out for us in London.

'That's a laugh,' he said sourly, 'it was supposed to kick off for us when we first came up here. Now Gordon's completely skint. It's a bloody joke. It's pointless staying another minute in this shit hole. You can stay Vern but I'm going back home.'

I tried to explain that if he did that he'd be letting us all down. I reasoned with him that we might not get another chance, 'you'll regret not wringing it out to the bitter end. You'll curse yourself for not ever knowing if it might have worked out.'

I suggested we do the rounds of all the local pubs in the area that night to see if we might drum up some gigs to help support Gordon and ourselves. As far as I was concerned the 'no playing London' policy was now dead in the water.

'Gordon won't mind us playing anywhere now that he needs every penny he can get hold of. The North Star and The Bush have live music. We'll all go up for a nosy around later, Tom.'

That seemed to cheer him up a little, 'Come on let's get out of this dump. The band is waiting for us down at Pete's. Let's go and get you some grub.'

It was true that if Tom had crumbled then we would have all been breadcrumbs, that's a fact. But we did manage to secure some gigs in Shepherds Bush later that evening and he was okay after that.

Gordon was down but far from out. He needed every penny to stop the ship from sinking. He got to hear about Tom's

Notting Hill incident, which must have left him with many a sleepless night. Really desperate measures were now called for. Gordon's only option was to bring on board some money men in exchange for a stake in the band. Gordon was inherently a greedy man, and he would have been at pains not to go down that particular avenue, but what choice did he have? As luck would have it, when he was exploring potential investors, a much welcomed royalty cheque arrived. It was enough to get us out of the 'Calcutta' and Ladbroke Grove. I think he'd realised that Tom and the band were close to the edge and the freezing damp flat wasn't helping matters any.

We packed our belongings and headed for Shepherds Bush and Lime Grove. What a change in environment. Lime Grove consisted of elegant bay windowed Victorian houses set along a wide tree-lined road. The BBC studios were at one end, its massive presence hidden behind the terraced bay windows of two of the houses. It looked ever so ordinary to anyone passing by. The only clue to what was going on behind the scenes was the familiar face of a newsreader rehearsing his script in the window. The studios were situated in the labyrinth deep behind. Top of the Pops was filmed there and we all dreamed about appearing on that show one day.

Directly opposite the studios was the Lime Grove Baths where you could have a good scrub for a small fee. Not that we ever used the place, for we now had our own bathroom, what luxury! We were chuffed to bits.

A friendly Polish family was our landlords. They lived on the ground floor and we had the run of the second floor to ourselves. The rooms were large, with a spacious lounge and three bedrooms. We split up along similar lines to the 'Calcutta'. Well almost, Tom claimed the smaller bedroom for himself, I doubled up with Dai in one room and Micky Gee and Chris Slade took the other bedroom. We even had a black and white television set. There were only two stations in those days, BBC and ITV, but who was complaining! This was a real step up: we even had a three-piece-suite to sit on, we felt like kings.

Goodbye dry rot, wall fungus, grubby carpets and dodgy gas fires. We were still getting by on our one pound food allowance, but it was bearable now that our spirits had risen out of the depths of despair. We scoured the area for another greasy spoon as good as Pete's. We had become used to dining on Greek egg and chips and now we got used to Turkish egg and chips. We had discovered a Turkish café and just like Pete the Greek's menu there wasn't a foreign dish in sight!

Things were definitely on the up alright. One morning Gordon came around banging on the door. He had a song he wanted us to record. I let him in and he came rushing up the stairs carrying a tape recorder, 'I want you all to listen to this song I've written: 'It's Not Unusual'. I've booked a twenty minute slot at Regent Sound Studios for 2:30pm so listen carefully, you'll only have one crack at it.'

Gordon played the new tune, he was accompanying himself on piano and providing the vocal. The melody was quite catchy but the lyrics sounded a little effeminate, 'I wanna cry, I wanna die,' and so on. After playing it through a couple of times we headed for the studios in Denmark Street.

When we arrived at the tiny demo studio there was a guy sitting at the baby grand rehearsing the song. His hands were spread all over the keys. I think he was using every digit and he was producing these almighty chords. It was an early run at the rousing introduction to 'Not Unusual'.

It was inspiring, Gordon's piano interpretation back in the flat earlier had sounded more like the comedian Les Dawson's famous piano lessons. Suddenly the little tune had come magically to life and with a real awe-inspiring riven intensity. In that moment it really struck me how a twee little melody could be transformed into something very special by a gifted musical arranger. His name was Les Reed and he was the co-writer of that now famous song. I learnt a lot from Les, he really enlightened me on what's possible with the right arrangement.

We hurriedly set up our gear. There wasn't even time for Chris Slade to get his drum kit together, so he grabbed a tambourine instead. We had time for one quick run through and, I have to admit, Dave Cooper, on rhythm guitar, and me, on bass guitar, hadn't paid quite enough attention to the song back at the flat. There was no time to go through it again. The clock was ticking and we only had five minutes of studio time left. It was left to Micky Gee, lead guitar, Chris on tambourine, Les Reed on piano and the voice of Tom.

We were told after that the song had been especially written for Sandie Shaw. We thought nothing more about it, it was just another demo to record. Gordon told us to go and grab a pint in The George around the corner on Shaftesbury Avenue. He wanted to get an acetate of the demo there and then and told us he would follow us later. Once settled in The George we came to the conclusion that 'It's Not Unusual,' was indeed very unusual thanks to Les Reed's deft use of chords and fillings.

We convinced ourselves that this could be the breakthrough we had been striving for. By the time Gordon had arrived we had set our hearts on releasing it. We all believed we had a real chance of making a breakthrough with this song.

When Gordon pitched up, we told him our thoughts. It would be crazy to give the song to Sandie Shaw when it could be the making of us and Tom. Disappointingly he told us that his hands were tied. Les Reed had co-written the song and it was his intention that it be presented to Sandie Shaw. He went on to explain that it had been especially written for her. After having a hit with 'Always Something there to remind me' Les wanted to present her with a song that had a similar beat. With its laid back Motown feel and 'shuu, shuu, shuu' rhythm they thought this was that song. If she had a hit with it then, Gordon explained, he'd have more money to invest in developing the band. It all sounded a little near sighted to me, why bother having the band under contract if he was going to give away all the best songs to other artistes? It just didn't make any sense.

Mickey Gee and I were always the most confrontational members of the band, and we ended up having a blazing row with Gordon. All our frustrations from the past year boiled over. Tom took a back seat. When it came to confrontations with Gordon he was a bit of a shrinking violet, he'd stoke us all up beforehand, but he wouldn't say a word in Gordon's presence.

The argument ended in a stalemate with us threatening to pack it all in and head back home, and Gordon promising to do his best to persuade Les Reed to let us release the song. But Tom didn't want to leave it there, he'd set his heart on that song. He took to visiting Gordon two or three times a day trying to coax him into letting him release the song. Tom thought it would be less confrontational if it was just him doing the asking, or so he told us anyway. What we subsequently learnt was that he was lobbying hard for a solo release and was putting some distance between himself and the band. He thought Gordon might go for that. But Gordon stuck to his guns and insisted the song was for Sandie Shaw.

But then his hand was forced and he had little choice. A few days later Les and Gordon had a meeting with Sandie Shaw's famously volatile manager, Eve Taylor. Gordon presented Taylor with the acetate of 'It's Not Unusual', telling her it was a sure fire hit. After listening to the track for all of twenty seconds she asked, 'Which of my acts is this for?'

'Sandie Shaw,' Les and Gordon answered.

'This record will never be a hit,' Eve Taylor informed them bluntly and turfed them out of her office.

On hearing the news we were jumping with joy. This is it we thought he has to give it to us now. But we were to be sadly disappointed. Gordon informed us that Les Reed had arranged a big-band sound for 'Not Unusual'. They both thought this was the best way forward and a tight-knit group sound just wasn't part of the arrangement.

'To put it bluntly,' said Gordon, 'You boys are not going to be on the record.'

Gordon began lining up session musicians for the recording instead. At first we couldn't quiet take it in. We had spent years playing with Tom and had our own distinctive sound. Now we were being sidelined, shoved into the background. It was a bitter pill to swallow. Tom and Gordon tried to put a spin on it, saying we would all benefit if the record was a hit. But after all we had been through together it just didn't seem right or proper. Whichever way you looked at it just didn't make any sense. If Gordon's intention had always been to push Tom as a solo act then why go through the rigmarole of signing the whole band and dragging us up to London? In retrospect it was probably his intention all along to ditch us eventually, we were a means to an end. That end being: Tom under contract and settled in London under Gordon's wing.

We were pretty demoralized. But what could we do? Go on strike? Send Tom to Coventry? Tom told us if we had a hit on our hands we'd all be sitting pretty. So we got over our disappointment and all got behind the decision for a 'big band' sound as opposed to our sound.

The first recording session was a total waste of money, it was a complete disaster. The arrangement was just all wrong. That session was recorded at Decca's studio in West Hampstead and Tom's verdict was, 'It wasn't really happening. The music was all wrong.' So it was back to the drawing board and another session was booked. This time the arrangement was changed from a jazz feel, smooth and silky, to something far funkier and with a more positive beat. There were plenty of brass instruments, trumpets, trombones, saxophones; it was a big raucous dance band sound. I remember thinking at the time that it was pretty meaty and brash.

There were around twenty musicians, gathered around Tom. He was in a small recording booth, no bigger than a shower cubicle, and that helped muffle the awesome sound of the orchestra. I was fascinated by the actions of one particular musician. He'd been booked for the session and paid an equal fee to the others, but all he did for the entire duration was rub a sheet of sandpaper in a circular fashion on a wooden stool. It made a distinctive 'shh, shh, shh' rasping rhythmic sound into the mike.

Our old friend Peter Sullivan was there, we still hadn't entirely forgiven him for over producing our earlier track 'Chills and Fever'. But he was a good record producer and a complete perfectionist. I remember him giving Tom a really hard time during the session. He wasn't entirely happy with Tom's singing. Time after time he kept pushing him to give a bit more. Take after take, again and again. He saved every single take in case Tom's voice packed in. But it was the final take of the day that finally nailed it.

It was a real tense evening's work. Back then the singer and the backing had to be in real time. We didn't have the recording facilities we take for granted today. Every take was a fresh combination of both elements. I felt sorry for the brass musicians, they're lips must have been red raw the following morning. I'll always remember Peter Sullivan addressing the orchestra from the control room, at the end of the session, via the intercom, 'Thank you gentleman, for your patience and co-operation. I do believe we have a hit record. Goodnight.'

With Christmas only six weeks away Decca decided not to release the record until the New Year. There was far too much competition with other artistes fighting for that elusive number one slot on Christmas Day. Gordon was at the end of his tether, he was coming apart at the seams. No one knew what the future might yield. It's fair to say that if the record didn't work out it would have been the end of everything; it was the last roll of the dice.

Gordon confided in me that he owed the bank £1000 as it was; this was a bloody large amount in those days. He had already sold off everything of value that he owned and was just getting by on the essentials. Although, as I pointed out at the time, so were we. We were starving on a wage of one pound a day and all the revenue from gigs was going directly to him. We both agreed we were all in it together and when we finally made it, as we all hoped we would, the spoils would be distributed evenly. It was the first time that Gordon had really opened up to me on an emotional level. He went on to tell me that Jo was having problems with her second pregnancy. She was ill and in hospital at the time. It was all very worrying, especially for a young couple. They were still only in their late twenties.

Christmas arrived and everyone was feeling a bit depressed and on tenterhooks. The euphoria of not losing the song to Sandie Shaw had long dissipated. We all realised the chances of having a hit record were still comparatively remote in the grand scheme of things. No one was kidding themselves. Gordon was broke, we were broke, and all our gig money seemed to go into the black hole of keeping the whole venture afloat. Gordon turned up at the flat sheepishly and admitted there would be no Christmas dinner that year, he couldn't even afford boiled rice. There was nothing else for it but to head back home to Wales.

It was a nail biting time for Gordon, he had put all his eggs in the one basket. 'It's Not Unusual' simply had to be a hit. The pressure was getting to him and he took me aside before we all broke up for the hitch hike home. He was a little worried that we all might enjoy ourselves a bit too much at home, what with decent regular food and being amongst family and friends. He thought we might not come back. I assured him he didn't have to worry; we had come too far and suffered too much to pack it all in now.

D-Day was fast approaching alright. What I didn't know back then, but obviously recognise now, was that 'Not Unusual' was truly unique. Put in perspective the charts at the time were strongly biased in favour of pop groups. The whole Liverpool bands scene had fostered a certain climate: The Beatles and The Rolling Stones had spawned a whole generation of artistes and the charts had been teeming with them for years. The public was receptive to something a little bit different.

And suddenly this 'hybrid' song was released into the mix: a blend of Motown and traditional dance band, with cutting rhythm guitar and biting lead guitar. There was a hint of Latin rhythm sexing it up and coupled with Tom's contribution of soul and pop vocal it was really out there. Tom's jarring machismo actually offset the feminine lyrics in a really powerful way, adding an extra level of depth. Gordon's wife Jo had composed most of the lyrics with Sandie Shaw in mind, but Tom made them his own.

It was one of those happy accidents that strike the right chord at the right time. The lack of macho lyrics became advantageous. Tom's big drawback at the time was that he didn't fit the typical pop star profile. The press cruelly described him as 'the brick layer singer'. All the solo singers back then were Elvis and Cliff Richard clones, good looking, silky smooth rock n rollers and balladeers. Gordon was no mug. He took this all on board and went about softening Tom's image.

'It's Not Unusual' was released at the end of January 1965. It was promoted on radio with a couple of appearances on television. Tom's stage wear for those appearances was black leather. Gordon quickly realised that was a big mistake, the audience weren't receptive to that side of Tom. Then came the big one: Top of the Pops. That was the make and break appearance during that era. It was a short hop up the road from our flat in Lime Grove. Tom made his appearance on that all important show dressed entirely in white: virginal wool sweater, trousers and white patent shoes. He looked so clean and pure it was if the show had cut to a commercial break for Persil washing powder. One of the boys piped up that he was surprised that Gordon hadn't made him get his hair dyed peroxide blonde just like Joe Meek's buddy Heinz.

The song hit a chord and went into the charts at number twenty-two. Then it started climbing and by a quirk of fate it got to number one on St David's Day. You couldn't have made it up! How about that for the hand of God or Kismet or whatever your belief. It was obviously written that the boy from Wales would smash the charts on our patron saint's day.

8

IT'S NOT UNUSUAL

A number one hit record. We all cracked the bubbly at Gordon's flat at Campden Hill Towers. The champagne was flowing, it was a massive relief and celebration all rolled into one. All of Gordon's friends came along to join in the celebrations: Englebert Humperdink, Les Reed and the money men who had helped him out when things were really bad, Mike Bradley and the agent Phil Solomon. Those guys were especially pleased, knowing they'd invested their money wisely. The Welsh singer Dorothy Squires was there as well. She'd had quite a bit to drink and was swearing like a docker, turning the air blue.

Tom and the band were knocking back the beer and helping themselves to the buffet. Gordon was walking on air, he was in the clouds. He was wearing a left-over paper hat from a Christmas cracker and wandering the room with a grin plastered to his face. He was merrily topping up everyone's champagne glasses. His eyes were wild with excitement, he had finally pulled it off.

'It's Not Unusual' was being played over and over again, much to Tom's delight. Although Dorothy Squires wasn't particularly enamored and told Gordon as much, 'For fucks sake Gordon, change the fucking record will you. Put one of my fucking songs on.' Up to that point I don't think I'd ever heard a woman swear and here was Dorothy Squires peppering her speech with expletives. I was pretty shocked, let me tell you. Tom said as much to me and told me he'd never heard such foul language coming from the lips of a woman. We both reckoned even the call girls we had befriended down at the Grove would have been shocked.

Dorothy was married to the suave and sophisticated film star Roger Moore at that time, and this made it even more shocking somehow. She was certainly a character was our Dot.

As the evening wore on we were all getting pretty rowdy, surfing a wave of elation. Quite suddenly Gordon approached me a little the worse for wear and he snapped something with his fingers, directly under my nose. Suddenly I was reeling I felt as if I'd hit a brick wall at a hundred miles an hour. Momentarily stunned, I then felt an incredible rush that sent me soaring. Gordon wagged his finger at me and roared with laughter. My legs were giving out under me and I staggered to a nearby chair. Tom and the boys gathered around fearful that I'd had a heart attack. Gordon slurred drunkenly, 'I bet that blew you're bloody head off Vernon. Don't worry, its only Amyl Nitrate, you'll soon feel okay,' and with that he wobbled off, tossing the empty Amyl Nitrate phial into an ashtray.

The aftershock left me feeling queasy and on top of all the beer and champagne I'd consumed, really nauseous. I just about made it to the toilet before throwing up. It affected me for the rest of the evening. Amyl Nitrate is a powerful stimulant that causes the heart to pound extremely fast. The veins and arteries dilate and blood rushes through the body at an accelerated rate. This often causes dizziness. Medically it's used in the treatment of angina, where the heart isn't receiving enough blood, due to narrow veins and arteries. Notably it has the same effect on the system as Viagra.

I wish Viagra had been discovered in 1965. Gordon wouldn't have needed to be using Amyl Nitrate to get his kicks and I wouldn't have had a bloody bass drum pounding inside my head. Later I told him in no uncertain terms never to pull a trick like that on me again.

At that stage, Chris Ellis, our former roadie from Wales and blessed bringer of food parcels, came to join us in London. He was now enlisted as our permanent official roadie. When 'Not Unusual' first appeared in the charts Gordon decided we needed a full time driver to take us along to all the gigs that were springing up. We were now very much in demand. Up until that point, Tom and the band had been taking it in turns to drive the van. Looking back it was madness, none of us carried a license to drive, we were all of us breaking the law and had been for quite a while.

Gordon had set his mind on hiring an old friend of his as our roadie. But I argued that Chris Ellis had been with the band almost from the outset. In addition to that he had always been there for us in our times of greatest need. Gordon was having none of it. Stubborn as a mule, he refused to take Chris on. One evening we were changing into our stage gear in the toilet of the venue we were performing at. Gordon and I started arguing over the roadie position. Things got heated very quickly. The issue had dragged on for some time at that point. Both our voices were echoing off the tiled walls, which seemed to magnify the argument even more than usual. He finally cracked and gave in, which was most unusual as Gordon never gave in. The band were pleased that Chris was now our official roadie and all slapped me on the back. Gordon's face was a picture, he was giving me daggers when he left and cursed me under his breath. I remember thinking at the time that I'd better watch my back. I was later to be proved right in that regard.

Tom's arch rival at that time was the American heart throb, P.J. Proby. He was a handsome, pony-tailed Texan. Proby had decided to try his luck in the United Kingdom and already had three chart hits under his cowboy belt. He was top dog alright and had become used to hogging the solo-singer limelight. The girls would go crazy for him. They loved his powerful slow vibrato voice and suggestive stage antics. P.J. wore velvet blouses and extremely tight velvet trousers. His trademark was a black velvet bow that held his pony-tail in place.

Proby had landed a plum spot on a major Cilla Black tour which started at the end of January. The tour was booked into all the major UK cities and the bill included The Fourmost, Sounds Incorporated and the American Singer, Tommy Roe.

Things didn't get off to a good start. Within a few performances Proby's tight pants split wide open, from his bum to his thigh. It was something he had a penchant for, especially when he wanted some serious screaming from his female fans. He used to drop suddenly to a squat and the trouser seams just couldn't take the strain. They would split wide open and Proby would shamelessly milk it for all he was worth.

It happened once too often and the wild American singer was fired. Rules back then were as tight as his pants. Things were pretty stringent and it's sufficient to say less broad-minded. So there was a gap to be filled on the tour and opportunity came a knocking. We joined the tour during the first week of February, just as 'Unusual' was shooting up the charts like a rocket. It was perfect timing for adding the song to our usual set. Tom sang it at every venue in every city and it went down a storm. Gordon balked at the cost of providing an orchestra for the song so there was no big band sound. We pared it back to a four-piece arrangement and made it really tight. The reaction from the audiences was electric, they loved it. I remember mentioning to Gordon at the time that, due to the reaction we were getting from playing it live, what was the reasoning for going with the big band sound in the first place? He just shrugged.

On that tour we roamed far and wide, we were constantly on the move. Up and down the M1 in and out of London we hardly had time to pause for breath. Sometimes in the early hours of the morning we'd stop for breakfast at Watford Gap Services, which we christened 'Gobblers Gulch'. On a few occasions we bumped into Elton John and his band, who had decided on post-gig bacon and eggs, the same as us.

It was around 4am on the 21st February when Chris Ellis parked the van outside a greasy spoon restaurant. There was a gang of tired lorry drivers huddled around a smoky coal burning stove outside. They were sipping their mugs of tea and scanning the early editions of the morning papers. What they must have made of us mop-haired musicians God only knows. They all rolled their eyes as we trooped past.

We crowded around a table and ordered five sausage sandwiches with five piping hot teas. Chris checked the budget and we had just about enough to fill our faces and fill the van with petrol to get us back to Lime Grove. We all ate in silence we were so tired, we just wanted to get some food in us and then to flop into bed. On the way back to the van Chris cheekily asked one of the truckers if he could borrow his newspaper for a second. The great big bear of a man reluctantly obliged.

Chris hastily flipped through the pages. We all knew exactly what he was searching for: the current record listings. Suddenly he gave out a whoop of joy, 'It's Not Unusual' was at number twenty-one and climbing. Tiredness forgotten we were all running around like maniacs, whopping and hollering. The gang of truckers just stared blankly at us thinking we were nuts. Chris showed them the chart listings and pointed at us and Tom, and told them we were on the way to a number one single.

The truckers all barred our way back to the van and insisted we sign every newspaper with our autographs. We all piled back onto the van elated, dawn was rising when we got back to Lime Grove and suddenly none of us felt like going to bed.

Gordon was beside himself. Having written a number one hit with Les and having it performed by a singer he was managing, he was on a roll. It meant double bubble, he was raking it in and for once his bank manager was a very happy man. It was all such a turnaround from a couple of months previously. He rushed down to the flat to show off his new watch, he'd had to sell the previous one to keep the band going. Then he dropped the bombshell.

Gordon thought it was best that Tom now moved into his own place, obviously the band would keep Lime Grove, but he thought Tom needed to be in his own space. We were all a bit taken aback; up to that point in time we'd been a very tight knit bunch of mates looking out for each other. It was a bit of a wrench to suddenly separate just like that and with no advance warning. I remember looking at Tom to gauge his reaction and was surprised to see his suitcase already packed and sitting at his feet. They'd obviously already discussed it beforehand and this was the send-off. Gordon and Tom trotted off to his blue Jaguar XJ6, turned it over with a roar, and sped off with a little wave.

We all felt a little deflated. It was unusual with Tom no longer with us twenty-four-seven. We'd all got so used to having each other around through all the turmoil and hard work. It just didn't seem the same after that.

Later Gordon called a band meeting with me, Chris Slade, Dave Cooper and Mickey Gee. He announced that things were on the up and we should all be very happy. Then he soured the mood somewhat by announcing that from now on we were all to be paid the princely sum of twenty pounds a week. We all knew that money had been flooding in through the success of 'It's Not Unusual' so you can forgive us for being a little taken aback. At that time twenty pounds was considerably less than the average weekly wage. I pointed out the fact that we'd been starving up to that point waiting for our break, and surely we all should share a bit in the success of a chart hit. Gordon wasn't having any of it. He went on and on about how he had to reinvest the profits to keep the band moving forward. Gordon pointed out that he'd have to spend an awful lot on a full make-over for Tom, stardom demanded it, and handmade shirts, suits and stage wear didn't come cheap.

The real sting was in the tail though; we were utterly stunned when Gordon informed us that out of our twenty pounds a week wage he was deducting one pound at source to pay back our food allowance from the time spent at the Calcutta. Not only that, we would now have to pay for our own accommodation on the road, as well as taking on the rent for the flat in Lime Grove. You could have heard a pin drop. We realised that we'd soon have to find cheaper lodgings as there was no way we could finance the flat as well as accommodation on tour; it was a real kick in the teeth.

Gordon's parting shot was to inform us that we'd have to be responsible for our own tax affairs as he didn't have the time to sort all that out. As for being responsible for paying our own tax, filling in returns and paying stamp, we didn't know where to start.

What was going on? Tom and Gordon were doing very well for themselves and the band had been kicked into touch. We tried to get hold of Tom to see what he thought about all this but he'd decamped to Gordon's flat and moved Linda and his son Mark in with him. He kept promising to meet up and discuss the issue, but kept making excuses as he was house hunting with Linda at the time, and viewing potential properties was taking up all his time. He eventually moved into an ultra-modern house in Shepperton, 89 Manygate Lane, for which he paid £7,000 in cash. After Tom failed to show up for yet another meeting the band asked me to go and speak with Gordon, which I duly did. After explaining our grievances and asking for a more equitable share in the success of 'It's Not Unusual', Gordon was his usual charming self and said, 'If you don't like my terms, you can all piss off back to the valleys.'

Considering that's where both he and Tom had also come from, it was a bit demeaning to say the least. Go back to Ponty?

Go back to what exactly? We had all sacrificed our jobs to get this far and struggled through the lean times together. Now there was a chasm opening up with Gordon and Tom on the one side and the band on the other. It caused a hell of a lot of bad feeling. What an awful way to be treated, especially as Gordon and Tom were on a spending spree and took every delight in showing off their new acquisitions to the band.

Tom's appearance changed dramatically in a short space of time. As that summer rolled on so did his taste for the good life. He took to wearing expensive handmade suits cut by top West End tailor, Dougie Millins. He'd drop by the flat to show off handmade shirts, ties, shoes and jewellery. He had a bunch of gold rings, identity bracelets and neck chains, one of his favourites had a huge chunky gold cross attached. Tom's humble Woodbines had been replaced by expensive Havana cigars. Gordon had also finally sorted out Tom's driving test; rather than take it in London, it had been arranged in Bristol, where it was assumed he'd stand more chance of passing. He duly did and turned up at Lime Grove in a gleaming new white Volvo sports car, the same model that Roger Moore had made famous in the television series 'The Saint'.

Happily stunned by the success of 'Not Unusual', we were now unhappily stunned by the way things were moving. It was great for Tom and Gordon but not so great for the rest of us. We all discussed packing it all in, but decided to muddle on in the hope that after another hit we might actually share in the spoils. Looking back we were young and naive. But on the upside we were certainly getting a lot of attention and there were a lot of amorous distractions along the way that cushioned the blow somewhat, we were certainly really hot at that time and took full advantage.

Around that time we paid a visit to our old stomping ground in Ladbroke Grove. Not because we missed the 'Calcutta' but because Gordon had asked us to set up our gear for a session at All Saints Church, close to Clydesdale Road. It was mid-afternoon and Gordon was being all mysterious. He wanted Tom and the band ready on stage for a good jam session. Gordon finally arrived accompanied by one of the world's greatest composers, Burt Bacharach. He was there to audition Tom for the soundtrack to a new Woody Allen comedy. The film that was in production at the time was 'What's New Pussycat', starring the great comic actor Peter Sellers.

Even at that stage of his career, Burt Bacharach was a living legend. He'd had a precarious start to his career with his songs rejected time after time. But he finally scored a major hit with Perry Como's 'Magic Moments' and went on to write one hit after another for the cream of American talent, along with his lyricist Hal David.

It was a magic moment for us and we belted out a number of songs from our act: 'I Can't Stop Loving You,' 'Stand By Me,' and 'The Midnight Hour'.

Burt Bacharach was a slight figure of a man, he stood stony faced throughout the audition, and he left as quietly as he had arrived. But he gave the nod to Gordon on his exit, Tom was in. Gordon played Tom a demo of the music he was to record for the film and he was less than impressed. He was down the Grove in a shot complaining to us all about it, he described it as, 'humpty dumpty music, all over the place.' Even the title had put him off, 'What's New Pussycat'. I had to agree with him wholeheartedly, everything about it sounded gay. Nevertheless Gordon had set his mind on it and would brook no dissent. Tom enlisted our help in trying to dissuade Gordon but he was adamant and would not budge. Gordon wore Tom down as he always did and Tom took the credit for singing the hugely successful films title track. It was a huge hit and Tom had Gordon to thank for his persistence in making him record the song.

We were still on the road and enjoying the adulation. We started to gather quite a sizeable female following at this stage. You can imagine the results on a bunch of kids from the valleys of South Wales. From our teens up until this point girls had been exotic foreign creatures, always difficult to score with. Chapel preachers back in Wales were always warning them about the perils of copulation and the inherent sins of being, God Forbid, loose. Now it felt like we had struck gold, they were throwing themselves at us and, well I must admit it was pretty difficult to say no. Well I'd be lying if I said we didn't get stuck in, we were young and full of energy after all.

We were all recognized from being on television with Tom and from playing venues up and down the whole UK. Scoring with girls quickly became a bit of a sport amongst us and helped take our mind of the fact we were getting shafted on the pay front by Gordon. Tom quickly decided to muck in with the boys. Gordon had bought a new Commer van for the band and booked us into B and B's up and down the county, which we had to pay for ourselves. He'd planned for Tom to travel separately and be in far more salubrious accommodation. But as soon as Tom realised just how much fun we were having he chucked those plans in and threw in his lot with us. He didn't like being on his own and there was always more fun to be had with the gang and the copious amount of groupies which were orbiting us. It allowed him the vanity of playing 'top dog' and boy did he enjoy it.

Mid tour Gordon dropped another bombshell. He'd decided to add three more musicians to our line-up; trumpeters Tony Mabett and Australian Frank Chapman, and Doug Firth on tenor sax. Our previous stage gear had been blue Marks and Spencer shirts, black trousers and black leather waistcoats. Now thanks to the new members to the band we were being measured for dark blue mohair suits. We all waited with bated breath for Gordon to send us a bill for the tailoring, but thankfully it never arrived, that's not to say he probably took it out of our wages at source.

At around that time we had our first major appearance on BBC television's 'Billy Cotton Bandshow' on March 13th 1965 and that was immediately followed by ITV's 'Beat Room', alongside 'The Kinks', 'John Lee Hooker' and 'Julie Rogers'. The phone lines back home to the valleys were red hot, letting everyone know to tune in and watch us.

Then we were off to Glasgow appearing on 'Scottish Round Up' and straight onto a converted church in Manchester to record 'Top of the Pops'. Then we were booked to appear on ITV's successful show 'Crackerjack' hosted by Leslie Crowther. We shared the bill with 'The Animals', and the risqué girls' dance troupe, 'Pan's People'. We went straight from that recording to appear on 'Blue Peter'.

In between all this crazy exposure the band pulled me aside and showed me a recent newspaper article they weren't particularly happy with. It was an interview with Tom, and he'd said, 'One of the biggest effects is that success gives you more confidence in your work. Before, the group was getting fed up and disillusioned but now we all have a contented feeling.' The boys asked me to pull him up on this statement, after all it was a case of them and us at this stage with Gordon and Tom raking it in and the rest of us getting squarely shafted.

From the very start back in Ponty, even before Tom had teamed up with the Senators, I had always admired the bloke, not only because of his singing voice, but also because of his charismatic 'jack the lad' street wise ways. More importantly he knew his music inside out and I always respected him for that. I always felt we had a strong bond between us, we had shared an awful lot together, and not just music.

It was pretty evident to me at that time that the friendship and all we had shared was pretty strained. From that point onward I felt a little like a 'Walter Mitty' character. I was on the payroll, and I played along with things as best I could, as did the rest of the band. We played our parts both musically and socially but at the end of the day we couldn't entirely mask our disappointment. We all felt let down by Gordon and Tom, and who wouldn't? Put yourself in our place, if you had struggled and scrimped and toughed it out, then two of your number sailed off into the distance with untold riches, and with a casual 'see you boys' flung over the shoulder, how would you feel? Many years later Robin Eggar was writing a biography on Tom and came to talk to me about it. I remember talking over this time with him and explaining our disappointment and I'll never forget what he said, 'Tom Jones is like a Ming vase Vernon, with an ugly crack running down its centre.'

Our first performance with the new brass section was on April 11th. We were booked to play at the NME Poll Winners' Concert in front of 12,000 screaming fans at the Empire Pool in Wembley. The bill comprised: 'The Beatles', 'The Rolling Stones', 'The Animals', 'Dusty Springfield', and 'P.J. Proby.'

What a line up! We could hardly wait to take our place on stage. It was a Sunday afternoon and backstage, seeing all those legends nervously waiting their turn to go on, and fiddling around with their appearances and instruments, well it was quite something. The stage was immense, it was mostly taken up with Vox amplification it was a real amphitheatre.

We raised our game when we went on to compete with the amount of talent around us. Straight after our performance we rushed across London to 'The Palladium'. We were booked to appear live on 'Saturday Night At The Palladium'. It was a real thrill to be standing on the rotating stage for the finale, waving to the audience both in the auditorium and back home via the television. We all knew our folks and friends back home were glued to the telly waiting for our performance, it gave us a real lift.

That was all but a taste, we went onto to appear regularly on television with Tom, and loved every minute of it. A real highlight was appearing on the 'Royal Command Performance' in November 1967. The lineup included Tommy Cooper, Lulu, and Bob Hope, and it was compered by Jimmy Tarbuck. The band was particularly pleased as finally we were credited for the first time on the credits at the end. Up to that point Gordon had managed to get us white-washed out of all previous appearances. We didn't realise at the time, but every time he got us white-washed he pocketed our appearance fees, and didn't have to pay us; he pocketed all the fees himself.

The first I got wind of it was when the tax man came calling. Having not bothered to fill in our tax returns after Gordon cut us loose on that score, I had no invoices, petrol bills, or expenses receipts when the tax man came. They hit me with an almighty bill, way more than was fair or affordable, and then they demanded extra on my undeclared fees from all my appearances on television shows. I didn't know what they were talking about as we hadn't been receiving any appearance fees; it turned out Gordon had been pocketing all our fees without telling us.

The TV companies were obliged to pay a standard fee for each appearance made, should the performers name appear on the credits. In other words we were being paid the same fee as Tom for each television appearance. I have no idea if Tom was in on this scam, but Gordon was raking it in on our behalf and paying us nothing in return. It later transpired that he was pulling the same trick with Englebert Humperdink, and fiddling him out of all his television appearance fees. I later found out that the money Gordon was raking in from the television fees alone was pretty substantial and amounted to thousands of pounds.

I remember Tom telling me at the time that, 'Roy Orbison deals with his own financial affairs, something I couldn't handle myself, what with being caught up on the road, singing and stuff.' He would have had a fit if he knew back then what Gordon was up to.

At that time Gordon had moved into a suite of plush new offices in Bond Street and formed a fledgling new company called MAM to oversee operations. He'd made himself and Tom directors of the new enterprise. I told the tax man in no uncertain terms to take his enquiries there, as I didn't have the foggiest idea about any television appearance fees. I was so angry I told him, 'Tell those greedy thieving bastards to deal with it.' The Inland Revenue must have taken my advice because they never got back to me.

Gordon had set his sights on the United States as the next target. The band had a brief respite and opportunity to take a break and take stock. 'It's Not Unusual' had climbed to number 10 in the US charts. Gordon had big plans for tackling the American market and had arranged a spot on CBS TV's 'The Ed Sullivan Show'. This was the same show that Elvis had famously appeared on almost a decade previously. They only showed him from the waist up as they thought his wild movements were too suggestive for the audience tuning in from coast to coast. Gordon was terrified of flying, but the financial stakes were too high to be ignored.

Gordon and Tom both flew to the states on April 28th and made the first of five appearances on television, earning a whopping £2000 per show.

A week later upon their return we were back on the road. Gordon had organized a month's variety tour of the UK, supported by Englebert Humperdink, comedian Dave Allen and a stunningly beautiful twenty year old singer from Abercrave.

Her name was Mia Lewis, but some considerable time later here surname would change to Hopkins, on our wedding day.

Mia Lewis was already living in London, staying with her uncle and aunt in Crouch End. She had left Wales at about the same time as The Senators to make it big in the smoke. Mia was under the same umbrella as the rest of the acts on the tour, the Acuffe Rose Agency. The London office of the agency was run by Colin Berlin and his understudy nephew, Alan Field. Mia had recently launched the first of six releases on a new London label and was getting good airtime. She was petite and vivacious with a lovely singing voice. The tour started at the New Theatre in Cardiff and was followed by concerts at the Theatre Royal and The Hippodrome Theatres' in Birmingham and Bristol.

Each venue was fully booked and the month tour positively whizzed by. I remember being in the foyer of the New Theatre meeting some of my family before the start of the show. I was taken aback when I caught sight of my old headmaster, Mr Railton, amongst the crowd. I must say it caused me to wince a little as I had an image in my mind's eye of him thrashing me six times with his willow cane. I never bothered to approach him and reminisce about my schooldays. The tour was a great success and the whole cast went their separate ways, including Mia. It would be almost a year before we'd bump into each other again.

Straight after the tour Tom flew back to America for another appearance on the Ed Sullivan Show. Whilst he was away Jo Meek came back to haunt us. The crazy record producer was still very much alive at that stage. Later in 1967 Meek killed his landlady Violet Shenton and then himself with a single-barreled shotgun. Joe was annoyed when he found out that Tom and the band had been signed by Decca Records. He released two of the tracks we had recorded with him back in 1963: 'Little Lonely One' and a B-side 'That's What Love Will Do'. This time he had no problem in finding a record company to release the songs. He sold them to Columbia Records (UK) and Tower Records (USA). 'Little Lonely One' reached number forty-two on America's Billboard chart. The UK release came out at around the same time as Gordon had decided to release 'Once Upon A Time'. Many of the fans decided they preferred the earlier Joe Meek recording and bought 'Little Lonely One' instead of our latest release, which got stuck at a dismal number thirty in the UK charts.

Gordon was furious and Tom went ballistic, calling Meek a 'thieving swine'. Tom told the media at the time, 'Little Lonely One is something I could well do without. I made it a long time ago and tastes have changed a lot since then. They were tough days when the group and I made that record. We were called Tommy Scott and The Senators back then and we really pinned all our hopes on that recording session with Joe Meek. I think it's dated and I want to disassociate myself from it entirely.'

Joe Meek was far from happy and came back with both barrels blazing, 'I have four other tapes which I would like to release. Tom and The Senators auditioned for me and nobody wanted to know about him because it was a time when the group scene was very 'in' and everyone said Tom sang too well. I originally did him singing 'Chills and Fever', the record Decca finally released and re-recorded. I wouldn't have released 'Little

Lonely One' if I thought it was poor. I think this is a very good record.'

Gordon and Tom were seething that Joe Meek had beaten them in the charts with the earlier recording, and that they were receiving no payments for the success of 'Little Lonely One'. Joe never did get to release those other tracks as two years later he committed suicide.

9

WHAT'S NEW PUSSYCAT?

The Joe Meek recordings weren't the only ones we did along the way. The band had missed out on recording 'Not Unusual' but just prior to the brass section joining us we went into the studio to record four songs for an EP (Extended Play): 'Bama Bama Bama Loo', 'I Can't Stop Loving You', 'Lucille', and 'Little By Little'. The recording was entitled 'Tom Jones On Stage' .Well there was no stage and all the screaming you hear in the background was added in the studio. In truth the title should have been 'Tom Jones In Studio'.

The EP was well received and became a big seller. Naturally the band didn't receive a penny for our contribution, but at least on this occasion Gordon had actually credited us on the record. The EP went out as 'Tom Jones and the Squires'. Whenever I raised this issue with Gordon he'd always fob me off with one excuse or another: he was re-investing profits, we were still paying off our food and lodging from 'Calcutta days', money was tied up in studio time etc. We received the same treatment two years later when we recorded 'Live At The Talk Of The Town'.

We played a month there in 1967 and recorded the show for release. It was hugely successful, but again we didn't receive a penny. Gordon just paid us an extra ten pounds a week on top of our wage of twenty pounds. It was a far from equitable split especially as both Tom and Gordon had recently moved to St. George's Hill, Weybridge's stockbroker belt. They had purchased palatial mansions complete with swimming pools and tennis courts. Gordon had even installed his own personal zoo. There were tigers, chimpanzees, orangutans, and a one-eyed silver back gorilla called Ollie. One of the band piped up that those animals were better treated than us.

At that time the band was living in separate accommodation a few miles from Weybridge. All we could afford was digs; my landlady was technically breaking the law by taking me in as a lodger in her council house.

When Tom returned the second time from America and his appearance on the Ed Sullivan Show, he began promoting 'What's New Pussycat'. By this stage we all knew our position with Gordon and Tom; we were all disillusioned with the state of affairs but just got on with it. We tried to keep our spirits up by having as many laughs as possible and simply riding with the tide. There was talk about touring Australia in the New Year, 'Chills and Fever' had become a big hit down under. Our mantra had become, 'Sod those miserly bastards, let's make the best of it and see as much of the world as we can.' It was pointless trying to reason with Gordon, he just had no intention of ever paying us properly for our efforts; he was far too busy lining his own pockets.

Around this time our roadie Chris Ellis broke his arm. It was just before we had to move out of Lime Grove. We had a golden rule that if one of the band got lucky and happened to bring a girl back for the evening then the others would move into another room to provide some privacy. One particular evening I got lucky and Chris moved into the room with Dave Cooper to afford me and the lady a little privacy.

We were in the back bedroom which looked onto the yard. Left of the window was an extension which housed a toilet. I noticed the curtains were half open but thought nothing of it. Pretty soon we had both divested ourselves of our clothes and were locked in a passionate embrace. Suddenly there was an ear-piercing scream followed by a dull thud from outside. I rushed to the window, below in the moonlight was our intrepid roadie. Chris was wailing and crying out in pain. It was around 11pm and suddenly the whole house came alive. Our landlord rushed into the back yard to see what all the commotion was about. Chris was in a bit of a state with a badly broken arm. He seemed badly concussed and kept muttering about having fallen out of the toilet window.

We took him to the nearest hospital and they checked him over and put his arm in plaster. By the time we got him back home and safely tucked up in bed, my girlfriend had upped and left. The following morning I was using the toilet and wondering how the hell Chris had managed to fall through the window. He would have had to have been standing on the toilet seat. I opened the narrow window and looked down. It was quite a drop. If Chris had fallen on his head he would have been a goner.

When I leaned out the window I could see Chris tucked up in bed, pumped full of painkillers. The dressing table mirror provided a perfect viewpoint. Then it hit me. Our broken-armed roadie had positioned the dressing mirror to get the best possible angle on the bed. He must have lost his balance while perched on the toilet and toppled out the window.

Later when he was well on the road to recovery we teased him mercilessly with hilarious one-liners about his escapade. Chris emphatically denied getting up to any mischief, insisting that he wanted to get a bit of fresh air. He reckoned someone had stunk out the toilet before him. Well he got a little more fresh air than he bargained for that evening. He continues to deny having a peep, even to this very day, and of course we all believe him. Our poor roadie drove the Commer van for the next six weeks, steering with just the one hand.

Pretty soon we had a little band celebration; Tom and Gordon were not invited. We had finally paid back every penny that Gordon had spent on us at Clydesdale Road (The Calcutta). I still think it was really mean of him to claw back that money from us, especially as we were under contract and he was raking it in at the time. We did wonder what Gordon was paying the new brass section. After all they were all members of the Musicians Union, so we assumed they were getting a better deal than us. Unfortunately we never got to the bottom of it as Gordon had strictly told them not to tell us, on pain of dismissal.

August was upon us and we were on the move again. Before making the move to Weybridge we took on a ground floor flat in Fulham, it was considerably cheaper than Lime Grove. The place was quite shabby, but after the Calcutta we were used to slumming it and anywhere was an improvement on that place. With no more deductions we were now earning the princely sum of thirty pounds a week. I even managed to save a few quid. The brass section had really pumped up our sound, and our live shows were eagerly anticipated, we were packing them in up and down the country.

Tony Mabbett had learned to play trumpet as a bandsman in the Army. He was a hell of a nice guy, as was Dougie Firth on tenor sax. The other trumpeter, Frank Chapman, was a bit of a slimy character and none of us took to him. Tony and Dougie didn't like him either. Gordon had brought these three together; none of them had worked with each other previously. We nicknamed Tony 'The Phone King'. He practically lived in a phone kiosk and must have spent most of his wages in them. If mobile phones had been around back then Tony would have had one glued to his ear twenty-four-seven. One moment you'd be having a conversation with him, but if you got distracted for even a moment, you'd turn around and he would have disappeared to the phone kiosk. Dougie Firth was the complete opposite to Tony. Thin and quietly spoken, he wouldn't say boo to a goose. All three were incredibly talented musicians. Now with the band numbering seven individuals Gordon decided we needed an element of discipline, so he chose Frank Chapman as the new bandleader. The position went to Frank's head and he started to throw his weight around quite a bit. The first person in the firing line was poor old Tony Mabbett. I'll never forget Frank scolding him with his broad Australian accent, 'You can cut out disappearing round the corner to use the phone every five minutes, Mabbett.'

'What's it got to do with you?' said Tony.

'Gordon has made me bandleader and he wants to keep a tight ship. I like to know where everyone is at any given time. I don't want to be having to search for you, cobber, especially when we're due on stage or whatever.'

'Don't tell me when or not to phone, you Ozzie prick. I was

in the army, I don't let people down.'

It degenerated from there and we had to separate them, or Tony would have knocked his block off. Frank's new position hadn't got off to the best start. The fault lay in his condescending manner. He'd squint his eyes shut and stare narrowly at you as he spoke on any given subject he professed to be an expert on. It was mildly irritating to say the least and it used to drive Tony half up the wall. Eventually after one altercation too many and a constant tide of verbal challenges from the band, he told Gordon to stuff his bandleader position up his arse, unless he was paid double for putting up with all the abuse from the rest of us. Gordon of course refused and that was the end of the matter.

Tom's stock in the US was soaring, especially on the back of 'Not Unusual'. From August right through to the end of 1965 he would fly the Atlantic on numerous occasions. Dick Clark, the American host of ABC's long running TV show 'American Bandstand', was also involved in running a live tour throughout the States. The Dick Clark Caravan Show comprised of a dozen acts that would tour from coast to coast taking in over thirty-six cities. Gordon had managed to get Tom on board the Greyhound bus known as the 'Caravan of Stars'. He was cramped up alongside a host of stars: Sonny and Cher, The Turtles, The Shirelles, Peter and Gordon, the Jive Five, Ronnie Dove and Jackie DeShannon.

The Squires were left behind and went back to Ponty for a month, on a retainer of twenty pounds. Tom used the tour band which backed all the other stars on the bus. By the sound of things we didn't miss much by not going. Tom told us on his return that, 'it was bloody murder. The bus was packed to the seams with uncomfortable seats. We did a show and then got straight back on the bus again travelling through the night. We were sweating like pigs during the long hours' drive through the desert onto the next gig.'

Tom also complained about the tour band as they were unfamiliar with our material. The only highlight of the tour had been meeting Elvis on the set of his new film, 'Paradise Hawaiian Style'. 'It might have been paradise for Elvis,' moaned Tom, 'but it was Paradise Lost for me.' He told Gordon in no uncertain terms that he didn't want to do another tour like that.

Back in London after Tom's return we continued playing the clubs, theatres and ballrooms up and down the country. Dave Cooper had found himself a pretty dark-haired girlfriend. The rest of the band nicknamed her 'the Governor'. For the life of me I can't remember why. She wasn't bossy or demanding, she was rather petite and around the same height as him. They looked very comfortable together and Dai could hardly wait to get back off the road and into the Fulham flat to meet up with her. I was quite the reverse for the rest of us, we couldn't wait to get out of the grotty Fulham flat and back on the road gigging.

Dave's new found happiness was about to be cruelly shattered. Gordon, obsessed with money matters as always, felt that having to pay for the new brass section was a burden that would be less costly if there wasn't a rhythm guitar involved. Gordon's reasoning was that the brass filled out the overall sound and made rhythm guitar redundant. In one word Dave was expendable and was promptly informed of that fact by

Frank Chapman. But not before Frank had pleaded with Gordon to sack me instead and have Dave take over bass guitar.

Frank's reasoning for singling me out was pretty apparent. We had recently almost come to blows backstage at a theatre in the north. I'm a bit of a slow burner by nature but Frank wore me down. He was really getting up my nose with his high and mighty ways, lording it over the rest of us. He just wouldn't let up and continued his habit of giving everyone an unnecessary hard time. But his pleas to Gordon fell on deaf ears. Frank wasn't like the rest of us; we were all gutted to see Dave leave the band. Frank was gutted that it wasn't me leaving.

Dave had been with us since taking over from Keith Davies, long before we left for London. We all fondly recalled the days when we'd roll him out into the audience hidden in a drum case and he'd jump out dressed in a gorilla costume. How could Tom stand idly by and watch his loyal guitarist get blown out, without a whimper of protest to Gordon? He left without a penny of compensation for all his loyal contribution along the way. I felt really angry with both Tom and Gordon, it was merciless. We all now knew that the writing was on the wall, any one of us could be next for the chop. We were all expendable and when there was no further use for us we'd be turfed out without a second thought.

It was heartbreaking to see Dave pack his tatty suitcase containing all his worldly belongings and leave the flat with his girlfriend. With Christmas just around the corner it would be the last time any of us would ever see Dave again. He went back to Ponty and tried his hand at a number of different forms of employment, eventually emigrating to South Africa. I bumped into a mutual friend many years later who told me Dave 'couldn't stand being in the same country as Tom and Gordon, he didn't want to breathe the same air.' He was incredibly bitter about the way he had been treated and who could blame him.

Wherever he is, I hope that he's safe and well and doing fine for himself. Dave was a loveable character and a great musician. We all lost a great friend when he went. He deserved far better treatment from Tom and Gordon. Not long after Dave had gone Gordon had another bright idea. In January 1966 he decided to get rid of the brass section.

Gordon had settled on a cheaper alternative. Vic Cooper, no relation to the recently sacked Dave Cooper, was keyboard player with Johnny Kid and The Pirates. Vic was a lean, fair-haired twenty-three year old, and just like Tom his hero was Jerry Lee Lewis. Born in Battersea, south west London, Vic went to school with the legendary lead guitarist, Mick Green, who also played with Johnny Kid and the Pirates.

Gordon had been pestering Vic for weeks and weeks. He wanted him to join Tom and The Squires. At first Vic declined as he was happy with his current band and hadn't even considered leaving. But Gordon being Gordon refused to take no for an answer and kept hounding him, trying to wear him down. Gordon offered him the opportunity to tour Australia with us in the spring and dangled a forty pounds a week fee in front of his nose. Vic duly took the bait, and thanks to him we all got an extra ten pounds a week in our pay packet, Gordon realised he wouldn't be able to keep that one quiet for long.

Vic Cooper had a typical south London accent, flavoured with a touch of cockney. He was the original 'Mr. Smooth', always sharp in dress and wit. He'd recently passed his advanced driving test and was swanning around in a powerful blue Austin Healy sports car. Vic was an expert in chatting up the women, a real smooth talker just like Tom. The both of them were rampant pursuers of the opposite sex. Being from Wales we were all partial to beer and a lot of it, Vic on the other hand preferred Bacardi and Coke and was partial to smoking a lot of pot.

So we had come full circle and were now back to being a four piece band again. With a great keyboard player and singer we were rocking and used to belt out our set with gusto. Tom particularly loved the new Jerry Lee piano sound supplied by Vic and was in his element. We went back to knocking out rock n roll numbers: Joe Tex's 'Show Me', Wilson Picket's 'Land of a Thousand Dances', and 'Midnight Hour'. It was great having Vic around, he really boosted our moral.

One of Vic's first appearances with the Squires was on TV's 'Ready, Steady, Go', and this was followed by 'The David Nixon Show'. Vic hadn't appeared on TV with Johnny Kidd and The Pirates and was initially a bit taken aback by the sea change, but after clocking up a load of appearances he soon acclimatized and really took to it.

A few weeks after Vic joined the band, we were booked to appear at De Montfort Hall in Leicester. On the supporting bill were The Who and skiffle king Lonnie Donegan. While Lonnie was firing up the audience with 'My Old Man's a Dustman' and 'Rock Island Line', The Who were backstage fretting about their bass guitarist. He hadn't shown up and they were due on stage immediately after Lonnie Donegan. I was in our dressing room with the rest of the band; we were getting changed into our stage suits. Suddenly there was an urgent knocking at the door. I opened it and was confronted by a clearly agitated Roger Daltrey, 'Can I have a word with your bass player?'

'Sure, that's me,' I said.

'Do us a favour mate, our bass player hasn't turned up. Would you fill in for him?'

'What, you mean go on stage with the Who?'

'Yeah, mate, you must know 'My Generation' surely?'

'Well yeah, but I don't know all your songs, Roger.'

'Nah, well they're a doddle. Townsend will shout out the chords if you get stuck. We can't go on without a bass player, will you do it?'

It didn't take me long to chew it over, 'Christ, yeah okay.'

'Great,' and with that Daltrey turned and disappeared back to his dressing room. I was glassy-eyed and my heart was thumping. I remember thinking, what have I let myself in for? The Who were down for a forty minute spot. I spent the remainder of Lonnie's set feverishly practicing the bass solos from 'My Generation' and trying to remember all The Who's hits.

Standing in the wings watching Lonnie and his band take their final bows, my heart was going like the clappers and I was in a cold sweat. I ran my sweating hands up and down the neck of my Epiphone bass guitar getting myself ready. I felt a sudden tap on my shoulder. It was a beaming Roger Daltrey; he told me that Entwhistle had arrived just in the nick of time.

To be quite honest I gave a huge sigh of relief. But watching them perform a few moments later I did feel my moment of glory had been snatched away. They were electric and Townsend smashed his guitar to smithereens at the end of the set. We were also amused to see them hurling their amplifiers and loudspeakers down the fire stairs when they left the hall. You can imagine Gordon's reaction if we had ever tried something similar.

Vic was partial to rolling a joint before going on stage. It didn't seem to affect his ability to perform; he used to play great piano, or in this case Hammond organ. Vic was and always has been a complete wind-up merchant, the 'Gotcha' type. It was all harmless fun, although one time his humour went a little too far. Not long before we were due to depart for the month's tour of Australia we played a nightclub in Stoke-on-Trent. It was quite a mediocre club with a small stage and packed to bursting point. We were playing the Bailey circuit of small nightclubs all over the north of England. Each club included a casino and Tom and the boys would make a beeline on arrival straight for the croupiers. They would always be attractive young girls. I think it was part of the job description that they had to be knockout stunners. We'd lay on the patter with a trowel and try and line up some fun post gig.

Tom would always book into a small hotel and we would all pile into the nearest bed and breakfast nearby. We were normally booked to appear for a week in each nightclub before moving onto the next town. It was quite a hectic schedule at times, playing an early spot at one club and then racing across country to another venue, sometimes over thirty miles away. It did wear you down a bit.

Tom had released 'What's New Pussycat' by then along with a

number of other songs previously. But none of them had taken off like 'Not Unusual'. He was still riding on the success of that particular hit, and it was always our most eagerly anticipated song at all our gigs. Tom had also released 'Thunderball' at around that time for the James Bond film but it had bombed. It reached a dismal thirty-five in the UK charts and then sank without trace.

Still here we were packing them in nightly. We were performing all these heavily produced and orchestrated songs as a four piece band. Gordon hit on the idea of getting Vic to play Hammond organ instead of piano. This had the benefit of filling out the sound and the fill-ins on the records. It worked a treat and everyone, including Tom, felt very comfortable with the new arrangement.

Tom would be out centre front of stage with us nestling behind him. We were all so well-rehearsed at that stage of our careers that we could have performed the set blindfolded if required. But then came the crunch. I have no idea what Stoke-on-Trent is like today but back then I recall it being a very depressing and drab town. On that particular winter's day there was a steady icy drizzle, it was pretty bleak. We were due on stage at 10pm and we were getting ready after finishing booking into our bed and breakfast at around 7pm.

Just before we left Vic collared me and offered a drag on his monster sized spliff. I'd never tried it before, and really didn't fancy trying it now, so I declined. But Vic being Vic was incredibly insistent:

'Go on Vern, you look on a bit of a downer, this will cheer you up.'

'It's hardly surprising Vic, what with the weather and this town being a dump and all. But no it's not for me,' I remember telling him.

'Come on, take a drag or two,' I shook my head, 'It'll make you play better Vern, honest. Go on, take a pull.'

Vic went on and on at me, he was relentless, and I finally gave in, 'Go on then, pass it over.'

I took a tentative puff and felt nothing unusual, so I took another longer pull and handed it back. We all climbed into the van and headed for the club. We had sound checked earlier that afternoon so all we had to do was change into our stage gear.

Making our way toward the club entrance, I began feeling a little light-headed. Then Vic started getting up to his tricks, he told me we were being followed by a police officer, it was starting to make me feel really paranoid. By the time we were due on stage I was feeling wave after wave of light-headedness. I felt as if I was on a boat rocking on a turbulent sea. I told Vic I was feeling really strange. He had a devilish glint in his eyes and told me that two puffs wouldn't have much effect and not to worry.

On we went, performing a couple of openers before Tom sprang on stage. Everything was going smoothly until about half way through the set. We were mid-way through 'What's New Pussycat'. We used to provide the backing vocals to the chorus. Tom would sing, 'What's New Pussycat' and we would reply, 'Whow, whow, whow, whow'. That was when I lost it. I came in well behind the rest of the boys. Everything seemed to be going slow in my head; it was as if time had stopped. Tom turned to stare at me with an incredulous look on his face. The band never made mistakes, everything was second nature, and he was shocked.

I turned to Vic behind me. I was panicking and so was he. I didn't make another mistake during the number. But as soon as the song ended I began to walk off stage. I thought the show was over. I'd only got a couple of yards before Vic grabbed me and walked me back to my microphone stand. Tom hadn't seen it happen, he was busy introducing the next number.

I got through the rest of the set in a cold sweat. By the time I came off stage my head was more or less back together. Nothing was said about my strange behaviour. But when we got back to London, Gordon went ballistic. He confronted Vic and gave him a real dressing down; he went on to tell him, 'I know you're on it. But don't you dare let any of the boys try it again.'

That was the last time I saw Vic smoke a joint before we went on stage. I was under no illusion, Vic was a seasoned smoker and could handle it, but two puffs had almost sent me into orbit. I was never stupid enough to be tempted again, especially before going stage. I fully understood Gordon's concern. But it was a bit ironic that not long before he had snapped a phial of Amyl Nitrate right under my nose.

We continued playing the Bailey Clubs right up until going to Australia. It was essential that we had all the relevant jabs against tropical diseases. Our first stop on the tour was to be Sydney. We were all excited and couldn't wait to get started on the tour.

We finished the last of the UK tour in Blackburn and one

afternoon we all traipsed down to the local hospital for our jabs. The five of us mop-headed musicians caused a bit of a stir. We were all dressed in leather jackets and jeans, and were immediately recognized from all our TV appearances. The male nurse preparing to inject us made quite a fuss and told us he was a big fan. Job done, we were preparing to leave when the nurse pressed a clutch of disposable needles into our hands, 'don't tell a soul boys,' he whispered, 'they may come in handy.'

We all stared at him blankly when we filed out. It was only later that the penny dropped. As we climbed into the van Chris Ellis piped up, 'I told you to get your bloody haircut,' he moaned,' that nurse thinks you're a bunch of drug addicts.' We got shot of the needles but we didn't get our haircut.

10

AUSTRALIA

The flight from Heathrow to Australia took at least forty-eight hours back in 1966. We anxiously climbed aboard the notorious Boeing 707. I can't recall the amount of times those particular airlines had crashed during the sixties, but it was a lot. We stopped over in Berne for an hour while the Swiss transit passengers left the plane. That first stop was one of eight on the journey. With nothing else to relieve the boredom and tension we got thoroughly pissed. By the time we arrived in Australia we fell out of the plane looking drawn and shattered.

After landing in Darwin, the Boeing re-fuelled and then carried onto Sydney. The plane had to circle the airport for ages waiting for a slot to land. Our pilot informed us that the delay was down to another Boeing having lost its wheels on landing.

For the month long tour we shared the bill with Herman's Hermits, a lightweight group from Manchester. They had been blessed with a string of hits including, 'No Milk Today,' and 'Henry the Eighth I Am.' we were riding high at the time as 'Chills and Fever' had been a massive hit down under. There was a great deal of squabbling as to who would close the shows. It didn't quite come down to a fist fight, but it wasn't far off.

Tom stayed at the Sydney Hilton and, believe it or not, The Squires landed a very nice hotel too. It was courtesy of the Australian promoter, who had also kindly paid for our air fare. Throughout the tour, which included a New Zealand leg, we stayed in respectable hotels. It was a real turn-about from the way we were used to being treated by Gordon back in the UK.

I remember playing a massive venue in Sydney on a revolving stage. We performed bang in the centre and the stage revolved 360 degrees so that all the audience would have the opportunity of seeing us play. The place was packed to the rafters with thousands and thousands of fans. On that particular evening we appeared with The Four Tops, with not a Hermit in sight.

There was a bit of a farcical end to the evening. Tom and the band were signing autographs from the stage. Suddenly Beryl Evans jumped up and joined me on stage. Beryl was the gorgeous elder sister of my ex-girlfriend Jean from back home in Wales. The stunning blonde had emigrated to Australia with her footballer husband, Colin Gale. We were happily chatting away when I noticed Tom staring daggers at me. He was busily signing autographs as loads of attractive girls swarmed around him, but he had eyes for just me and Beryl.

The band was always aware that Tom had a jealous streak running right through him. Back in Wales he was always lusting after Beryl, he fancied her something rotten from way back. Now here she was the other side of the world, married and chatting away to me, ignoring him completely. Tom shouted over, 'Hey Vernon, stop farting around over there and put your fucking guitar away.'

My jaw dropped and so did Beryl's. I remember saying, 'I'm just having a little chat with Beryl, you do remember Beryl from back home?'

'Yeah well hurry up, they want to clear the stage. Let's get out of here, me and the boys are off in a minute.'

The band all looked away sniggering. It was blatantly obvious that Tom was turning green with jealously. He didn't like to be ignored and he could never disguise it. Just then Beryl's husband joined us on stage and Tom looking sheepish went back to signing autographs.

Gordon was back in London and had decided not to accompany us on the tour. But he was busy scanning the daily newspapers back home in the UK. Virtually every day there was a news report about Tom's antics down under. He was rubbing his hands with glee at all the publicity.

The Australian authorities were rather prudish about Tom's sexual antics on stage. They didn't care for his tight trousers and his thrusting pelvis was causing consternation. The British press were busily reporting that the Australian police had been ordered to mingle with the audiences and form their own opinion as to whether he was breaking any laws with his suggestive performance.

On one occasion they threatened to close the show when Tom took his shirt off and began swinging it around his head. Tom later joked to a Daily Mail reporter, 'I only took my shirt off because it was too hot.'

The police didn't take too kindly to such flippancy. The next performance was filmed by the Sydney police and handed over to a magistrate for inspection. It's my guess that it was a female magistrate who studied the film, as the report back was that it just looked like Tom dancing, and the magistrate was looking forward to seeing his next performance.

On one of our nights off during our dates in Sydney, we went down town to have a nosy around. We found ourselves in a basement club in the Chinese district. Celebrations for Chinese New Year were well underway, and we settled down to watch the colourful entertainment. There were huge dragons, animated from within by crouching Chinese dancers. They circled and twisted around the dance floor to a deafening cacophony of Oriental music. We sat there mesmerised by it all, we'd never seen anything like it back home.

Later three guys appeared on the small stage, one of them was far taller than the others. They started singing three-part harmonies and playing guitars. Along with us they must have been the only other non-Orientals in the club. They were mostly singing Everly Brother's songs and other harmonious melodies. I distinctly recall that one song particularly stood out, as it didn't fit with the rest of their set. They knocked out Lonnie Donegan's classic, 'My Old Man's A Dustman'. The roomful of Chinese didn't know what to make of it at first, but soon got into clapping along.

I thought they were quite entertaining, although it was pretty mild non-adventurous music. After they'd finished their set they came over and introduced themselves. They were the Gibb Brothers, later to find worldwide fame as the Bee Gees, with their distinctive disco hits.

Barry Gibb recognised us and asked, 'Hey you're the Squires, where's Tom?'

'Probably back at the Hilton, chatting up some bird,' I replied.

'We've got some demos back in the dressing room, Vernon, a few songs that my brothers and I have written. I wonder if you could pass them onto Tom's manager when you get back to London.'

I remember telling them just how difficult it was to try and get a break, having already been through the mill myself. Our 'Calcutta days' were still fresh in my mind at that stage. But we went back to the dressing room to get the demos, chatting about how to get on in the business. They were a nice bunch of lads and I wished them all well.

I returned to join the boys and showed them the three demos and some black and white publicity photos. I'd promised the Gibb Brothers I'd pass them to Gordon upon our return to London. I did exactly that and told Gordon they were a talented trio. But Gordon being Gordon dismissed them out of hand; he said they'd, 'never amount to anything.' Gordon tossed the demos in the rubbish bin. But it was his loss and their gain as they achieved super stardom. The following year, in 1967, the Bee Gees released the first of their many number one hits, 'New York Mining Disaster'. It was all legend status after that and the hits just kept coming.

I remember bumping into them again at Elstree TV Studios in late 1967. I told them about Gordon's reaction to the original demos. Whether they believed me or not, I'll never know. But they were three very happy guys, everything was on the up for them. The Chinese basement club in Sydney was a very long way behind them.

Many years later I was searching through my attic in Shepperton having a clear out and I came across one of the publicity shots Barry had given me in Sydney. I remember keeping it back as a memento before passing the rest along with the demos to Gordon. It's a good job I did or Gordon would have binned that as well.

The Australian tour took in Brisbane, Adelaide, Melbourne and Perth and then on to New Zealand. Looking back it was a wonderful time and we all thoroughly enjoyed ourselves. We were made to feel like super stars the attention we got was like a drug. I have very fond memories. But soon it was time to head back home to the UK.

Tom took the Pacific route back to London via Los Angeles and across to New York, where he stopped off to promote his latest single. Chris Slade and Mickey Gee stopped off in Singapore to sample the delights of that particular city. Vic decided on heading straight home to London. Chris Ellis and I plumped for staying in Perth for a couple of extra days. It was bliss, lazing on the beach. When we had soaked up as much sun as we could possibly take we decided to follow Slade and Mickey to Singapore. When we arrived in Singapore we had just missed them. But they had left us a message at Singapore International Airport. The note read:

Vernon, Chris, look out for tall thin Oriental bloke. He's got horn-rimmed glasses, can't miss him. Gave us a great time but conned us. Be careful.

Best,

Mickey and Chris

Sure enough as we walked out of the airport to hail a taxi, up steps 'Mr Horn-Rimms'. He promised us a cheap ride into the city and a cosy cheap hotel. After reading the note we were on high alert but accepted his offer. He drove us to a decent hotel, apparently the same one Chris and Mickey had stayed at. Chris checked out the price for a three night stay, and it looked pretty reasonable, being just a few Singapore Dollars each. Mr Horn-

Rimms had promised us it would be cheap and it was. He didn't even charge us very much for the cab fare from the airport.

Chris and I both had spacious separate rooms with a single bed in each, mosquito nets and massive rotating fans hanging from the ceiling. The hotel had a laundry service and we deposited our spent tour clothes there. They were returned washed and ironed to perfection. All for the price of a couple of pints back home in London.

We went out that night to sample the night life. Hung over the next morning I swept back the mosquito net and almost jumped out of my skin. The bare white washed walls were alive with millions of bright green lizards, each about six inches long. I let out a croaky yell and they all scattered, disappearing into narrow cracks in the wall. I checked in on Chris and he was holding one of the lizards in his hands, sitting on the edge of his bed. He'd found they were harmless and great at keeping the mosquitoes at bay.

Later that day Mr Horn-Rimms came a calling and suggested we take a, 'nice cool bath and massage with honourable geisha girl, who work in public relations.' Considering the temperature was in the high nineties, humid as hell and we were nursing hangovers, I looked at Chris and asked if he was up for it. We were both sweating buckets so we readily agreed.

'How much for the massage?' I asked.

'Very cheap, just five pound each, include cool bath and 'flaglant' oils massage. Very refreshing you enjoy,' he said.

'Where,' asked Chris.

'Not far, just little way. You ride in white Mercedes, same car as airport drive.'

Chris and I hopped in the Mercedes expecting a short drive. We found ourselves being driven way out of the city and over the border into the dense Malaysian jungle. 'Not far' was obviously an understatement. Natives kept appearing from mud and straw huts to peer at us as we drove deeper and deeper into the jungle along a dirt track. After about an hour the car finally stopped in a jungle clearing right next to a white bungalow, with a noisy generator humming beside it.

Mr Horn-Rimms led us into a clinically white room and sat us down at a table. The jungle was steaming hot and there was vapour rising off our clothes. He suggested we have a few ice-cold beers to chill out. We both readily agreed and a very old, feeble Malaysian woman brought us a tray of beers. I asked Mr Horn-Rimms why we had to cross over to Malaysia for a massage and bath. He told us the clinic was not licensed to operate in Singapore, which I must admit made us feel a little uncomfortable.

Pretty soon our masseurs entered the room. They were two stunningly beautiful Malaysian girls, one petite and one slightly taller. The shorter girl took me into a small room. There was a single bed and a tin bath. On a shelf next to the bath was a line of small bottles of oil in various colours.

She pointed to the ridiculously tiny bath and motioned for me to get undressed. I crammed myself into it and she poured a jug of cooling water over me, then handed me a bar of soap. After washing away the jungle sweat I got the full massage treatment, and it relieved the tensions of months spent on the road on tour. This was followed with the oil treatment which had me dozing off to sleep, it was incredibly relaxing.

We were there for about an hour and a half. I remember thinking, not bad for a fiver. After lining up the bottles of oil, back on the shelf, she undid her white housecoat and let it fall to the floor, standing there naked. I must admit she was absolutely stunning and it wasn't just my eyes standing on stalks. Being young and carefree the inevitable happened.

Afterwards back in the main room I was still waiting for Chris to appear. He was certainly taking his time. I was then presented with the bill: £5 massage, £10 extra services, £20 four beers, £5 taxi ride. In total £40 each. I broke out in a cold sweat as we'd blown a whole week's wages in one afternoon.

We both obviously protested but to no avail. Mr Horn-Rimms threatened that if we didn't pay up he'd leave us there stranded in the jungle. We both paid up and chalked it up to experience. Slade and Mickey had tried to warn us, after all.

We flew out of Singapore back to London. The flat in Fulham had been kicked into touch and we'd rented a small detached house in West Hounslow. It had worked out cheaper to rent a small house as opposed to the four of us all paying the same rent on the flat in Fulham. The house was directly opposite West Hounslow Tube Station. It was sparsely furnished and needed a good make-over, but you couldn't argue with the rent. I had taken the front box room and the rest of the boys fought over the other two bedrooms. The back garden was overgrown and had been left unattended for years, but who cared, none of us ever went out there. In an echo of earlier 'Calcutta' days, when we first moved in we spent days trying to catch a mouse that had taken up residence rent free. In the end we didn't have the heart to set traps and it quickly became tame and was adopted as band mascot.

Chris and I were the first to arrive, as Slade and Mickey had gone straight back to Wales upon returning from Australia. London was freezing when we got back, especially as we had become acclimatised to the temperate southern hemisphere. Shattered after our long flight from Singapore we let ourselves in the front door and were confronted by a mass of icicles hanging from the ceiling. Some of the icicles were at least six feet long and stretched the entire length of the hallway. The pipes had burst in the bathroom due to the extreme cold. The floor of the hallway was like an ice rink. We turned on our heels and jumped in the van. Unfortunately the battery was flat as it had been sitting parked outside for over a month. We called in at a local garage and they came and charged the van. We booked into a bed and breakfast until our landlord sorted out the leak.

Pretty soon we were back on the road again, playing gigs the length and breadth of the UK. We had regular TV appearances and this ensured all the venues were booked out well in advance. Tom was a bit down in the dumps as he was finding it difficult to produce another number one single. Although he didn't have much to moan about as there was an enormous amount of money flooding in from the venues, and some of them were cash-in-hand jobs.

At that time Mickey Gee was becoming increasingly disenchanted with the way Gordon and Tom were treating us financially. Mickey had joined the band days before leaving for London, almost two years earlier. He'd struggled through those early days when we were scrimping to get by, and now the money was flooding in we weren't in any real better shape. On the other hand Gordon and Tom were living like millionaires. What brought matters to a head was the fact that we were back on the road yet again and it was costing us whatever we made in wages. We were running to stand still. What with paying for digs, rent on the house back in London, petrol for the van, meals up and down the country, and all the expenses involved in touring, we were flat broke. Mickey decided that we should make a stand and ask for a tenner more a week to cover all our tour expenses.

We were playing a venue in Southampton and Gordon happened to make a rare appearance. Increasingly he'd been spending more and more time in his plush new offices in Bond Street and directing the MAM Empire from there. Gordon was in conference with Tom, in his dressing room. Mickey elected himself spokesman, with our backing, and went to discuss matters with Gordon. It was agreed that Mickey would ask both Gordon and Tom for a ten pounds raise and our tax paid, or a twenty pound raise and we'd have to sort out or own tax and stamps.

Mickey was gone some time and upon his return he reported, 'Tom was stood next to Gordon, wearing sunglasses with his arms folded, and Gordon was all stern and business-like. It was like a scene from a Humphrey Bogart gangster film. I thought I was going to get whacked!'

After considering our request for a small rise and help with our tax and stamps, Gordon had sent Mickey back to get the rest of us. He wanted us all in Tom's dressing room pronto. In we all filed and Gordon produced one of his big pronouncements, he was relishing it, 'I was in a band once. We were called the

Viscounts, and when I didn't like being in the band anymore, do you know what I did? Well let me tell you, I left. You can forget about this money you're asking for, you're not getting it, and if you don't like it, then you can all piss off back to Wales.'

Tom just stood there expressionless behind his sunglasses, puffing on a big cigar. He didn't utter a word of protest to Gordon for cutting us down so coldly. Looking back with hindsight, what we were asking for was a minuscule amount of what they were both raking in on a daily basis. They wouldn't have even noticed such a small amount, and yet it was a great deal to us, after all we were doing all the donkey work promoting and gigging, and we were the ones paying for it too. Tom had come up on the hard rail with us, he really should have said something to support us then and there. But he didn't.

Gordon issued an ultimatum, 'Mickey, what are you doing, are you staying or going?' Mickey looked at Gordon and then Tom. Then ignoring Gordon completely he said to Tom, 'I'm going Tom, I'm not going to leave you in the lurch. I'll back you on tonight's gig and I'll stay on until you find a replacement. That's what friends do for each other. After all we've been through together Tom, have you got nothing to say?' Tom Jones didn't say a word, and we all filed out of the dressing room, as Gordon slapped him on the back.

Mickey was disgusted, more with Tom than Gordon. I thought it was very brave of Mickey and noble of him to stay on until they found another lead guitarist. The rest of us decided to stay on, we could see which way the wind was blowing, but thought we'd stay for now and start looking for new opportunities. I couldn't bring myself to leave at that stage. I was the founder member of The Senators, I'd been the one to enlist Tom in the first place. I'd put an enormous amount of my life and soul into the band since its inception six years previously. I just couldn't walk away from it all now, it would have broken my heart. Obviously that's what did happen eventually.

Mickey later told Stafford Hildred and David Gritten in their biography, 'Tom Jones', that, 'the only reason we went up to forty pounds a week was because we had started to work with session musicians and found out what the proper rates were. Even then the other guys in the band were pretty easy-going about the session men getting more than us. I kept saying, 'for God's sake, they never starved with you, or went on the road to all those awful places. Tom and Gordon are paying them session rates, let them pay us session rates.' Mickey went onto to tell them that, 'Of course Tom and Gordon got rid of the rest of the band in the end, as I knew they would. But the thing that really pissed me off was that after I left them, they did all get to tour America and meet Elvis. It was always my dream to meet Elvis, so I missed out in that way.'

That time in Southampton was a real watershed moment. We all saw a very different side of Tom that day. Prior to that confrontation with Gordon, whenever we had asked Tom why we were being treated so badly, he had put it all down to Gordon, and told us he was fighting our corner. Now we had all seen him in his true colours. In the midst of the conflict he had stood there stony-faced puffing on his big cigar, and taken Gordon's side. And to not even say a word to Mickey, well that was pretty rotten behaviour. It was hard to believe that less than a year previously we had all been holed up together in the

'Calcutta', sharing two sausage rolls between the five of us.

The whole situation was very sad. I remember thinking about an occasion back in Wales before we left for London. Tom was going on and on about how much he hated the police, and how they were the scum of the earth. It probably had something to do with him being clobbered for thieving or fighting. He was ranting and raving when I reminded him that my brother, Norman, was a copper. Tom instantly quipped back, 'I'm more like a brother to you than he is.' We were certainly very close back then, but now we were oceans apart, and I didn't understand then how he could treat us all like that. All these years later, and I'm no closer to understanding it even now.

Tom lost a fine musician and a good loyal friend when Mickey left. He also lost the respect of the rest of the band. Mickey went on to appear with a lot of great bands during the years that followed, 'Plum Crazy', 'Love Sculpture', 'Micky and the Gee Men', and he also worked with Dave Edmunds, Shaking Stevens and the legendary Bruce Springsteen.

The effects of the Australian tour, coupled with his liking for woodbines and cigars, had put a major strain on Tom's voice. It was decided that he check into hospital and have his tonsils removed. The surgeons would check his throat at the same time. The prognosis was not good. If he didn't stop smoking woodbines immediately his voice would crack up. Gordon suggested that he cut out the woodbines and just smoke cigars, but not inhale. As for drinking alcohol, the specialist recommended that beer and spirits be completely avoided at all costs. Gordon had the perfect solution, champagne. Tom took some convincing to give up the pints, but Gordon played on his vanity, telling him that he didn't want to end up with a big fat beer belly, after all who would pay to come and see him then?

I remember Tom gave an interview at the time where he said, 'I've always smoked woodbines and drank beer. My manager told me that one day I'd be smoking cigars and drinking champagne. I told him at the time 'I love woodbines and beer, and that's that.' So what am I doing today? Drinking champagne and smoking cigars, when you can afford to do that, what the hell. Lots of people say I've changed. The only change in me is that the real person has come out.'

He had changed and not for the better, the band were all testaments to that, those of us left anyway. Mickey's departure also had the knock-on effect of us losing our rented house. With only Chris Slade, Chris Ellis and me now living there, we couldn't afford the rent and had to hand in our notice. The only option was to split up and each look for our own accommodation. Chris Slade's girlfriend Lynne packed in her job in Ponty and she and Chris rented a small flat in London. Chris Ellis and I went looking for somewhere near Tom and Gordon. Gordon wanted us to be close and within a few miles of his home, in Shepperton, to be available when needed. Shepperton is near the River Thames, an up-market area of West London. We both got digs a few miles from each other in Molesey, close by.

I've got Tony Cartwright to thank for helping me find the digs. The band had befriended Tony when we lived at Ladbroke Grove. Tony was part of a young Liverpool band that had migrated to London on their quest for fame, just like us. He was their singer and rhythm guitarist. Tony was a bit of a character, like most Scousers he had the gift of the gab, and I can only describe him as the spitting image of the movie star Tom Hanks. His Liverpool accent was sometimes impenetrable and he was seriously streetwise. Having grown up in the poorer part of Liverpool he had elevated 'blagging' to an art form.

Sadly we had lost touch after leaving the 'Calcutta' at Ladbroke Grove, but amazingly, when I went back to Ponty when Tom was in hospital having his tonsils out, my sister said he had been in touch. Well it was a bit more than just getting in touch. Tony being Tony had got his band put up at my Dad's house. They had been on tour playing all the dance halls up and down the Welsh valleys. Tony remembered me mentioning my address at 2 Glyndwr Avenue, and along with his fifteen year old drummer, who had absconded from school to take part in the tour, knocked on my Dad's door. The cheeky bugger talked Dad into putting the band up for a few nights. Tony told him they were too skint to afford accommodation. My kindly father duly obliged and they all slept in the front parlour, where Tom and the Senators used to rehearse all those years before. The diminutive drummer, mitching off school, would go on to great things. He eventually became one of the most famous and celebrated musicians in the world. His name was Mitch Mitchell and he became the drummer with The Jimi Hendrix Experience.

Tony had heard on the grapevine that Chris Ellis and I were looking for lodgings, and got in contact. He was holed up in West Molesley at the time, three miles from Shepperton. He was lodging with a family in a council house on a small new estate in Tonbridge Road. Tony told me he was lodging there illegally, council red tape had banned the taking in of lodgers. It was a four bedroom house and there was a room going spare for five pounds a week, with an extra couple of quid for laundry and joining the family for evening meals. I jumped at the offer and Chris Ellis found lodgings with my new landlady's sister in Thames Ditton, a mile or two away.

It would turn out to be the best move for both of us. After all the dumps we had bedded down in over the previous few years, this was a real step up, and we were made to feel part of the family. Muriel McKenna and her ten year old daughter, Jill, lived there with Mu's elderly mother, Nancy. There was also a yappy little Jack Russell, called Julie. The house was cosy and spotless, Tony and I went back away so got on like a house on fire. Tony's Liverpool humour always used to crack me up. It was a manic laugh a minute with Tony, you never knew what he was going to come out with next, and he had the whole family in fits of giggles. Tony was out on a limb at the time, he'd finished playing with the band and was on the dole. But he was always on the make, looking for opportunities to make a few bob or two. Gordon took him on eventually, getting Tony to drive him around and do the occasional odd job.

I really took to my new family. Muriel was about forty years old, tiny in stature, thin and a little old for her age. She had short fair hair and could produce a cackle that could haunt a house. Mu was always stressed out and her language could be quite ripe at times, as could her considerable bark. But it was all very theatrical, she was one hell of a character, with a heart of gold. Mu's daughter Jill was born a love child. Her black American father had been stationed at an American Army base nearby and Mu had met him at a dance hall in Walton-on-Thames. When he was drafted back to America, Mu and her daughter had moved back in with Nancy, and subsequently they had managed to secure the tenancy on the council house. Mu had a job as a house cleaner in nearby Weybridge. Her most famous client was the pop singer, Adam Faith; she used to clean house for Adam and his stunning wife Jackie and was treated like one of the family.

At that time Gordon had arranged for a new band member to join us. Lead guitarist Dave Wendals was a former member of Lulu's band, 'The Luvvers'. Dave was a tall good looking twenty-four year old and lived with his mother in Central Hounslow. Dave's house is ingrained in my memory. I had recently passed my driving test (at last) and had bought a clapped out old Ford Anglia. The very same model made famous in the Harry Potter movies. I'd driven over to Dave's house to catch up and have a cup of tea or two. Stepping out of the house I was dismayed to find that the offside front wing of my car had been damaged by another car which hadn't stopped to exchange insurance details. After surveying the damage, my attention was caught by a nearby news stand. The headline on the bill board read: South Wales Tip Tragedy. Over 100 Schoolchildren Buried Alive. It was the day of the Aberfan tragedy in October 1966 and it stopped me dead in my tracks. My dismay about the damaged wing was quickly forgotten, I was shocked and numbed at the terrible news, and went to find a phone kiosk to call home to Wales. I can still see that road and news stand as if it was just yesterday.

11

SHEPPERTON

It was now almost the beginning of summer. On the 15th May Tom and The Squires were booked to appear for a charity concert at Blackpool Opera House. On the same bill were Dusty Springfield and The Mindbenders. Immediately after the concert we boarded a plane for Brussels to make a television appearance. Then we went by train to Paris to appear on another television show being filmed at the famous Paris Olympia.

Gordon was there to meet us. After the show Gordon had arranged to meet Tom at a Paris nightclub and asked me if I'd like to come along. We were both offered a lift to the club by a journalist and hopped into his battered old Citroen C5. It was a tight squeeze with Gordon and I both being six-footers. We felt every bump in the road rattling across town in that tin can of a car. Stopping at some traffic lights, another car pulled up alongside us. It was a powerful red sports car, a convertible with the hood up. At the wheel was a stunningly beautiful brunette and she was giving Gordon 'the eye'.

Gordon would down his window and smiled. He asked if she would mind giving us a lift. 'Of course,' she purred in a sexy French accent. We squeezed ourselves out of the Citroen and hopped into the sports car. Gordon was in the passenger seat and I was in the back. We explained where we were heading and invited her to join us for the evening. The convertible sped off with the tires screeching.

Curled up in the back I was barely able to move. We shot across Paris at breakneck speed. Gordon seemed to be enjoying the thrill of it. I was beginning to wish I'd stuck with the C5. I could see some traffic lights up ahead turning red. The woman put her foot to the floor and drove straight through. Suddenly she lost control of the car and it smashed into the side of another vehicle. I blanked out.

When I came around I was hanging out of the front passenger door with my head resting on the tarmac. Dazed and confused I struggled to my feet. Lights were flashing, there was hissing steam everywhere and the unmistakable smell of petrol. The car we had hit was overturned, resting on its roof, a complete write-off. The red sports car wasn't in any better condition, it was smashed to bits.

I saw Gordon standing on the pavement nearby, his clothes was torn and he was bleeding from a facial wound. He was yelling at some Police officers, 'But I'm British, I'm British', he seemed very animated and a little concussed. The beautiful brunette was lying at Gordon's feet, completely out cold. He had placed his jacket under her head as a pillow. Moments later an ambulance arrived and Gordon helped lift the women into the back.

I stumbled over to Gordon. I was very unsteady on my feet after being knocked out cold and my vision was swimming in and out of focus. He turned to me with a look of utter disdain on his bloodied face. He was livid and snarled, 'Where the fuck was you when I needed you?' I tried to explain that I had been knocked out cold but he just scowled at me.

After giving our details to the police and explaining as best we could what had happened, they let us go. We found our own way back to the hotel. I helped Gordon up to his room the full effects of the accident were starting to bear down on him. I inspected his wounds. His trousers were completely ripped apart revealing a nasty gash to his shin. He looked pretty well shook up as I bathed the wound with a flannel. I seemed to have got off quite lightly with just a few cuts, bruises and a pounding headache.

It was gone midnight at this point and the phone suddenly rang. Gordon reached over and answered it. He seemed to turn an even whiter shade of pale than he'd been earlier. It was his wife calling from Shepperton, apologizing for waking him up. Fair play to Gordon, he instantly recovered his cool. 'That's okay Jo. I was just about to turn the light off. I've been tucked up in bed reading a novel. Yes, everything's fine...What!'

Jo had decided she wanted to join Gordon in Paris and enjoy a little of the 'Parisienne highlife'. She promptly informed him she would be arriving in about twelve hours' time. He was in a right old panic. Only the night porter was on duty at that hour and his only suit was the one he had been wearing. He'd left his jacket at the scene of the accident. His white shirt was covered in blood and the trousers were ripped apart.

Putting down the phone he threw his shirt at me and begged me to have a go at cleaning the blood off. There I was, in the bathroom, attempting the impossible while Gordon paced the bedroom, limping like a car park attendant.

'How am I going to explain this one, Vernon?'

'Well Gordon, you shouldn't have told her you was tucked up in bed with a book,' I said

'You're right. I'm in a bit of a pickle here.'

'Why not tell her you fell down the hotel lift shaft,' I cracked.

'No she'd never believe that. What if I tell her I was mugged and I didn't want to upset her at this time of night?'

I left him to it and crawled back to my own bed down the corridor. When I awoke my entire body was aching from head to toe. God only knows how Gordon must have felt. As for the beautiful brunette, we made some enquiries and were informed that she had survived but was still in intensive care.

We were back in France not long after for a month's tour of concerts along the south coast. Gordon had decided to make the thousand mile journey in his new blue Jaguar XJ6. He didn't want to drive across France on his own so asked me if I would accompany him on the journey over. Tom and the rest of the band had already flown down to the south of France, apart from Chris Ellis who drove the van down to the Riviera with all the equipment in back.

Gordon and I boarded the ferry from Dover and practically raced through Paris. We caught up with Chris Ellis not far from the city. He'd pulled the van into a lay by and was cooking some food on a portable stove. The poor guy look completely knackered and yet he had hardly got half way there. I told Gordon I should share the driving with Chris, but he was having none of it and told me I needed to share the driving with him, forget Chris, he was doing what he was paid for.

I really started to regret not joining Chris and the equipment when I had the chance. Gordon was completely overbearing the whole journey. About half way there Gordon got bored of driving, tossed me the keys and stretched out in the back for a nice kip. Up until that point I'd been map reading and I couldn't drive and study the map at the same time, but Gordon just told me to get on with it and fell fast asleep. Gordon only awoke to tell me to pull over at the next restaurant. Luckily I was carrying some French currency because when it came time to settle the bill, Gordon threw a couple of francs on the table, and strolled out. 'See you back at the car,' he tossed over his shoulder.

There I was fumbling around with foreign coins trying to add up my part of the bill. Of course Gordon had woefully underpaid and left it to me to make up the difference. This was a man who had just become a millionaire. 'Charming!' I remember thinking at the time. I fully expected him to ask me for petrol money next.

The mountain roads leading down to the south were baking hot and quite treacherous. This was long before motorways crossed the length and breadth of France. Gordon asked me to pull over as he was bursting for a pee. He had polished off a good few beers back at the restaurant and I'd had a couple too. We pulled over and both went for a pee.

I was blissfully relieving myself when I heard the throaty roar of the Jag's engine spring into life. Gordon had leapt back behind the wheel and roared off, shouting, 'You're taking too long Vernon. You can hitch a ride.' He disappeared around the side of the mountain in a cloud of dust, leaving me standing there with my flies open and my mouth gaping. I had figured out a long time earlier that Gordon was a bit of a joker. But this was taking the piss, quite literally. I was convinced that he would return after a few minutes of winding me up. But I stood there for hours. The sun was blazing overhead and I started to feel really dehydrated, the beers back at the restaurant hadn't helped any. I started walking along the mountain road. A couple of cars went by but no one stopped and offered me a ride.

I walked for what seemed like hours and hours cursing Gordon to kingdom come. I finally caught up with the Jag, it was pulled over at the side of the road. Gordon was fast asleep in the back. I shook him awake and had a real go at him, calling him every name under the blazing sun. Gordon being Gordon just smiled and yawned. He told me he was going to come back, it was just a wind up, but he'd fallen asleep. He tossed me the keys and said, 'You drive Vernon, those continental beers have knocked me for six.' I could have strangled him.

Arriving in Nice we teamed up with Tom and the boys. They had been waiting patiently for Chris Ellis to arrive with the equipment. But there was no sign of him. We were all beginning to get a little worried. There were no mobile phones back then so it was impossible to get in contact and check if everything was alright. Finally to our immense relief he arrived looking like death warmed up. He had great big shadows under his glazed eyes and was walking around in a trance. Chris always carried a bag of Dexedrine tablets in the van, so that he wouldn't fall asleep on our long hauls up and down the M1 on gigs all over the UK. But driving through France had been another kettle of fish entirely. Chris was pumped up to the eyebrows with uppers. He hadn't slept a wink since leaving London. He was flying but at the same time he could hardly stand up!

Chris mumbled something to Gordon about being held up

in traffic. He staggered off like a zombie and disappeared into a crowd of tourists. Before we knew it we had lost him entirely. The sun was going down and we organized ourselves into two search parties to go and find him. Thankfully we finally found him wandering the streets, bumping into people and cars and mumbling incoherently. He didn't even know he was in France, he thought he was back in London. We gently led him back to our hotel and put him to bed, where he slept for eighteen straight hours.

After the month long tour of concerts along the coast Gordon and Tom drove back to London in the Jag. I was thankful that I wasn't enlisted for the drive back with Gordon and hoped Tom fared better than me. There was no need for The Squires to return to London for a few days so we decided to jump in the van and explore the coast. We drove to Juan Les Pins, not far from St Tropez, Bridget Bardot's home town. We found some cheap accommodation, which we later learned was infested with ants, and spruced ourselves up to hit the town.

Juan Les Pins was a quaint little fishing village back then. It was very unassuming by day, but once the sun had gone down it exploded. It was full of live music resonating along the seafront. We went on a bar crawl and came across The Brian Auger Trinity. Their lead singer was Rod Stewart, he was unknown in those days. Brian Auger played Hammond organ and they also had a female vocalist, Julie Driscoll. They were on the cusp of stardom and we visited the bar every subsequent night, really enjoying the music. One evening the band quarrelled with the owner and moved to another venue close by. With no band to take their place at short notice the owner asked us if we would fill in.

That night we belted out all the rock n roll classics in the book and Rod Stewart's audience drifted on back from their new venue to watch us. The Brian Auger Trinity weren't very happy with that state of affairs. After the gig they challenged us to a drinking contest. We nominated our new lead guitarist, Dave Wendals, to uphold the honour of the band. Dave could consume a lot of alcohol without it affecting him very much. The choice of liquor was a bottle of vodka each, to be consumed within half-an-hour! It was decided that the dual take place at the new Trinity venue. Both bands gathered around a table and faced off.

It's no easy task sinking a bottle of neat vodka in such a short time. A good twenty minutes in and Auger's lead guitarist was swaying like a pendulum. Dave seemed to be holding his own, glassy-eyed and poker faced. A little while later, with both bands cheering them on, Auger's guitarist fell off his chair and was counted out. It was a great shame as he only had to finish a couple more tumblers of vodka and he would have won.

We all congratulated our champion. He was looking a little the worse for wear and was completely cross-eyed as he staggered across the bar in search of the toilet. We all settled in with Rod and Auger's band and got down to some serious drinking. Dave Wendals was nowhere to be seen for the rest of the evening and we assumed he'd gone back to the hotel to sleep it off. The bar finally closed and we all staggered out for a moon light wander down to the beach. Walking along the sea front we could just about make out a figure, about sixty yards away, leaning against the seafront wall.

I remember saying 'Isn't that Dave?' but before anyone could answer me a gendarme van pulled up, tossed him in the back and sped away. He had been whisked off to the cells. Rod said, 'They'll let him out in the morning after he's slept it off.'

Chris and I staggered back to the hotel a little the worse for wear and found our beds swarming with ants. They were everywhere, in our beds, under the beds and scampering all over the walls. There were millions of the little buggers. We were too pissed to deal with it so we both turned on our heels and ended up sleeping on the beach.

The next day there was no sign of Dave. The day wore on and we were due on stage in a couple of hours. Vic could speak a little French so enquired at the local police station. He explained that Dave had been arrested the previous evening for being drunk and incapable. A few minutes later the gendarmes escorted Dave from the cells looking in a right state. He was still completely smashed. They released him to Vic and how he managed to play that night I'll never know, but play he did.

When we got back to London we were booked to appear on Bruce Forsyth's new show on ITV. Directly after that we were off on our travels again, this time to record a TV special in Madrid. Dave Wendals managed to behave himself on this occasion, he'd sworn off the alcohol, and just the sight of a bottle of vodka was enough to make him turn green.

Tom had decided to buy himself a new car. He became the proud owner of a gleaming red Jaguar. It was the same shape as the revived S-Type and incredibly sleek and powerful. On our return from Madrid Tom, Tony Cartwright, Chris Ellis and myself all arranged to meet at The Cromwelliam Club. It had become one of our favourite haunts and we used to go there quite a bit. The Club was on the Cromwell Road directly opposite The Natural History Museum. Eric Clapton, Ginger Baker, Jimmy Page and a host of other yet-to-be-discovered musicians used to play in the Clubs basement and we enjoyed their company and the general vibe. It was also a great place for pulling girls and later that year I would bump into Mia Lewis again, my future wife.

That particular evening, Tom and Tony had latched onto a couple of air hostesses. Everyone was in fine spirits and it was turning into a bit of a raucous time. We all decided to head onto The Bag o Nails in the West End. This was the pub where Paul McCartney had met his future wife, Linda Eastman. I followed Tom in my little Ford Anglia and was finding it increasingly difficult to keep up with him. He was driving like a lunatic up Park Lane. One of the air hostesses in the back was giving Tom directions and told him to make a sudden right turn into an opening in the dual carriageway. Chris and I, travelling behind in the Anglia, watched the whole scenario unfold.

It was quite apparent that there was no chance the Jag was going to be able to cut through at that speed. Tom crashed into a wall on the reservation at considerable speed. The car was a write off. Chris and I pulled over and leaped out of my car. Tom and Tony were both in a bit of a mess, crumpled up in the front seats. Tom had a nasty gash above his left eye, there was blood everywhere. They stumbled out of the wrecked Jag. Tom mumbled that he was in the shit big time. He was drunk and he had two air hostesses in the back. We could all imagine the headlines in the morning newspapers.

I went to check on the girls in the back and make sure they

were okay; both seemed fine if not a little shaken up. Tom and Tony decided to make a run for it and sprinted off up the road. Unfortunately their escape attempt was foiled when a police car and ambulance arrived with lights flashing. They were all bundled into the back of the ambulance and taken to St. George's Hospital at Hyde Park Corner, just two minutes away.

They took Tony out of the ambulance on a stretcher, he was moaning and groaning and probably concussed. But after being checked over it turned out that thankfully there was nothing wrong with him. Tom on the other hand received fourteen stitches above his eye and was kept in for observation until dawn the following morning. Tom got off very lightly, there were no breathalyzers back then, and you just had to walk a chalk line and not topple over. Luckily the newspapers never caught a sniff of the accident and it went unreported.

Tony Cartwright and I were being spoiled rotten at Tonbridge Road. Mu was like a mother hen fussing over us. She fed us, washed and ironed our clothes, we had our own keys so came and went as we wished. Mu used to make the biggest Sunday dinners on the planet. A lot of our fellow musicians soon got wind of this and took to calling in at all hours of day and night to visit. Mu and her mum, Nancy, were so easy going they didn't mind a bit.

One of our most regular visitors was Mick Avery, The Kinks drummer. We had performed on the same TV show in 1964, BBC's Beat Room, and been friends ever since. At that time he was living just around the corner in West Molesly. We all used to meet at The Cannon pub in the village and Mick would invite himself back to Mu's for a cup of tea when he wasn't touring with The Kinks. He was a lovely guy and a very talented musician.

Another regular visitor was Noel Redding, who would become famous as the bass guitarist with The Jimi Hendrix Experience. He had joined the band along with my old friend, the drummer Mitch Mitchell, who had crashed at my Dad's house in Wales all those years before. Noel used to stay over at Mu's when he was out on a limb workwise. We'd put him on the couch and he was happy dossing there. However whenever we had him to stay it was a necessity that every downstairs window and door be left open. Noel had the smelliest socks imaginable, it was enough to bring tears to your eyes. The stench was overpowering. Even Julie the Jack Russell used to beat it out the back door to get some fresh air.

Sadly both Noel Redding and Mitch Mitchell died at a relatively young age. It was a great loss to show business, they were both incredibly talented musicians with so much to offer. I have very fond memories of the times I shared with them both.

Another regular visitor was Adam Faith and his wife Jackie, a stunning beautiful ex-dancer. Mu was their cleaner but had been adopted as one of the family. Looking back on those days at Tonbridge Road it's amazing the amount of people that used to drop in for a cup of tea and a chat. As well as Tom, Englebert Humperdink and Gilbert O'Sullivan we had a host of fellow musicians that would rock up unannounced because they knew they'd always be welcome. They were certainly very happy days. I remember one day returning home to find Freddie Lennon, John Lennon's estranged father, warming himself in front of the fire. He'd dropped in to meet with Tony Cartwright.

Tony was earning a few bob as Gordon's 'gopher'. As Tony explained to me at the time, he was using the opportunity to pick up as many business tips as possible. He had his sights set on becoming a successful manager, just like Gordon. One day he would realise his ambition and he went on to manage the comedian Freddie Starr, the singer Malcolm Roberts and eventually he took over the management of Englebert Humperdink from Gordon.

But during that lean spell he hardly had a shilling to his name. Gordon was notoriously tight with money and was paying him practically nothing for all his chores. He would have been better off on the dole, but he was biding his time and picking up as many tips on the business as he could. Tony's favourite drink was Guinness and Bitter mix and he was always on the scrounge for a pint, pleading poverty. He was such a colourful character no-one could ever refuse him. I knew what it meant to be skint and always helped him out when I could.

Tony used to wind Mu up something chronic. When Julie the Jack Russell came into season, Mu gave us strict instructions not to let her out of the house. She didn't want to have to be dealing with a litter of puppies. We gave her our solemn promise we wouldn't let her out. I remember being up in my bedroom and I happened to peer out the window. There was Julie across the road surrounded by a pack of five panting dogs. They were all taking turns to try and mount her. Tony, of course, had left the door open after collecting a parcel from the post man.

I rushed downstairs and Tony was sat on the couch with his nose in the newspaper, the door wide open. Mu's mum, Nancy, was fast asleep in the chair opposite. I shook him, so as not to disturb the old girl, and urgently beckoned for him to meet me outside. It was too late. The Jack Russell was being mounted by a flea-bitten mongrel and they were stuck together, bum to bum. Poor little Julie was yelping whenever the larger dog swung her around, desperately trying to get herself unstuck.

Boy we were in trouble now. There were net curtains rustling up and down the street to see what the commotion was all about. By the time we threw a bucket of cold water over them, Mu's neighbours had all come out to see the show. The water did the trick and we shooed Julie back into the house and put her in the bath. Thankfully Nancy slept through the entire incident. We both thought we'd got away with it. But when Jill came home from school she went out to play with her friends and a few moments later came back clacking to her Mum. Mu predictably hit the bloody roof.

I used to think Dorothy Squires had a bit of a mouth on her, but she wasn't a patch on Mu. The air turned blue alright, 'Okay own up. Which one of you bleedin' tossers let my Julie get raped by a pack of mongrels? The poor little fucker, she's in bleedin' shock. Mum, did you see any of it?'

'No Mu. I must have been kipping. Didn't hear a thing,' said her Mum.

'Tony I bet it was you. You never remember to shut the fuckin' front door. You're the worst lodger I've ever 'ad. I know it was you that poured half a bottle of bleedin' aftershave over the dog because she was niffin'. All dogs smell after they've been in the rain, you pillock. The poor little fucker went bald because of you. She looked like a piglet for months after.'

'Calm down Mu. I did pay for the vet to have a look at her, didn't I?' squirmed Tony.

'Yeah, I know you did Cartwright. But who had to pay for all the fuckin' ointment? Not you, you're always fucking skint. I know it was you Tony, 'cos you haven't denied it,' she raged, 'You can't put the blame on Vernon this time, like you did when you set the fuckin' chimney on fire.'

That was news to me, that one, and I stared narrowly at Tony, 'I told you, Mu, I had nothing to do with that,' he piped up in his scouse accent.

'Course you did, when the bleedin' fire brigade turned up you was the only one in the bleedin' house. Our next door neighbour told me Mick Avery and Vernon was up at the Cannon for a pint at the time.'

Tony was backpedalling furiously and realised he was going to have to come clean on this one. 'I'm really sorry Mu. There was a bloody great bee hovering around Nancy while she was having her kip. Her mouth was wide open like, and the bee was buzzing, so I chased it out the front door. That must have been when Julie slipped out,' lied Tony convincingly, even I started to believe him and I'd been there to witness him reading the paper nonchalantly.

'Bee, fuckin' slipped out. You can slip your bleedin 'and in your pocket, the one with the imaginary hole in it rent time. You is paying for the bleedin' abortion let me tell you.'

I don't know how I kept a straight face. It was all true of course, Tony Cartwright did cause the Jack Russell to go bald, and it was him that had set the chimney on fire. It was just his luck that Julie must have been sterile because to his great relief she never did have a litter of puppies. As for Mu, it was all soon forgotten, she never usually swore like that.

Although Tom and The Squires were now a million miles apart in financial terms, Tom still sought out our company socially. We were most of us based in and around Shepperton so it was always easy to meet up. Tom still liked being considered 'one of the boys'. Tom had an aversion to being cooped up in his mansion. He didn't like being indoors with Linda and Mark when he could be out on the town. We used to meet regularly in the village, knock back a few pints and go on the pull. Chris Ellis and I would frequent The Anchor, one of four pubs located in Shepperton village square. Many years later my daughter Tara and her husband would be married in St Mary's Church directly opposite.

The whole area was steeped in history; the church was over a thousand years old with the Anchor standing on the same site for not much less time. The oldest pub in the area was The Kings Head, built during the reign of Henry the Eighth. One of his many mistresses was reputed to have stayed there to be close to Hampton Court Palace.

The Anchor was a bit of a celebrity hang out and was often frequented by film stars. The pub was within shooting distance of Shepperton Studios and many a famous actor would stroll over for some refreshment after completing their scenes. Some of the more memorable people we met there was Peter Sellers, Richard Burton and Elizabeth Taylor. The film star John Gregson was a regular. John had played the leading role in the classic film 'Genevieve', about the London to Brighton car race. He had a house close to the square in a lovely riverside setting. John would often prop up the bar with his great pal, Ian Hendry. Ian was famous at the time for being the villain chased by Michael Caine at the end of the gangster movie 'Get Carter'. Tom and the band would stay drinking to the early hours with them both. They were great raconteurs and would have us in fits of giggles listening to all the tales about their film careers and personal lives.

John Gregson was a real character. After a few whiskeys he'd start in complaining about his wife. According to John she spent all of her time at the bottom of the garden worshiping a shrine. We could never get to the bottom of which deity the shrine was dedicated too. But when he started whining about the situation it was pure comedy gold.

Ian Hendry on the other hand was a raucous alcoholic and sometimes our small company of after-hours drinkers would have to suffer his boorish behaviour. Ian would get paralytic and end up insulting everyone within earshot. When he got really bad his long suffering wife, the actress Janet Munro, a reformed alcoholic, would come and collect him and cart him off. She would come and get him in a rowing boat from the other side of the Thames and coax him back home.

One particular evening in The Anchor, Tony Cartwright, Chris Ellis, Tom and I were propping up the bar until the early hours. Parked outside was Tom's white Volvo, Chris's Commer Van and my clapped out Anglia. Everyone was well oiled and nobody had any intention of turning in anytime soon. Suddenly I remembered that my driving test was arranged for 9am the following morning. The boys had been nagging me for ages to take it and get it over with and I'd finally relented. I didn't fancy driving my old conked out motor and asked Tom if I could borrow the Volvo. Stumbling out of The Anchor much the worse for wear, Tom told me to collect it from his garage in the morning; he'd leave the keys in the ignition.

I managed to get in a couple of hours sleep and Tony accompanied me to pick up the Volvo. We transferred the L-plate from the Anglia and drove to the test centre in nearby Weybridge. I had never driven the Volvo before and it was a real beast, very slick and fast. I'd made sure I had familiarized myself with the test route through Weybridge town centre and the surrounding area. I had my fingers crossed that it would all go well. Although it didn't get off to the best of starts when I accidently collided with my examiner and caused him to stumble into the gutter.

One thing was for sure, he was very impressed with the gleaming sports car and said as much. I was still feeling a little tipsy from propping up the bar at The Anchor earlier. But everything seemed to go very well. My hill start, reversing and emergency stop all passed without comment. But the examiner wasn't very happy with my gear changing. He kept asking if I was in the correct gear. I assured him that I was, but I have to admit the Volvo felt sluggish as though I was in top gear and yet driving at around 20mph. He seemed puzzled by the way the car was handling and when we got out of the 30mph limit asked me to open it up and give it some stick. I felt a little paranoid about the way the car was behaving, it made me hesitant, and I told him it wasn't advisable to be giving the car some welly on a provisional license. He remained silent and jotted down some notes in his pad.

Back at the test centre I sat the theoretical test and the Highway Code. I got all the questions correct until the very last, which threw me a bit. What's the first thing to do after being involved in a road accident with another vehicle? I rattled off a number of replies: exchange insurance details, check for injuries, and phone for an ambulance. The examiner kept shaking his head to all my answers. I thought well that's it, better luck next time.

Tony was waiting for me outside. He took one look at my face and patted me on the back, 'Well done Vernon, first time and all.' I'd passed my test. Whilst ripping off the L-plates I asked the examiner what the answer was to the last question. He gnomically told me to consult the Highway Code when I got home. I did and there it was, just one word...Stop!

I returned the Volvo to Tom and thanked him. He piped up that I must have bribed the examiner. I advised him to get the car checked as it seemed a little sluggish at 30mph, and the examiner had commented on it. Tom checked the gears and told me I'd been driving the Volvo in 'overdrive'. Back then 'overdrive' was completely alien to me, I'd never come across it in a car before, especially having only driven old bangers.

Tom was acquiring a real taste for cars at that time. Not long after he had an olive-green Rolls Continental delivered to Manygate Lane. It was a monster of a car a real status symbol number. Tom swung by the Archers to show it off and our jaws hit the floor, it was pretty impressive. I remember him complaining later that Linda had burst into tears when he showed it to her. He told me she had preferred the red Jag, the one he wrote off in Park Lane, and pleaded with him to ditch the Rolls and get another one of those instead. Tom couldn't understand it, the Rolls status seemed to mean nothing to her. Naturally he refused. I pointed out that with the money he was now making he could afford to buy her a fleet of Jags, one for every colour of the spectrum. He just looked at me like I'd taken leave of my senses.

12

THE GREEN, GREEN GRASS OF HOME

Toward the end of 1966 we were working the club circuit in the North of England. We happened to be playing in Leeds when it was brought to our attention that Tom's idol, Jerry Lee Lewis, was performing at a hall in the same city. It wasn't just Tom that idolized Jerry Lee Lewis, we were all great admirers and loved the man and his music. There was hardly any discussion, we all decided to descend on 'The Killer' and take in his show

Vic Cooper was pressed into service to drive Tom to the gig in his new Rolls. He wanted to make an entrance. The rest of us piled into the van and were driven there by Chris Ellis. The hall was packed to the rafters and we all stood at the back. Jerry Lee made his entrance backed by his four musicians and launched into a cracking start, he went down a storm.

Some of the audience noticed Tom standing with the band at the back of the venue, and heads started to turn as the message rippled through the audience. Pretty soon they began chanting for Tom to get up and sing. This didn't pass unnoticed by Jerry Lee Lewis, he wasn't called 'The Killer' for nothing. Not only could he beat a piano to death, it was well documented his wild streak ran deep. He was reputed to have a vile temper and at that moment his face was like thunder. But the chanting just got louder and louder.

Finishing 'Great Balls Of Fire' midway through the song, he kicked over his chair and glared at the audience, staring them down. It looked as if he was going to reach down into the audience grab someone and throttle them to death. Jerry Lee told the audience they were welcome to Tom Jones and then he stormed off stage.

That was the cue for the audience to push and hustle Tom up on stage. Tom, being Tom, was basking in the attention, it was evident he was relishing it, and allowed himself to be manhandled up onto Jerry's recently vacated stage. We were all shocked, and even more shocked when he grabbed the mike and called for us all to join him onstage. I was cringing and I turned to the rest of the band and could see they were mortified too. Jerry Lee Lewis was our hero for goodness sake. I remember motioning to the exit and we all started edging toward it.

Then Tom asked the audience to help get The Squires up on stage, and they duly started chanting and hustling us forward. We had no choice but to join him onstage. It was even more embarrassing when Jerry's band handed over their instruments to us and left the stage to join Jerry in the dressing room. I remember thinking at the time, you just don't do that sort of thing to a fellow artiste. I think in Tom's case he wanted to prove that he could outshine his hero.

We launched into a load of rock n roll songs ending with 'Not Unusual' and left the stage to thunderous applause. The audience stayed rooted to the spot waiting for Jerry to come back on, but they would have a long wait. The venue manager had to eventually inform them that Jerry would not be finishing his act. There were loud catcalls and boos all around. But you could hardly blame him, he'd been undermined big-time.

We all felt incredibly guilty and traipsed backstage and

knocked on Jerry's dressing room door. He called us in. There he was sitting in a chair looking utterly miserable. Tom apologized for being 'forced to override Jerry' and went on to gush about how he was such a massive fan, and how Jerry had been his inspiration. The Killer responded with a glare that could have peeled paint. Needless to say our visit to the dressing room was very short lived, some of Jerry's band could see which way the wind was blowing and hustled us out. Jerry obviously never forgot the experience because many years later he confronted Tom and they almost came to blows.

Tom and Gordon were both down in the dumps during that period. There was no sign of another chart hit on the horizon. What had made matters worse was that Wilson Pickett had berated Tom both personally and through the press, telling him to, 'stop recording the crap he's bringing out and be a soul brother.' Tom's voice was as soulful as any black singer and if he had taken Pickett's advice he might have found a real rich niche at the time. Gordon wasn't convinced and wanted to keep chopping and changing: blues, soul, country and western, rock n roll, jazz, folk and a mixture of mainstream pop. It was pretty dizzying for us, God only knows what it was like for Tom.

In the end, funnily enough, it was Jerry Lee Lewis he had to thank. In the Autumn Tom was going through his record collection and came across an album of country songs by Jerry Lee. He was really taken with one of the tracks and played it over and over. He told me later that he'd played it so many times that the grooves on the vinyl were almost worn right through. The track was called 'The Green, Green Grass of Home'.

I remembered that back in Wales Tom had a yearning for country music, almost as much as he loved rock n roll. The culture of the Welsh valleys identified with that whole mid-west American sound, the open scenery, the psyche, the whole ambience struck a real resonant chord.

'The Green, Green Grass of Home,' was a track from an album entitled, 'Country Songs for City Folks'. The song had already been covered by a host of stars in America, as well as Jerry Lee Lewis. Most of the earlier arrangements were mild, toned down instrumental affairs. Les Reed on the other hand gave Tom's version a much lusher makeover, complete with a string section and vocal backing. Tom said at the time, 'It was the right song. Some numbers are so personal they can hardly fail. There is an immediate bond between the singer, the lyrics and the audience. What makes me especially proud is that it was chosen by me alone. I knew instinctively that it was right for me.'

The song had been written by Claude Curly Putnam Junior, Inspired by a film called 'The Asphalt Jungle'. The film starred Marilyn Monroe, and one memorable scene depicts a gangster who wants to return home to his farm before he dies. At the end of the movie he collapses, bleeding and shot through with bullet holes, onto the green, green grass of home.

The song was released in November 1966 and went to number one in the charts in December of that year. It sold over one million copies in the UK alone and went onto to eclipse that figure when it was released in America. The song appealed to a far broader audience than previous hits and because of this Gordon decided to 'spruce up' Tom's image. Gordon got him to wear beautifully handmade suits and large bow ties. Colourful shirts, jeans and black trousers were now banned. The Squires were also smartened up with dark blue suits. The jackets had high collars, which was my idea, based on the seventieth century coats that local squires would have originally worn back then. Elvis commented on the suits when we met him in Las Vegas in 1968, he told us he was going to get himself some jumpsuits made with similar collars. He certainly did, I remember seeing his white rhinestone encrusted jump suit and the collar was enormous, it dwarfed ours.

Tom and Gordon were now back on a roll. With two number one hits under their belts, things were definitely on the up. This hadn't gone entirely unnoticed by the ex-editor of the New Musical Express, Chris Hutchins. Chris was in his mid-twenties back then, slightly-built and fair haired, he was quick minded and softly spoken. He had a comprehensive knowledge of show business from his time at the Express and had recently set up his own public relations company. Chris was on the prowl for stars to represent and he had Tom in his sights.

Gordon had employed a PR man, John Rowlands, when 'Not Unusual' went to number one. John represented Tom for some time after but Gordon felt he was getting Tom's image all wrong. John was thin and tall and looked a bit geeky with his heavily framed spectacles. He'd set up a series of publicity shots with Tom washing the dishes in the kitchen at Manygate Lane. Gordon thought this cut across the grain of Tom's macho image. So he replaced him with a new guy called Max Clifford.

Max was a good looking man, in his mid-twenties at the time. He was the polar opposite to John Rowlands. Whereas John was a bit of a snob, Max was really down to earth with a fantastic sense of humour. The band really warmed to him. Especially as for the first time he started to bring us a little into the limelight. We weren't invisible to Max, and, whenever he thought it would benefit his duties as Tom's PR man, he'd include us in interviews and TV spots. He was incredibly professional and diligent and would always advise us beforehand on just what to say.

Max lived in Raynes Park and after leaving the press office at EMI he worked, a couple of years, for Chris Hutchings and Syd Gillingham, before going out on his own in 1971. Max would sometimes invite us over to an upstairs room in his local pub. He had a little enterprise going on there, blue movies! Max had set up a small movie screen and charged a few friends to join in the fun. Never mind the hot films, the air was always blue with cigarette smoke, as a dozen or so randy blokes pulled hard on their cigarettes, staring intently at the screen. You could have heard a pin drop, none of us had seen anything like it before.

None of us knew what happened, but there must have been some kind of falling out between Gordon and Max, as the next thing we knew he'd been replaced by Chris Hutchins. The band was really sad to see him go. But he did alright for himself, just look at him today: the guru of Britain's PR men and a multimillionaire to boot.

Chris Hutchins was another kettle of fish entirely. Chris came across as a very good manipulator, which is essential in the PR business. He eventually went on to represent a host of stars including Englebert Humperdink, The Bee Gees, Eric Clapton and many others.

With Tom now firmly established and with Chris running his PR, Gordon had some time to devote to another of his acts, Englebert Humperdink. I can still remember when Gordon first told me that Gerry's stage name was going to be Englebert Humperdink. I thought he had lost the plot. It was a ridiculous name for a tall, dark and handsome pop singer. It sounded like something from a children's story book. But hats off to Gordon, it certainly seemed to work.

Gordon asked me to take a listen to a track on a portable tape recorder. We were setting up for a gig in Birmingham at the time. I listened to the song and thought it a very pleasant country song, not unlike Ray Charles's 'I Can't Stop Loving You'. Being a bit of a country fan I told Gordon about the similarities, especially the female backing vocal, singing one line in the chorus and the lead in the other. Gordon went back and changed the arrangement and 'Release Me' was released in March 1967. It went straight to number one. It was the biggest selling single of that year. Gordon was beside himself, he had the Midas touch. Englebert was ecstatic, all those years of struggling were now starting to pay off.

It's fair to say that Dickie Valentine was partly responsible for the song's meteoric rise. Dicky Valentine was a major heart throb of that era, and was destined to die in a terrible car crash a few years later. He was due to appear on 'Sunday Night at the London Palladium'. The audience back then for the show was over twenty million television viewers, and it was every artiste's dream to appear. The exposure was invaluable. As luck would have it for Englebert, Dickie had to cancel his spot due to a throat infection. Gordon got wind of this and managed to get the virtually unknown Englebert Humperdink to replace him.

I remember watching the show on television. Englebert came on looking like a million dollars and groomed to perfection. Gordon had learnt all his lessons with Tom, and he had put Englebert in exactly the same stage wear: tuxedo, low cut waistcoat, white frilled shirt and a large bow tie. Before Tom had started the fashion, bow ties used to be small and narrow, now they hung there like bloody great enormous black butterflies.

Gordon was grooming Englebert to follow in Tom's shoes, quite literally. Right down to the same kind of material. Gordon had seen the success that Tom was getting with an older audience and wanted Englebert to plough the same furrow. Both singers were poles apart vocally but they became intertwined through Gordon's management. He had hit on the right formula for Tom and now wanted to replicate it with the new kid on the block.

Tom didn't seem entirely happy with this arrangement but he didn't make any protestations to Gordon. They had many similarities, Gordon saw to that, but their personalities were like chalk and cheese. Englebert was like a Chardonnay, smooth with delicate undertones, sweet yet crisp. Tom on the other hand was more your full bodied Tarragona, a wine stamped on by wild Spanish gypsies

I have backed them both on stage and to my mind; Tom was by far the better star, both vocally and visually. Performing on stage with Tom was always a thrill. Right from the very first day he joined The Senators I used to get a kick out of working with him. He had a phenomenal stage presence. Englebert, on the other hand, was full of insecurities. He was a very sensitive character and always seemed concerned about something or other. I guess everyone has a bit of that in their makeup but Englebert took it to extremes he was a real worrier, if he had any nails left they would have been bitten to the quick.

Englebert was very proud of his sideburns, he considered them his trademark. Not long after 'Release Me' was launched I bumped into him leaving the Acuffe Rose Theatrical Agency, close to Bond Street. Both Tom and Englebert were represented by them. We had a little chat and caught up on all the latest news. Suddenly he pointed to his sideburns and asked me what I thought of the new look he had given them. To be entirely honest they looked dreadful. They were grown down below the earlobe, which wasn't unusual as Elvis had done something similar. But Englebert had sliced a gap halfway down, exposing about an inch of bare skin. It looked absolutely ridiculous. I told him I didn't think it was a very good idea and the sooner he grew them back together again, the better. He didn't seem impressed with my honest answer and sloped off.

That was the last I saw of him until about a year later. Tony Cartwright had taken over from Gordon as Englebert's manager. Tony called me and asked for me to come and meet him at The London Palladium. I turned up ahead of time and was taken to wait for him in Englebert's dressing room. It was a bit uncomfortable to say the least as I was sat there waiting for Tony to arrive and Englebert just ignored me completely. Talk about the cold shoulder, he just turned his back on me and my greetings went unanswered.

I stayed put in the dressing room in silence, wondering if

Englebert would eventually acknowledge my presence. But after what seemed like an age, he never did. I made my excuses and left him staring blankly into his dressing room mirror. I've often wondered what on earth this childish behaviour was all about. We went back a considerable way together, I used to visit him and his wife at their flat in Hammersmith, and we had both come up together through Gordon's management. Maybe he now saw me as being in the opposition camp after leaving Gordon on bad terms. I'd hate to think it was over the fact I didn't like his sideburns stunt. Thankfully cooler heads had prevailed there because that look was never launched on the British public. I guess I'll never really know because that was the last time we would ever meet each other.

After the success of 'Green Grass' Tom decided on a house move. He put Manygate Lane on the market and moved Linda and Mark into a larger mansion in nearby Sunbury-on-Thames. The property was at the end of a posh cul-de-sac and had excellent privacy. Springfield House was a sprawling palace with five bedrooms, two bathrooms, four toilets, countless lounges and a study. Tom also had a den, where he set up a screen and film projector to watch his favourite films: mostly Cowboy and Indian movies with the odd American Civil War adventure thrown in for good measure.

Tom used to invite the band over to watch some of the movies. We were always in awe to see the luxurious furnishings. Ivory coloured calfskin sofas and easy chairs, expensive paintings in ornate frames, a monumental colour television, the technology was still in its infancy back then and it was a rare sight. There was every kind of luxury imaginable, wherever you looked. We were all still living in digs and as you can imagine we were mesmerised by all the trappings of stardom.

At that time we were performing regularly on 'Sunday Night at the Palladium' and Tom had become very friendly with the compere, Jimmy Tarbuck. Every time we called in at Springfield House Jimmy would be there, he'd become a bit of a permanent fixture. He was desperate to raise his profile at the time and having Tom as a close pal certainly helped in that regard. Jimmy was a shameless name dropper, and littered his conversation at every opportunity, letting you know he was a friend to the stars. It could get tiresome after a while and the band thought he was overly cocky, self-opinionated and a complete loudmouth. He could be very boorish, it was like he was always on stage, and he just couldn't switch off.

Around that time our guitarist, Dave Wendals, was in Gordon's bad books. Dave had become a bit too laid back for Gordon's taste. I got on great with Dave, but admittedly he was a bit of a dreamer and sometimes his attention wandered. Whenever I visited Dave, at his mother's house in Central Hounslow, the front room would be chock-a-block with models of Count Dracula. There were even toy bats dangling from the ceiling. Every surface was covered in models of Frankenstein, ghouls, zombies and every imaginable character related to horror movies. The walls were decorated with voodoo masks and witches' brooms. Although his mother had managed to retain the upper hand with one particular wall which was decorated with three innocent flying ducks, a bit of a 60's style classic. They looked quite bizarre surrounded by all that horror. Sadly Gordon fired him and we were all sorry to see him go.

I've lost touch with Dave. I heard on the grapevine he moved to South Africa, just like Dave Cooper, our previous band mate. I would dearly love to catch up with him again and swap tales about our time together.

Gordon began looking around for Dave Wendals replacement. It was arranged for us to meet with a new potential lead guitarist, Bill Parkinson. Bill was a northerner from Morecambe Bay. I remember the venue was somewhere on the banks of the Thames, on the way to Hampton Court. It was a bit of a rickety building, a hotel-come-nightclub. Bill was a six foot muscular guy, with a broad Lancashire accent. Gordon introduced us and we got straight down to business, running through Tom's stage act and getting a feel for our new lead guitarist. Bill fitted in great and he could read music to boot, which was always handy.

Bill settled into the band very quickly. He was married to a lovely girl, Jenny, and they had two beautiful daughters. The family was living in Muswell Hill, North London, at the time. Bill had completed his National Service in the Army, where he did a bit of boxing for his regiment. He was a keep fit fanatic which was very unusual back then. Most musicians were into booze, fags and sleeping in until noon.

It was during this period that I met up with Mia Lewis again. We bumped into each other at the Cromwellian Club one evening. Mia was staying with her aunt and uncle in Muswell Hill. Her uncle Vivian was headmaster of Muswell Hill Senior School, and his wife Margaret taught there also. We got talking and it went from there.

Mia had got her first break with a singing residency at

Swansea's Townsman dance hall, fronting a local band. She was one of eight children. Arthur, her father, was a coal miner and Razzie, her mother, a very busy housewife. The family lived high up the Swansea Valley in Abercrave, near Dan-yr-Ogof Show Caves, a stunning part of the Brecon Beacons National Heritage Park. Mia had been spotted by Welsh pop singer, Larry Page, who also had a hand in artiste management. Larry had persuaded her to make the move to London. That was the only way to make it in the business at the time. Mia had packed in her job at a watch and clock assembly factory and made the move. She was immediately signed to Decca Records.

Stunningly pretty, she made the front cover of the New Musical Express on the release of her first single 'Wish I Didn't Love Him'. With such striking good looks, the eighteen year old blonde bombshell was in constant demand for TV appearances. She went on to release a further four discs, 'It's Goodbye Now', 'Nothing Lasts Forever', 'No Time For Lovin', and 'Woman's Love.' The tracks never made the top 10 but her TV work really picked up. Mia appeared on the panel of 'Juke Box Jury', and her down-to-earth honesty struck a real chord with the viewers and won her many plaudits.

Mia appeared on 'The Simon Dee Show' with Ken Dodd, singer Vince Hall, and Roy Hudd. The ratings for the popular show were averaging over twenty million viewers at the time but still that all important hit single eluded her. In my opinion the problem she had was with the record company. She had no say in what songs were released. The only voice she was allowed to project was her singing voice. It was a real shame because some of the B-sides were far more commercial than the A-sides.

The Acuff-Rose Agency, part of the American organization that represented a massive slice of country and western stars, kept her very busy with work. She was booked in venues from one end of the UK to the other. It would be crazy now for a young girl to be constantly on the road all alone, travelling from city to city by train and coach. It was a different age back then and you were expected to just get on with it. Our drummer, Chris Slade, got married to his long term girlfriend, Lynne, at the time. It would be another five years before Mia and I would tie the knot. We saw each other whenever possible, most of the time passing like ships in the night. I'd be travelling up the M1 for a gig and she'd be on her way back to London for another gig.

Tom had been booked to appear in London's famous 'Talk of the Town'. Peter Stringfellows' 'Hippodrome Nightclub' now occupies the site of the once famous venue. At the time 'Talk of the Town' was the jewel in the crown of the capital's nightspots. To say it was plush would be an understatement. The cabaret room was absolutely massive and the colour scheme was all red and gold, with huge glittering chandeliers. The vast majority of the clientele was very well-heeled and would enjoy a sumptuous meal followed by the cream of international talent. The house orchestra would top off the evening, providing dance music into the early hours.

'Talk of the Town' was managed by Bernard Delfont, a close relation of Lew Grade. They were two of the most powerful men in show business. Lew would come along to watch the acts and then decide whether they were good enough to appear on television. The lucky ones would then go onto become household names. Simon Cowell is doing a very similar thing today with 'X-Factor' and 'Britain's Got Talent'. Give them plenty of TV exposure, turn them into stars and smile all the way to the bank.

Tom was booked to appear at 'The Talk' for a month and we were booked to augment the orchestra. On the opening night the place was jam packed with celebrities. There was a real buzz in the air and everyone was looking forward to Tom's appearance. But you could have heard a pin drop when Ava Gardner swept in with her entourage, and took a table at the front of the stage.

Ava Gardner was Hollywood royalty. She was considered a legend along with Marilyn Monroe, Barbara Stanwyck, and Bette Davis. At one time she had been married to Frank Sinatra. She had appeared in numerous movies: '55 Days at Peking' with Charlton Heston, 'The Night of the Iguana' with Richard Burton, 'The Life and Times of Judge Roy Bean' with Paul Newman, 'The Barefoot Contessa' with Humphrey Bogart. The list is endless, she was a real superstar alright. Ava would have been in her mid-forties at the time and the whole place was in awe of her fame and beauty. Word soon reached the dressing rooms and Tom and Gordon were delighted by her attendance. Gordon said, 'It's great copy for the morning papers.'

The orchestra struck up and the resident troupe of dancers appeared on stage, complete with legs up to their armpits, skimpy rhinestone costumes and ostrich-feathered head-dresses. They went through their high-kicking routine and eye-watering splits to warm up the audience. The curtains closed and The Squires leapt on stage and took up our positions behind

Tom. The resident bass player, guitarist, keyboard player and drummer all gave us beaming smiles as they disappeared across the road to the pub for an hour.

The curtain swished open and a clearly nervous Tom charged onto the stage to thunderous applause. He went into his opening number and the audience really responded. Lew Grade was sat at the back of the room watching Tom, and Gordon was watching Lew intently, trying to gauge his reaction. There was a lot riding on it. Gordon was convinced that if Tom went down a storm Lew might offer him his own TV Show.

After the show we went back to our dressing room next door to Tom, and changed out of our stage gear. Tom had invited us to join him in his room for some champagne. We knocked on the door and were ushered in. The room was full of dense cigar smoke and tinkling champagne glasses. Lew Grade was amongst the guests, puffing on a large Havana. Cliff Richard and The Shadows were there also, but all eyes were drawn toward Ava Gardner. She was dressed in a slinky black gown, and was chain smoking and knocking back the booze.

Ava tottered toward me, giving me the once over with her alluring green eyes. I stood rooted to the spot, mesmerised. 'Don't feel nervous honey,' she quipped, 'I won't eat you.' I thought about what to say back, but my mouth was dry and my throat had seized up. 'I'm staying at The Dorchester, room 101,' she smiled and winked at me. Then squeezed my arm and moved on.

The raven-haired statuesque beauty had left me speechless. I watched her make her way through the room and rejoin her entourage. A few minutes later they all swept out, probably back to The Dorchester. After knocking back a few drinks I thought about heading over to The Dorchester and knocking on room 101, but imagined 'Ole Blue Eyes' opening the door and demanding an explanation. Somehow the thought of one of Hollywood's hottest stars and a 'boyo' from an obscure mining town, illegally renting a bedroom in a council house and driving around in an old banger, didn't quite cut the mustard. Besides I'd recently started getting serious about Mia, and she was less than half Ava's age and far prettier!

Tom's stint at 'The Talk' proved a huge success. Gordon had also used the opportunity to record an album, 'Live At The Talk Of The Town'. I think Tom was at his best both vocally and physically. That year he managed to get five hit singles under his belt. 'The Green, Green Grass,' had been the catalyst and had undoubtedly sealed his reputation as a superstar.

13

LENNON

My good friend and housemate Tony Cartwright had taken his first steps to becoming a 'manager to the stars'. He'd picked up as much as he could from Gordon and was now setting out on his own path. One of the first 'artistes' on his books was Freddie Lennon, John Lennon's estranged father. My first proper meeting with the old rascal was marked by a funny turn of events.

My landlady, Mu, was under the impression that I would be on the road with Tom and the band for over a month. Mu always liked the idea of me being away on tour, she still got her rent money, it was one less mouth to feed and no washing and ironing chores. But on this occasion I returned to Tonbridge Road earlier than expected. Some of the venues had been taken off the tour due to Tom's television commitments.

I arrived at the front door, only to find I had misplaced my keys. This was unusual for me as it was normally something that always happened to Cartwright, the bane of Mu's life. I didn't want to wake everyone up as it was the early hours of the morning. I noticed that my front bedroom window was open and decided to shinny up the drainpipe and climb in. My bed was directly under the window and with my legs half hanging out I flopped in, landing on the bed. There was an almighty scream! It was piercing enough to wake the neighbours. I was so startled I scrambled over the bed and switched on the light.

Sitting bolt upright in bed, her hands wrapped around her nightie, was Mu. I should have been the one screaming. She had a thick white pancake of night cream on her face and her hair was a mess of pink curlers. What a bloody sight, she looked like a vampire bat!

Mu's eyes were shut tight and she had no idea it was me in the room, she kept hollering for her mother. Before I had a chance to say anything and calm her down, the door burst open and little old Nancy staggered in brandishing a poker. One of the neighbours was banging on the front door enough to break it down. Then Cartwright arrived wiping the sleep from his eyes. Mu finally stopped screaming and was calling me all the foul names under the sun.

After she had calmed down and everyone else had gone back to bed, Mu told me she hadn't expected me back for another week, and had moved into my bed to give her daughter, Jill, and Mum, Nancy, a bit more space in the other room. Mu also informed me we had another unexpected visitor, 'Freddie bleedin' Lennon's downstairs sleeping one off on the settee. Cartwright's aiming to manage the scruffy bugger and turn 'im into a star. He'll be bleedin' lucky. The old scrote's only got about three teeth in his head, 'e's as fat as a pudding, 'ardly any hair and he's got a bloody nose like Fagin.'

The following morning I woke early and found Freddie still asleep. Both Mu and I stood over his slumbering form, and I had to admit Mu hadn't been exaggerating, he was certainly no oil painting. Mu gave him a shake to wake him up. His clothes were dishevelled and a bit whiffy.

Lennon had deserted his young family and run away to

sea. He had joined the Merchant Navy when his son, John Lennon, was just a young kid. John never forgave his father for deserting him. Freddie had recently returned to England and was living like a vagrant, sweeping floors and collecting glasses in a pub in Surbiton in exchange for lodgings. At closing time he'd empty all the ashtrays, looking for dog-ends to smoke. Tony Cartwright had heard that his fellow Scouser had come back home to roost and signed him up. Tony had big plans, what with Freddie being John's Dad and all. He made him lose weight until his clothes were practically hanging off him, dabbed some self-raising flour on his face and roughed him up a bit. When Tony was satisfied that Freddie looked the part, he marched him up to John Lennon's front door. At that time Lennon was living in a sprawling residence at St Georges' Hill, Weybridge.

John Lennon answered the door and Tony laid on the sympathy, after exhausting his fiddle, he asked John if he'd help his father out financially. The three Scousers became involved in a proper Liverpool conversation and it ended with Lennon telling the pair of them to piss off or he'd set the dogs on them. Tony took Freddie back to the local pub to drown their sorrows and it was there they hatched their next plan.

Tony accompanied Freddie to a local dentist and had the last of his rotten teeth removed, leaving him completely gummy. Then he had him fitted with a set of false teeth, big shiny tombstones. God only knows how Tony paid for it all as he was always skint. I'll never know how he managed it, sheer blag more than likely, but Tony then managed to get him a recording contract with a German record label. Not only that, but Freddie's first single with the label was a massive hit in Germany. It never made it outside that country, but Tony and Freddie were over the moon.

Of course Freddie's new career as a pop star didn't last very long. He was a bit too fond of lazing around and smoking and drinking himself to death. But at least Tony had made enough money out of the venture to continue his management company and set up a publishing company to boot, 'Winterfold Music'. Poor Freddie Lennon passed away aged sixty-two, a victim of cancer, and sadly his relationship with his son was never resolved.

At that time Tom and The Squires were booked to appear at 'The London Palladium' for a four week stint. The comedians Mike and Bernie Winters were the supporting act. We played six nights a week, also a matinee performance on Saturday afternoon. Sunday was normally our day off and 'The Palladium' would book a top-flight star to fill the gap. One particular booking was the legendary comedian George Burns. George was famous for his dry wit and used to wise-crack his way through the set smoking cigar after cigar. Every visiting performer would be given the number one dressing room, the star's room. This was Tom's room for the duration of our stay at 'The Palladium'.

Monday night came around and Tom rocked up along with Chris Ellis. He was just about to change into his stage gear when he did a double take. 'Some bugger's nicked my bloody cigars. I left a full box here on the dressing table.' Chris picked up the empty Monte Christo box and a note floated out which he handed to Tom. Scribbled on the note was, 'Nice dressing room Tom. Thanks for the cigars. Keep the change. George.' Tom was spluttering with fury, 'what does he mean keep the bloody change?' Chris picked up a pound note from the floor which had fallen out of the empty cigar box and handed it to Tom. 'Is he bloody joking or what, he's nicked all my Monte Cristos, a pound won't buy one of the buggers.' Chris pointed out to Tom that George was a comedian after all, but Tom was cursing him for days afterwards.

With two shows a night and three on Saturdays, there was a good deal of hanging around between sets, so we took to nipping across the road for a pint to kill time. The pub was about twenty yards from the backstage door. One evening we were all sat there enjoying a pint. Chris Slade and Vic Cooper finished their drinks in double quick time and sauntered off back to the dressing room. I glanced at my watch and noticed that Bill Parkinson and I had plenty of time to get back before the curtain went up. We were both sat there chatting away and I happened to glance at my watch again to see what time we should make a move. The bloody thing had stopped. I looked around desperately and asked someone the time. We had about three minutes until we were due on stage.

Panicking we dashed across the road, oblivious to the traffic and honking horns. We charged through the stage door and hurtled up the endless flights of stairs. Back in the dressing room we quickly changed into our suits, grabbed our instruments and literally threw ourselves back down the stairs and into the wings. The curtains were closed and Mike and Bernie Winters were out in front going through one of their routines. They had been quickly summoned back from their dressing room to fill in, whilst Chris Ellis had gone searching for us. The pair of us were sweating buckets and quietly crept across the stage. We got to our stage positions and plugged in our guitars. Every eye in the orchestra watched us with disdain. The conductor practically had steam coming out of his nostrils, he looked livid. It was all very embarrassing and I just wanted the earth to open and swallow me.

Getting animated signals from the wings, Mike and Bernie wound up their routine and introduced Tom. The curtain went up and Tom leapt on stage as if nothing was amiss. The audience seemed unaware of the delay and thought Mike and Bernie were part of the second half of the show. Bill and I called in on Tom afterwards and apologised for not being on time. Naturally my wristwatch took the blame for the whole lousy episode. It was a real wind-up job, the watch I mean. I cursed that watch, during my eight years in the band with Tom it was the only time I was ever late on stage.

With five hit records, Tom and Gordon were now seriously rich men. The rest of us were still slumming it, but at least we had regular work. Tom decided he had enough new cars and decided he wanted a new nose. Tom had always been obsessed about the state of his nose. Before joining The Senators his nose had taken quite a bit of bashing. Back in the dance halls and clubs in and around Ponty, Tom was forever getting into fights and his 'conk' was a bit deformed due to it being 'nutted' so often. Gordon agreed that he was overdue a make-over and arrangements were made for him to enter hospital. Gordon also came up with a complete fabrication to bamboozle the press, 'troublesome sinuses', and after the operation Tom duly reported,

'I had an operation for sinus trouble. When I came out I noticed the nose was shorter. They must have cut something out of it.'

Pinocchio would have been amused. Tom later came clean and admitted to the 'Evening Standard' that, 'I don't think I could have done so well if I hadn't had my nose altered. I think it doesn't look as offensive as it did beforehand. Some people might have thought, 'Well I quite like his voice but I don't like his nose', so you have to eliminate all those things that put people off.' Tom also took the opportunity to get his crooked teeth capped. I don't believe he had any other facial alterations until many years later.

Autumn had set in and The Squires found themselves augmented again with a full blown orchestra. This time it was the Ted Heath Orchestra, and Gordon had arranged a British tour, taking in Ireland. Ted Heath had passed away but the orchestra kept on, keeping his name alive. Some of the musicians were stars in their own right. The drummer Ronnie Veral and trumpeter, Stan Reynolds, were legends in that field of music. The orchestra comprised of the cream of big band musicians performing in the UK at that time. We soon discovered that they all liked to knock back the booze in copious amounts.

Some of them carried hip flasks filled with their tipple of choice. I remember playing a theatre in Dublin and we had a break between shows. The Squires followed the orchestra into a pub near the Theatre. The pub featured a very long narrow bar with barrel after barrel of Guinness on tap. Being in Ireland this was the real deal, black as tar and smooth as a fermenting swamp. The seasoned musicians got stuck in and they were knocking back pint after pint, just as quick as the bar staff could fill them. The average age of the orchestra was around fifty and us youngsters could hardly keep pace with them.

Pretty soon it was time to get back to the theatre for the second show. The trumpeter, Stan Reynolds, who also fronted his own band when not on the road with the orchestra, was a bit of a character. Slightly built and balding with a pencil-thin moustache, he was one of the old troupers, and had seen it all and done it all. Positioned at the back with three other trumpeters and the brass section, Stan sat directly behind me on bass guitar. He always had a mischievous twinkle in his eye, and whenever I happened to glance over my shoulder he would be pulling funny faces and that sort of thing.

On that particular night Stan was feeling the after-effects of all the Guinness he'd knocked back at the pub. Midway through Tom's act Stan's eyelids began to flutter, his head sagging during the gaps in the musical arrangement. The musician sitting next to him had to keep giving him a dig in the ribs whenever they were due to come in again. Toward the end of the show Tom sailed into 'Not Unusual' and Stan was almost out for the count. Suddenly I heard a muffled crash. Stan had fallen backwards off his chair and straight off the back of the stage dais. He had fallen a good five feet to the floor below. I turned around and watched incredulously as he rolled into the curtain backdrop. I looked around me my mouth flapping open, but no one had noticed, not Tom or the audience. Stan lay there sleeping it off, we finished the set and Tom took his bows. The following evening Stan Reynolds was propping up the bar as usual as if nothing had happened. He was knocking back the Guinness as usual, although we were now in Belfast.

I was using a new bass guitar during that period. When we had toured Australia one of our support acts was an Australian band. The bass player fell in love with my Epiphone guitar. Apparently you couldn't get hold of one for love nor money down under. America didn't import the model there. As I recall he was using a white Fender Precision Bass, and he begged me to make a straight swap. Gordon had been on at me for some time to ditch the Epiphone and get myself a Fender, as he thought it had a better quality. Gordon thought the sound was 'chunkier' and fitted better with the material Tom was producing.

I made the swap, but what I wasn't aware of at the time was that the Fender had been rebuilt, using some parts that weren't designed for that model. I was playing a hybrid and not a genuine model. I wasn't really happy with this state of affairs and wanted to get rid of it. Tom was due to travel to America at the end of the Irish leg of the tour, and as every musician knew at the time, guitars were much cheaper over there than in the UK, on account of the import duty. I asked Tom if he would bring me back a Fender Bass, and I'd sell my dodgy hybrid to pay for the new one. He readily agreed as it was also in his own interests that the band sounded the best it could be.

I was chuffed to bits when he returned with a beautiful Sunburst Fender Precision. Tom told me I could pick it up from the Acuff-Rose Agency whenever I liked. But before I could get my hands on it we were off to Birmingham, booked for a week at 'The Castaway' nightclub. It was an amazing venue. The club was a life size model of a wrecked pirate ship with a huge cannon hole shot in the side. The audience would enter through the cannon hole and walk into a cabaret room with all the fixtures and furnishings connected with seafaring. Tom always looked forward to playing there. It was a very special place and the owner was a real gem, he would always give us a hearty welcome and really looked after us.

Before the tour to 'The Castaway' I'd traded in my battered old Anglia for a green Austin Cambridge. It had a lot of mileage on the clock but the engine seemed sound. I'd taken advantage of Tom being away in America and driven it home to Wales to visit Mia and her family in the Swansea Valley. I felt refreshed and a little in love when I said my goodbyes and pointed the car toward Birmingham. The drive was faultless and the Cambridge behaved admirably, even though the suspension seemed to be stiffening up the closer I got to Birmingham.

I have always found Birmingham a bit of a nightmare for drivers trying to find their way around. I kept getting lost and the engine started boiling over. I recognised where I was finally, a little over a mile away from 'The Castaway'. Suddenly the car started making a hell of a racket and then stopped dead in its tracks. I raised the bonnet, steam and hot water was spurting out of the radiator and the smell of burning oil stung my nostrils. The engine was searing hot and there was a mess of ruptured hoses hissing steam.

Stranded on a main road I was fortunate enough to find a telephone kiosk. I phoned the club and managed to speak with Chris Ellis who came and collected me in the van. I arranged for a garage to come and collect the Cambridge. Later that day I was informed that the engine had completely seized up and I would need a replacement. In all, parts and labour amounted to

£175 including towing charge, four weeks wages! The evening wasn't any better. I shared a bedroom in a flea bitten bed and breakfast with a grizzled ex-seaman down on his luck, just like me. The old tar stank to high heaven and just like Freddie Lennon he had breath like a constipated crocodile. I was now in no position to be able to afford a regular bed and breakfast and had to cut my cloth accordingly.

Along with my wages and Mia sending me the rest I was just about able to settle the garage bill. I took Tom aside and explained I was in a tricky spot and would have to tighten my belt. I asked him if he would let me have the Fender on spec and I'd pay him back out my future wages. But he refused to release it until I coughed up all the money.

The Fender was propped up in the corner of Acuff-Rose Agency whenever I called in for a cup of tea, tantalisingly close but out of reach. It just sat there gathering dust. I thought it pointless to try and get Tom to relent and let me use it. When his mind was made up, that was the end of the matter. In a way he was shooting himself in the foot, surely it would have been to his advantage to have his band sounding the best that they could? But he obviously didn't see it that way.

When we had some free time in between tours and gigs, the band would hop in the van and Chris Ellis would take us for a wander around Denmark Street in Soho. We'd always visit the 'Gioconda' café in Tin Pan Alley where musicians would all gather and exchange gossip about the London music scene. There was a clutch of music shops in the immediate area and still is to this very day. We called in at one of our regular stops, a musical shop run by Mike, a charming Jewish guy who used to cater for all our musical needs. He knew all about the story of my hybrid Fender and the new Sunburst, 'in custody' at the Acuff-Rose Agency on Tom's orders. Just like the rest of the band he couldn't understand the logic behind it all. He asked me, 'Vern, has Jonesy let you have that guitar from the States yet?' I shook my head and told him about my money troubles and Tom wanting cash up front for the guitar. 'Look Vern, me and the wife watch you guys on TV all the time, give me the crap Fender and you can have whatever you want from the shop.' I was too shocked to speak and swear I felt my eyes welling up. Mike reached up, took down a pristine Fender Precision Bass and handed it over to me. It was snow white, with a tortoiseshell scratch plate and the beast felt nice and heavy hanging from my shoulder. I objected to Mike that it wasn't a fair swap, but he wouldn't hear about it and shooed us out of the shop, complaining he had other customers to serve. What a wonderful gesture and what a wonderful man. I hope he's still kickin'.

Poor old Tom was spitting feathers when I told him I wouldn't need that bass after all. It's probably still sitting there propped up in a corner of the Acuff-Rose Agency, for all I know.

It took me awhile to clear all my debts for the Cambridge's new engine. But I finally got back on my feet again. Everything was getting along fine, I was motoring and my new Fender was a real treat to play. Gordon called us into his office for a band meeting around that time, and we went with some trepidation wondering who was next for the chop. But as it happened it was really good news. Gordon informed us that Tom had been chosen to appear before Her Majesty Queen Elizabeth and the Duke of Edinburgh for the Royal Variety Performance. Back then that was a real signifier that you had finally arrived. Gordon saved the best for last; we were going to appear with him!

We were all elated but also a little shocked. This was a very sudden about turn and a lot to take in all at once. Up until that point in time there hadn't been an awful lot that Gordon had wanted us to be included in. Quite the reverse, he'd actually always gone out of his way to put us down and treat us like the hired help. We had all come to terms with that a long time ago. Now he was offering us a Royal Command Performance, this wasn't just any run of the mill TV programme, at that time it was the TV programme'. We were all a little baffled about this sudden 'hand of friendship' gesture. After all there had been an aching chasm yawning between the band and Tom and Gordon for some time.

We were incredibly excited to be appearing at such a prestigious event with Tom. The band discussed amongst ourselves why Gordon hadn't booked session musicians for the performance or relied on The Palladium's orchestra, as he had done so many times before. It was very unusual to offer us any of the limelight. The only reason we could come up with was that Tom was dead nervous about the whole occasion and didn't want to be up on that stage all on his own.

On the evening of the performance we were all back stage rubbing shoulders with all the stars of the show. Everyone was a bag of nerves, Tom was really worried. The only person who seemed remotely calm was the American comedian, Bob Hope. There was a great line up including: Rolf Harris, Lulu, Sandie

232

Shaw, Val Doonican, Tommy Cooper, Harry Secombe, The Rockin' Berries, Ken Dodd, Vikki Carr, Mireille Mathieu and of course Tom Jones and The Squires. Everyone had butterflies. Easily the most nervous was Lulu. She couldn't stand still for a moment and was nibbling her fingernails to the quick. Every once in a while she'd blurt out, 'Oh my God!'

If Lulu had been wearing hobnail boots, the poor girl would have worn a deep furrow in the backstage floor. She was incredibly relieved to get her five minute spot out of the way. There was a variety act on directly after her, Tanya the baby elephant. Tanya had the audience in fits of laughter, even the Queen was tittering, especially when the elephant dropped a few dollops on stage. Luckily the stage hands were nearby to clear it all up. Tanya wasn't the only one feeling nervous. There was a queue for the backstage toilet a mile long.

We enjoyed our moment in the limelight. Sadly it was to be our last Royal Performance. Tom had got over his nerves and from then on he was happy to go it alone for all future Palladium performances.

With New Year bells still ringing in our ears 1968 saw Tom and The Squires really pushing the envelope. We were on a hectic European tour, taking in Scandinavia and Germany, we hardly paused for breath. Toward the end of January we were booked to appear at the Bambi Awards in Munich. At that time the Bambis were Europe's version of the American Oscars. We were performing alongside The Supremes. Our eyes were out on stalks; we had never seen so many movie stars in one place and were a bit nervous about performing to such a glittering crowd.

Sitting directly in the front row were Clint Eastwood,

Richard Burton and Elizabeth Taylor. Eastwood and Burton were filming 'Where Eagles Dare' and had taken a break from filming to attend the event. Eastwood was sitting at a different table to Richard and Elizabeth and it was clear to see why. They were going at each other hammer and tongs, knocking back the champagne and doing their best to out-curse each other. They were certainly a tempestuous couple alright. Eastwood looked very bored by the whole event, but we were all very excited to see 'Dirty Harry' in the flesh.

Backstage in the dressing room we started getting ready for the show. Just along the corridor we could hear The Supremes, laughing and giggling. Tom winked at us and decided to go and knock on their door to introduce himself. He had a bit of a glint in his eye that we all recognised, and the band started a sweepstake on which Supreme he was going to have a crack at. Tom knocked on their dressing room door and Mary Wilson answered and ushered him in. It was the beginning of a serious love affair.

After the performance we all let our hair down at the after show party. The place was jammed with A-list movie stars and celebrities, it was pretty breath-taking being in such exalted company. We were introduced to Henry Mancini, who had recently composed the music for the smash Peter Sellers movie, 'The Pink Panther'. The Supremes hung out with us and they were delightful, very shy and modest, but a lot of fun. We were all sorry to part company with them, but had to push on to the next venue.

We stayed at a reputedly haunted hotel on the next leg of the German tour. I was shacked up with Vic Cooper while Bill

Parkinson and Chris Slade shared a bedroom along the creepy, creaking corridor. Vic was the band's 'wind-up merchant', forever playing pranks on the rest of us. Although on this occasion it all got a little hairy.

After finishing our gig we all piled back to the haunted hotel for a couple of beers and Vic suggested we hold a séance. The hotel was reputed to be full of wandering spirits and Vic thought it would be 'a bit of harmless fun.' Vic marched us up to our room which he felt had the best 'vibrations' for making contact. He told us he had held a number of séances in the past, and seemed to know all about it. Vic had us all sitting around a table with our hands flat, and asked us to concentrate. Then he switched off the room lights and draped a hand towel over a bedside lamp, to create the right atmosphere. Pretty soon he was ready to begin and hollered, 'Is there anybody there? If there is anyone there, give us a sign.' Suddenly there was a sharp clanging sound a few feet behind Vic, and we all jumped out of our skin. 'Are you a friendly spirit?' said Vic, 'Knock once for yes and twice for no'. There was a single sharp metallic clang, and it cut across the silence. We were all feeling very uncomfortable to say the least.

Within ten minutes Vic had managed to connect each band member in turn with a long lost relative. It was all very convincing, especially as we were all knocking back the beers to steady our nerves. The following night we all settled down to another séance. Vic had let me in on his little secret. He had tied a piece of string to his cigarette lighter and placed it in a chamber pot under his bed. The other end of the rope was tied to his ankle, and with both hands flat on the table he would give his ankle a little shake, it was all very convincing. The band fell for it hook, line and sinker. Vic went through the same ritual for the rest of the tour and poor Bill and Chris were convinced they'd made contact with long lost relatives.

Back in London we hardly had time to pause for breath before Gordon was busy planning our assault on America. At that time I made the mistake of telling him I had some early recordings of Tom and The Senators. During the early years when we rehearsed at 2 Glyndwr Avenue, we were lucky enough to be able to listen to playback of our repertoire to help iron out the creases. My Uncle Billy had been the proud owner of a portable Phillips tape recorder. It was not much bigger than a loaf of bread and had twin reels on top with a detachable lid to protect it in transit. They were very rare at the time and hard to come by. My father persuaded Billy to part with it for £10 and presented it to me, the band were over the moon. I loved playing around with it and also used it to tape family and friends.

Gordon's ears pricked up and he said, 'Next time you're back in Ponty, bring the tape recorder back with you, we may be able to do something with the tapes.'

The day came around and I plugged in the tape recorder at Gordon's place. Jo was there and both seemed fascinated with this little piece of 'pop history'. Afterwards Gordon asked me to leave the recording with him. He wanted to listen to them through a few more times. 'Call in tomorrow afternoon and pick them up', he said.

I returned the following afternoon and Gordon made an appearance with two of his Siamese cats in tow, one of them had been christened Elvis. Gordon looked a little apprehensive, 'Come in Vernon, bit of bad news I'm afraid. Elvis has been a very naughty boy.' I was devastated to see my tape recorder in the corner of the room, surrounded by yards and yards of twisted tape, and two empty spools. 'I trusted you Gordon,' I cried, 'The only recording of my mother's voice was on those tapes, and my father playing the piano, how can a bloody cat do all this damage?'

Gordon just shrugged, 'That's Siamese cats for you, they're very clever,' he replied without a hint of remorse. I could have burst into tears. It looked as if both tapes had been crushed together and there wasn't an inch of tape that was salvageable. The tapes were destroyed beyond repair. I couldn't bring myself to pick up the recorder. I just left in a daze, suspecting that Gordon had deliberately destroyed the tapes and I'll never know why. Those tapes were a little piece of history. They captured all the banter between Tom and the band in between songs. They were priceless to me, and far more important than the band rehearsing was my mother's voice and my father knocking out Charlie Kunz and Winifred Atwell numbers on the piano. Sometimes you lose complete faith in human nature and that was certainly one of those days.

14

AMERICA

Gordon was determined to crack America. He hired a new musical director and arranger, Johnny Harris, to accompany us on the tour. Johnny was a fantastic musician and one hell of a character. He was around thirty-five years of age at the time, average height, thin as a rake and as mad as a hatter. He was affectionately known in musical circles as 'Johnny the Boot', having been born with a club foot. Gordon sometimes had to tell him to ease up on the acrobatics. On stage, conducting the orchestra, he would get carried away, stamping his boot and swinging his arms around wildly. Baton in one hand he would leap around like a man possessed. Tom didn't like it because Johnny was getting more attention from the audience than he was.

Arriving at Heathrow Airport, The Squires and Chris Ellis teamed up with Johnny, while Gordon and Tom flew business class. The Boeing landed in Miami and there was a black Lincoln Continental waiting for us outside the airport. We were chauffeur-driven to a two star hotel close to a beautiful sandy beach. I was the last out of the car, and following the band into the hotel, I happened to glance back and noticed the chauffeur cursing us for not giving him a tip. We were fresh off the plane and hadn't caught up with the American custom of tipping yet. I grabbed the band to see if we could club something together, but we all had empty pockets. The chauffeur gave us a dark look and sped off.

We caught up with Gordon later and he reluctantly agreed to pay us £80 a week for the duration of the tour, insisting that it would go back to £40 a week when we returned to the UK. But there was always a catch with Gordon and he told us we would have to pay our own way for hotel accommodation and all other expenses, including meals, taxis and transport. We were playing Miami, New York, Los Angeles and Las Vegas on the tour and none of those cities were cheap. Johnny Harris thought we were crazy and should have held out for more. He was getting £250 a week plus expenses. We had to explain Gordon's modus operandi to him, we would have been on the first plane home if we tried to get any extra. Johnny thought Gordon was a right cheapskate.

We performed for three nights at the exclusive Deauville Hotel on Miami's famous coastal strip and then headed for New York and a two week stint at the famous 'Copacabana' nightclub. Many years later Barry Manilow would immortalize the night spot with his massive hit of the same name. The 'Copa' was the equivalent of 'The Palladium' back home. In the States it was a signifier that you had made it in show business. Every major star had performed there: Frank Sinatra, Ben E King, Ray Charles, Dionne Warwick and our friends The Supremes. The stage there was tiny because the room was so small and the tables were lit by dreaded candlelight. The flickering candles gave the room a certain ambience, but the fumes that spilled from them stung the vocal chords, they were the bane of every performer.

It was no use complaining about it, either. The guy who

managed the 'Copa', James Bodell, was not only a friend of the stars, he was an even greater 'friend' of the New York Mafia. The Mafia frequented the club on a regular basis, it was notorious in that respect, and no one argued with Bodell, if they knew what was good for them anyway. It was said at the time that if the police raided the 'Copa' the streets of New York would have been clean of crime.

The 'Copa' was an intimate venue and only held about one hundred and fifty customers. We were booked for three shows a night, the first kicked-off at 9pm followed by another spot at midnight and the closing set at 3am in the morning. On Tom's opening night we attracted a crowd of celebrities and some of them stopped off back stage afterwards for drinks. I didn't know where to look, there were so many famous faces. We were introduced to Dionne Warwick, Gladys Knight and The Pips, Roger Moore and the country singer, Jerry Reed, who looked as if he was on something as he was completely spaced out. It was a real eye-opener regarding Tom's popularity in the States, he was really making inroads.

The booze at the club was very expensive, far too expensive for us to afford. One evening, thinking we were really clever, we got Chris Ellis to smuggle in some beers from the local liquor store. James Bodell had eagle eyes and spotted we were drinking a different brand from that sold at the club. He ordered one of the bouncers to confiscate the lot and warned us about trying a similar stunt again. Naturally we didn't argue.

We worked with a small orchestra at the club, and they were cramped in behind us on the tiny stage. Tom had no option but to stand teetering at the audience edge, he was so close to the tables he could have shaken hands without getting off the stage. We all felt a little sorry for the front rows as when Tom really got into his act he'd drench them with his sweat. The orchestra we worked with was red hot at the time. They had recorded the soundtrack for 'Mission Impossible', the original television series, with Lalo Schifrin, and it was a real pleasure to work with them.

I'll never forget one evening during the midnight performance. Tom had the audience in the palm of his hand. Every night was a sell out and the word was spreading like wildfire that Tom Jones was hot. There was one particular song in the set that used to have all the 'Mob' guys weeping into their silk handkerchiefs. 'Danny Boy' would ring out and the room would go completely silent, all you could hear was the constrained sobs of these big tough guys, it was hilarious.

But that evening there was a huge bear of a man seated at a table with a blonde woman. They were directly in front of Tom. The women had her arms draped around the man's thick neck, and she was yapping in a high screech, like a spoiled poodle craving attention. Tom was tenderly singing 'Danny Boy' and every verse was being tarnished by this unwelcome high-pitched intrusion. Every musician on the stage was glaring at her. I could see that Tom was being knocked out of his stride by this boorish behaviour. But he let things ride, probably with the intention of saying something to her after he had finished the song. The lyrics at the end of the song went, 'I...love... you...so', a soaring climax to end on. The woman was oblivious and kept on screeching and caterwauling. Tom leapt down off the stage and shoved the microphone under her nose, 'Hey', he barked, eyes blazing, 'are you going to finish this song or what, huh?' The woman sat there in stunned silence and Tom jumped back on stage to finish the song. The response from the audience was deafening, and the big guy and his lady friend slunk out enduring a cacophony of cat calls.

I always thought it took a lot of guts for Tom to do as he did that evening. Considering the clientele of that particular establishment, he had no idea who he was dealing with. The guy could have been a high ranking mobster for all he knew. It might have been a little rash of him dealing with the situation so dramatically. I certainly admired him for doing it, that's for sure.

During our stint at the 'Copa' we made the best of our time in New York and took in all the sights. Gordon had flown back to London after watching Tom's opening night at the famous venue. Gordon had booked Tom into one of New York's finest hotels and he reported to us he was being waited on hand and foot. We asked him before he left to recommend somewhere we could afford and he suggested 'The Goram Hotel'. It was housed halfway up a skyscraper, and you walked straight out of the lift into a classic 'film noir' dark and gloomy reception. The desk clerk tossed us some keys from a row on the wall and that was the last we saw of him.

There were three single beds in one room and two next door. I remember our rooms having massive heating pipes sweeping around the skirting. You couldn't touch the pipes as they were boiling hot. They threw off so much heat we couldn't sleep. The windows were bolted shut so we were unable to cool the room down. It was bizarre as it was like living in an oven and the temperature outside was well below zero. After a couple of days the heating broke down and we found ourselves freezing to death. Then it was miraculously fixed and we were back to living in an oven, it was unbearably hot.

We found a cosy little bar about five blocks from 'The Goram' and trudged through the snow to enjoy a couple of beers. Vic began rolling his lucky dice on the table, and for a bit of fun we started gambling for loose change. Suddenly a massive hand cracked down on the table and scooped up the dice and coins. The owner of the bar had a face like thunder and bawled at us, 'You're going to cost me my license, you crazy limeys!' We hadn't realised that gambling in public was taboo in America at that time. Atlantic City and Las Vegas were the only cities licensed for gambling. The owner turfed us out of the bar and sent us on our way with a right earful. The snow was about three feet deep at this time and rising steadily, with a blizzard raging. We thought about getting a cab back but they had closed all the roads. Getting back to 'The Goram' was like Scotts Antarctic expedition, luckily we were well fortified from our time spent in the bar.

In between shows the band would retire to the lounge bar to get our second wind. The bar was situated below ground in the bowels of the 'Copa'. It was always full of Mafia 'underworld' characters, ironically gathered underground. One evening we were relaxing between sets and there were about half a dozen tough looking and heavy set guys staring in our direction. It was a bit unnerving, to say the least. They were seated across from us, near the far wall, and kept muttering amongst themselves and glaring over. Finally one of them beckoned us to join them.

Tom nervously looked at the band, and we all piped up, 'It's you they want, Tom.'

'Jesus,' he moaned, 'why me?' We all urged him not to keep them waiting and he slowly rose to his feet and padded over to join them.

Tom found himself squeezed in between the lot of them. He was no shrinking violet, but he looked incredibly nervous as they gave him a grilling about his rise to fame and how much money he was raking in. Tom turned whiter than a sheet, it looked as if they were about to put the squeeze on him for some protection money. Luckily we were due back on stage and hustled him away, making our apologies as we sidled out.

As it turned out, they never got around to asking him for protection money, and by the end of our stint at the 'Copa' we had become great pals and they kept buying us drinks. We were quite sad to say goodbye to them all, but they all promised to come and see us play in Vegas. We were even sadder when we later read in the LA Times that two of them had been killed in a hail of bullets. It was unnerving to study the photograph on the front page of the paper and realise that they had died in the 'Copa' in their usual spot. The wall behind them was riddled with machine gun bullets and splattered with blood. We felt a long way from home right then.

Los Angeles was on the cusp of spring when we landed. Blue balmy skies and warm breezes, it was quite a contrast to New York. Everyone had been looking forward to arriving in the Orange State. After the gruelling three shows a night stint at 'The Copa' we had a relatively relaxed schedule. Tom was lined up to appear on a number of chat shows, and Gordon had organized lots of Hollywood meetings for Tom to discuss potential movie business. The best surprise of all was our hotel, it had a swimming pool on the roof.

One day we were sunbathing beside the pool and a bit part Hollywood actor, Lance Le Gault, introduced himself. He was a handsome, rugged guy with a growling voice. 'Knight Rider' creator Glen Larson described him as having 'a voice that was four octaves lower than God's.' Lance later appeared in numerous film and TV shows including The A Team, Dallas, The Incredible Hulk and The Dukes of Hazzard, and he was Elvis's stunt double in all his movies. Back then he was in his early thirties and he told us he was on a 'covert operation', which we all took with a pinch of salt.

Lance was a friendly and charismatic guy, and he seemed over the moon to have bumped into Tom Jones's band. He told us he was a big fan and showed us around LA. We visited the recording studio where the Everly Brothers laid all their hits and he introduced us to Mexican food, insisting on picking up the bill at some wonderful restaurants. We visited his up-market apartment complex. The walls of his lounge were adorned with sporting handguns, rifles and memorabilia from the American Civil War. The whole time we were with him he never let up asking questions about Tom. He came across as a fanatical fan, and by the time we left for Las Vegas he knew everything about Tom's life story.

When we arrived at LA international Airport, on our way to Las Vegas, we ran into quite a commotion. There was a crowd gathered to see Liberace. He was incredibly tanned, all teeth and dimples, and the most exaggerated smile in show business.

The flamboyant classically trained pianist was returning from playing a stint in Vegas. Liberace had been booked by the 'Flamingo Hotel', which was the same venue that Tom and the band were due to play for a four week residency. Tom piped up, 'I hope you left my dressing room in good order?' Liberace flashed him a dazzling smile.

When we arrived in Vegas, Tom was whisked away to the penthouse suite at the 'Flamingo'. The band and Johnny Harris found a motel, just a few hundred yards from the hotel. 'Empey's Desert Inn' was an updated version of the motel made famous in Alfred Hitchcock's film, 'Psycho'. The motel was a wooden built structure. One row of rooms stretched for about fifty yards, and running parallel was a two-tier row with a narrow landing running the length of the first floor. There were two beds in each room and it was cheap and cheerful. Chris Ellis and Johnny Harris stayed in the two-tier row, with Johnny directly above Chris's ground floor room.

Gordon had been working up to Vegas for months. He believed it could be the making of Tom in America. If he could win over the Vegas audiences, then America would really open up for him and his status as an international star would be sealed. Tom was being paid twelve thousand pounds for the month, which was a bit of a pay cut. The bosses of the 'Flamingo' were taking a bit of a gamble booking first-time artistes, and were only willing to pay a rock bottom fee. For once Gordon didn't argue, which was very unlike him, I think he recognized that a successful stint with Tom commanding the main showroom was worth more than money on this occasion. Gordon arrived in Vegas with Tom's wife, Linda. They were both there for the opening night. Gordon had bitten his fingernails to the quick. I'd never seen him so nervous. It was unusual to see Linda there as she very rarely came along to see Tom perform. The adulation from Tom's female fan base used to really put her off and at heart she was still a 'Valleys Girl' and didn't like mixing with theatrical agents, promoters and all the assorted hangers-on. Linda was incredibly shy and having known her for over eight years I liked her immensely. She just let Tom get on with it, as long as he came home after playing away, so to speak.

The first thing we all noticed, after arriving in Vegas, was the massive publicity drive surrounding Tom's appearance at the 'Flamingo'. There were billboards, banners and posters just about everywhere you looked. The marketing was all geared to promote 'Tom Jones Fever' and Radio Stations kept airing commercials at the end of their weather reports informing the listeners 'what the Tom Jones fever temperature was,' at any given moment.

Sadly 'The Squires' were missing our keyboard player for the Vegas performance. Vic Cooper had been asked to audition for a new group called, 'Toomorrow'. He had been approached by Don Kirshner, the creator of the 'The Monkees' and 'The Archies', the cartoon characters who had a massive hit with 'Sugar, Sugar'. The other person involved in the new group was Harry Saltzman, producer of the James Bond movies. It was an incredible opportunity and one that Vic couldn't really turn down; we were sad to see him go and wished him every success.

Don Kirshner and Harry Saltzman were about to shoot a science fiction movie, it was a tongue-in-cheek comedy and they wanted a great soundtrack. They had already cast Olivia

Newton-John, and wanted a cheeky Cockney type character for the group. Vic Cooper was perfect for the part. Vic had originally been approached in New York, but had sworn us all to secrecy; he didn't want Gordon or Tom getting wind of it until he was sure he had got the part. Harry Saltzman had flown Vic to London for an audition. Tom was busy making TV appearances and interviews so it was easy for us to cover for his absence.

Vic had finally heard that the part was his, when we were in LA. We all congratulated him and threw him a going away party. Vic packed his suitcase and was on his way to the airport, but not before sending Gordon a telegram informing him of his decision to leave the band. Gordon naturally went ballistic and made all sorts of threats about blackening his name. He told Vic he'd never work in show business again and he'd make it his life's work to make him pay for doing this. Vic wasn't overly bothered, he phoned us in Vegas to let us know he'd been picked up from Heathrow Airport by a chauffeured white Rolls Royce and had five hundred pound handed him. They were to be his weekly expenses and didn't even include his wages. It was quite a turnaround from the forty pounds a week he was used to from Gordon.

There were plenty of musicians to take Vic's place, but what had upset Tom and Gordon the most was that Vic had left them, and not the other way around. Both of them were incensed but the rest of us were walking around with smiles plastered to our faces. Good old Vic, he'd certainly punctured their over-inflated egos. Gordon hastily recruited a new keyboard player from Cardiff, Mark Stevens. He was an accomplished musician, but he was a bit of a square peg in a round hole and never really fitted in. It was too late for Mark to join the Vegas tour at that stage, so Johnny Harris filled in by playing piano at the 'Flamingo'.

The bosses at the 'Flamingo' didn't want to try us out during high season, so we were playing before the season had begun and the venue wasn't exactly buzzing. The showroom held an audience of around five hundred. Our supporting act was American comedienne, Kay Ballard. She was a veteran in show business and, importantly for Gordon, relatively inexpensive. Kay had established herself as a musical comedienne in the 1940s with the Spike Jones revue of entertainers. She played broad physical comedy and stand-up, and was familiar with audiences through her many television and stage productions. Kay's famous catch phrase was, 'Good luck with your Mouth!' and she was the first person to record the song 'In Other Words', which was later renamed 'Fly Me To The Moon'.

One date on the tour, 6th April 1968, is forever ingrained in my memory. We were midway through our month's residency at the 'Flamingo' and the shows had been going really well. All the publicity about 'Tom Jones Fever' had done the trick and our two shows a night were packed to capacity every night. The first show used to start at 8pm and the second at 10pm. Tom was in terrific form, despite him complaining that the dry Nevada desert air was playing havoc with his voice. Tom had packed out his penthouse suite with humidifiers and refused to come down and join the band at poolside, when we were taking our breaks.

That evening we were killing a little time in between shows.

I was near the foyer of the 'Flamingo' chancing my luck on the slot machines. The area was mostly deserted as everyone had filed into the main showroom ahead of the second show. There were row upon row of slot machines, and I happened to be playing the one right next to the clearway that led from the foyer toward the showroom. I had pushed my last dime in the slot and yanked down the arm. I glanced over my shoulder and was dumbstruck. Heading right toward me was Elvis Presley and Priscilla, closely followed by their entourage, the Memphis Mafia. Elvis spotted the shocked look on my face and gave me a devilish wink as he swept on by. Elvis was met by one of the casino bosses and ushered into the showroom.

I rushed back stage to Tom's dressing room and instead of the customary knock, practically knocked the door down and burst in. Tom was seated at his dressing table, applying his stage make-up, and wearing his favourite white towelling bath robe. He was startled by my entrance and said, 'Bloody hell Vernon, you're meant to knock, you almost gave me a heart attack.' I told him I was glad he was sitting down, 'Elvis and Priscilla are here with the Memphis Mafia, to watch the show.'

'Vernon, stop winding me up,' he said.

'I'm deadly serious, Elvis is in the building.' At last it struck home and Tom leapt out of his seat. He flung open the door and started hollering for Chris Ellis. When Chris arrived to see what all the commotion was about, Tom sent him off to check that Elvis was really at the casino, he thought I was winding him up. I dashed back to the band's dressing room to let them all know the news. The excitement back stage was electric. We took up our positions with Johnny Harris at the grand piano. Tom was pacing up and down in the wings. The curtains opened and the orchestra steamed into Sam Cook's belter, 'Ain't That Good News.' Tom leapt across the stage, grabbing the mike from the stand. He was immaculate in a dark blue tuxedo, with white frilled shirt and bow tie. The room was pitch-black, with the only light coming from the stage.

I was desperately trying to locate Elvis in the audience. I finally saw him, directly below me, sitting at a massive table with Priscilla and his entourage. Elvis was puffing away on a cheroot. They had quietly seated themselves as soon as the house lights had dimmed and hardly anyone in the audience was aware of their presence.

It was mind-boggling performing in front of 'The King'. Elvis hardly ever went along to see other artistes perform. Tom had met him a year earlier on the set of one of his movies. It had made a huge impression on Tom, meeting one of his heroes, and now we were performing for him, we gave it our all that evening and didn't hold back. Before we had got on stage, Tom had nervously coughed into his hand and said, 'We got to make a good job of it tonight boys, for Elvis.'

Chris Slade's drums almost crashed off the podium, he was giving them so much stick. Johnny Harris, looked a little frustrated sitting at the piano, you could tell he wanted to be out in front of the orchestra, conducting for all he was worth. Bill Parkinson and I tucked in behind Tom and gave everything we had. Tom belted out every hit in his armoury. He discarded his jacket and bow tie and his white shirt was clinging to him like a wet Pontypridd Observer. The audience went wild at the end of the show, and Tom waited for the applause to die down and thanked the audience. Then he introduced Elvis:

'Ladies and gentlemen, the moment has come to introduce you to a man I have long admired, and who has been an inspiration to me for many years. When I was starting out back in South Wales, where I come from, he was my guiding light, and he's here tonight. Mr. Elvis Presley!'

The room exploded with five hundred hysterical voices practically taking the roof off. The room was in darkness and the audience didn't know where to look. A searchlight beamed around the audience, pretending to frantically search for 'The King'. The audience played along turning wildly around to follow the spot and search out Elvis in the audience. Finally the powerful beam came to rest on Elvis and he stood up, sending the place into meltdown. It was an unforgettable moment.

The audience was in raptures and there was no end to the cheering and applauding. I caught Tom's eye and made a subtle finger slash across my throat. He read it and shouted over the PA system, 'Okay, settle down, everyone settle down.' At last things started to calm a little and Tom thumped his chest, 'Hey don't forget I'm the star tonight!' The audience roared with laughter and Elvis got back to his feet to applaud Tom, and that set everyone off again going crazy.

Johnny Harris took the initiative and counted the orchestra in. We all steamed into 'It's Not Unusual' followed by Wilson Pickett's 'Midnight Hour'. Tom then introduced his new single, 'Delilah', which was flying up the UK charts at that time. We finished off with the explosive 'Land Of A Thousand Dances'. We left the stage to a standing ovation led by Elvis, it was magical.

Backstage in our dressing room we changed out of our stage

gear. We had made Tom promise to introduce us to Elvis on pain of death. True to his word, Chris Ellis came a calling and beckoned for us to follow him to Tom's room. We all filed in and there must have been over a dozen people crammed in there. Tom was in the corner in animated conversation with Elvis. Priscilla was seated near the door chatting to Linda. All the Memphis Mafia was present: Sonny West, Lamar Fike, Jerry Schilling, Red West and Charlie Hodge. They were all very friendly, if not a little guarded. They all had their individual jobs. Red and Sonny West were Elvis's bodyguards, although Red also had a talent for writing songs, some of which Elvis recorded: 'If every day was like Christmas' and 'Separate Ways'. Charlie Hodge used to harmonize with Elvis and specked out each stage before a concert. Lamar Fike handled all Elvis's stage lighting, and Jerry Schilling gave advice about what other groups were using for audio equipment.

Red West introduced me to Priscilla and I shook her hand. Her skin was almost alabaster white and was off-set by her stunning black beehive. She was absolutely stunning; Elvis was a very lucky guy. Everyone was smoking like chimneys and before very long the room was enveloped in a blue haze. Tom caught my eye and called me over. The rest of the boys watched as I excused myself from Priscilla and Linda, and eased my way through the guests. Elvis was wearing a black seaman's reefer jacket, white polo-neck and black trousers. I had planned to ask him if he had any intention of touring the UK, but that thought flew out of my head the moment he shook my hand. Tom introduced me, 'Elvis this is my bass player, Vernon. He's been with me right from the beginning.' I told him it was pleasure and an honour to meet him, and he said, 'You guys certainly laid it down out there. That was a great bass intro to 'Land Of A Thousand Dances', really cool.' I thanked him and told him that meant a great deal coming from him.

He smiled and said, 'You know I just can't win. I had this here outfit flown in from Carnaby Street, knowing I was going to meet you guys, and here's you guys dressed all American in T-shirts and jeans and all.' We all laughed and he shook my hand again, 'It was real good to meet you Vernon'. I turned, elated and almost bumped into Chris Slade. The rest of the band had formed an orderly little queue behind me, waiting patiently to be introduced to 'The King'. It was hard to believe that only a few years earlier, whilst working at the Pontypridd Observer, I'd been typesetting Elvis's name in countless articles.

Red West gave each of us an A4 size coloured photograph of Elvis and Priscilla. It was a beautiful portrait of them on their wedding day, cutting the cake. Elvis signed each of the photographs for the band, a personal keepsake from 'The King'. Pretty soon it was time for him to head back to Los Angeles. Elvis invited us all to take a look inside his Lincoln Continental limousine. It was as wide as a truck and capable of seating the whole entourage. Elvis was very proud of the Lincoln and took delight in showing us the built in TV, mini-bar and telephone. Watching the black beast speed away into the night, I turned to Chris Ellis and said, 'C'mon lets go and celebrate.'

Tom had gone back to the dressing room, but Linda overheard us making plans to visit the 'Aladdin Casino', where Little Richard was booked for the month. Linda had had a bit too much champagne and was a little glassy eyed. Quite suddenly she launched into a verbal tirade about us idolizing Elvis in front of Tom. She scolded us and said we shouldn't have behaved like that, making Tom feel small in front of Elvis, he was ten times a better singer. We tried to calm her down and explain we were more than loyal to Tom, but we had all just met one of our heroes, a once in a lifetime opportunity. The usually shy Linda Woodward could be incredibly protective of her husband.

A short walk from the 'Flamingo' and we were both propping up the bar in the 'Aladdin'. We had missed the end of Little Richard's set, but had caught it a few days earlier and even been introduced to the living legend by Tom's PR man, Chris Hutchins. It was way past midnight at this stage and the bar was almost empty. A smartly dressed lady, accompanied by a teenage girl, came and sat quite near us. After ordering drinks the elegant women turned to us both and said, 'You guys look like you've hit the million dollar jackpot.' We explained we were celebrating after meeting our hero, Elvis Presley, that evening. The women asked where we had met him, and we explained we were Tom Jones's band and Elvis had come along to watch us play. The women smiled and said the Memphis Mafia were no doubt tagging along, we asked her if she was an Elvis fan and she said:

'You could say that. I'm Priscilla's mom, Mrs. Beaulieu. Elvis is my son-in-law,' she introduced Priscilla's younger sister and said, 'We've been to the Sands to see Jerry Lewis. He's doing just fine without Dean Martin. The man is hilarious. Are you guys from England?'

Mrs. Beaulieu went on to explain that Elvis must be a big

fan of Tom's, as he never went to watch anyone perform live. She said she'd mention running into us when she met Elvis back at the suite. We were confused and said we'd just waved him off on his way back to L.A. Mrs. Beaulieu explained that Elvis wasn't due back on the set of his latest movie, 'Live A Little, Love A little', until the morning. He was staying in his regular suite on the top floor of 'The Aladdin', it's where he got married to Priscilla the previous year. Chris Ellis piped up, 'You're telling us that Elvis is staying here tonight?' We were both gobsmacked. We had a great evening chatting away with them. Mrs. Beaulieu told us all about Elvis's new song, 'A Little Less Conversation', which we couldn't wait to get our hands on. Finally they made their excuses, and we watched mother and daughter disappear into the lift heading for Elvis's penthouse suite. What an evening it had been, we were too wired to head off to bed and carried on celebrating. A good few hours later we were practically seeing double. A cowboy rancher had joined the party and was telling us all about rattlesnakes and desert critters.

The last I remember was staggering back to Empey's Desert Inn. I made it as far as the deserted swimming pool and collapsed into a sun lounger. I awoke the next morning, squinting up at a cloudless sky, with the mother of all hangovers. Around me was the sound of splashing water, happy chattering voices, and music blaring from portable radios. I was stretched out fully clothed on the lounger, my face redder than a lobster. I glanced at my watch and realised I only had two hours before we were due to rehearse our new song, 'Delilah'. It was climbing the UK charts and Gordon wanted it included in our set, especially after it was so well received by our audience the previous evening.

When we met for rehearsals, Tom told us that Gordon was rubbing his hands with glee. He had made sure Chris Hutchins contacted the British Press about Elvis attending our gig at the 'Flamingo'. The story was splashed across all the newspapers. Gordon told Tom that the all-important American tour was a huge success and would make them both multi-millionaires. However it wasn't such great news for the rest of us. Elvis had been knocked out with our drummer, Chris Slade, the previous evening. Elvis approached Gordon and offered him a substantial amount of cash to let Chris join his band. He thought Chris would fit in really well with James Burton and Glen Hardin. Gordon refused point-blank and Chris was mortified, it was the chance of a lifetime. Gordon told Chris he was under contract, and that was the end of the matter. Even to this very day, Chris still curses Gordon for not allowing him to take up the opportunity and advance his career.

Then it was my turn to be disappointed. A young producer had acquired the rights to a book, 'The Gospel Singer', and approached Gordon with the idea of Tom appearing in the movie. I remember walking through the floor of the casino with Gordon when the producer made his pitch. Gordon didn't go for it, he didn't think it was the right vehicle for Tom at the time. The producer wasn't discouraged and suggested me for the part instead. Gordon wasn't impressed with this idea at all and went out of his way to put me down. He told the producer that my broad Welsh accent would be a hindrance, and I was a little too green yet to be appearing in movies. We both stood there open mouthed as Gordon sauntered off, he tossed over his shoulder as a parting shot, 'Make sure you're not late for rehearsals Vernon, you don't want to keep Tom waiting.'

The biographers of 'Tom Jones Close Up', Lucy Ellis and Bryony Sutherland, capture it better than I ever could: 'Gordon thought he had the capacity to make an infinite number of stars. Nevertheless he was curiously reluctant to further the careers of The Squires, whether collectively or individually, regardless of the profit potential. In March 1968 a film producer approached Gordon with the idea of featuring Tom in a movie called 'The Gospel Singer', and suggested also that The Squires' bass player Vernon Hopkins should do a screen test. Taller and more classically handsome than Tom, Vernon was blessed with typical Hollywood looks, and perhaps better suited to the big screen than the singer's rugged profile. Gordon did not hesitate to block the move in order to protect his protégé's interests, and Vernon was sworn to secrecy 'for the good of the band'.

I'm blushing, it's very kind of them to describe me in those terms and I'm very thankful. I don't think for one moment that the film producer was thinking of me as an option to replace Tom. I believe he would have liked me to have played a role in 'The Gospel Singer' had it come to fruition. He also mentioned a screen test for another film project that he was involved in. Naturally I was very keen, who wouldn't be? But Gordon refused and offered me a decision between staying in the band or taking a gamble with the screen tests. There was no reasoning with him. I stuck with the band. Looking back with hindsight who knows what may have happened if I'd walked out then and taken my chance in Hollywood?

Tom also had another brush with the movie business. He

told us he had missed out on playing James Bond by a whisker. Harry Saltzman, the producer of the Bond films, had considered giving Tom the 007 role in the next movie. Tom duly reported through the press that he was up for it. But Saltzman had second thoughts, saying that Tom was too well-known as a singer. If it had come off I couldn't have imagined Gordon telling Harry Saltzman that Tom's accent was thicker than leek soup. The band had a chuckle about that one and the skits were flying fast and furious for weeks after, my favourite was:

'Watch it butt. Put that knuckle-duster away or I'll stick the nut on yew so 'ard, you'll be in 'ospital 'till the 'earse arrives! Now then place 'ewer 'ands against the wall an spread 'ewer legs. Any nonsense butt, 'an I'll squeeze ewer balls so 'ard, you'll sound like Mary 'opkin, yew bastud! Ow was that Mr. Saltzman?'

During our stay at the 'Flamingo' we made lots of friends. But one in particular stood out. Vince Silvestri was one of the 'suits' in charge of the casino. Vince was in his thirties, recently divorced, and in charge of emptying the masses of slot machines. He was fairly stocky and always wore a cowboy hat, along with his impeccable Italian-cut suits. Apart from watching us perform on stage, he thought we were a pretty miserable lot mooching around the casino on our time off. He thought we ought to be high-rollers living it large and having a ball. He was as sharp as a cut-throat razor and sensed that something wasn't right in our world. Vince pumped us for information; he wanted to know what was up. We told him our troubles and he was speechless. 'Our resident musicians are on more bread than you guys, and they get to go home every night.' Vince told us to leave it with him, we were going to have a fun time from now on. True to his word we were waited on hand and foot, if we were having a bite to eat in the restaurant, a word from Vince and the bill was lost. In between shows a beautiful waitress in fish-net tights would rock up with a tray full of beers, 'On the house, Vince says Hi.' He even arranged for a four-seated plane to fly us to the Grand Canyon.

There we were one morning climbing into this tiny Cessna parked on the apron of Las Vegas airport. It was so warm Chris Ellis was padding about in his flip-flops. Off we went into the wide blue yonder. It was amazing flying above the barren desert. The pilot started to climb so high, we found it hard to breathe as the air thinned out. We approached a landing strip on the Canyon's upper lip and were surprised to see pine trees heavy with snow. Although the temperature at the bottom is desert hot, it's Arctic-Alpine at the top and Chris was soon regretting his choice of footwear. The Grand Canyon is often referred to as one of the eight wonders of the world. As far as I'm concerned it's the first. Awesome! On the return journey the pilot took us on a helter-skelter ride through the canyon, diving right to the bottom and skimming the waters of the Colorado River. A good hour later we were back in Vegas and eternally indebted to our great friend, Vince Silvestri.

With our month's residency at the 'Flamingo' drawing to an end there was one final surprise in store. Johnny 'The Boot' Harris was a randy old sod who never looked a gift horse in the mouth. Skinny as a beanpole, his 'boot' weighed in at more than him. Bill Parkinson and I were practicing some chords for a new song that Tom wanted to include in the act. Suddenly

Chris Ellis burst into our room and told us to follow him. When we arrived at Chris's room we could hear one hell of a banging, and wondered where on earth it was coming from. Chris Ellis pointed to the ceiling. There was a maze of hairline cracks running through the plaster, caused by a consistent hammering on the floor above. Every once in a while the constant thudding would be accompanied by rapturous moaning.

The three of us stood rooted to the spot, craning our necks and watching the cracks get wider and wider. We heard bed springs squeaking and bits of plaster started dropping from the ceiling onto Chris's bed below. The motel was ancient and I guess the unrelenting desert sun had done its work; the place was falling apart under Johnny's onslaught. Suddenly the thudding stopped and, giggling, we all started to help Chris clear the plaster debris from his bed. Then it started off again and we were all covered in plaster from the ceiling as the thumping resumed.

By this stage we were all in hysterics and practically holding each other up. Chris piped up and started singing Trini Lopes's classic hit, 'If I Had A Hammer' and we all joined in. Pretty soon we were all in time with Johnny's 'boot' hitting the floor above. We managed to sing all of two verses in three part harmony before it all went silent again. The next thing we knew, Johnny Harris appeared in the open doorway wrapped up in a bath towel, 'Hey Chris, turn you're radio down a bit. I'm trying to concentrate upstairs.'

What a bloody liberty, priceless!

15

MARY WILSON

On the day we were due to fly out of Vegas, Tom told us we were stopping off in New York on the way back to the UK. We were all of us going to make an appearance on the Ed Sullivan Show. The program was a national event in the US, every Sunday evening, and was the first exposure for foreign performers coast to coast. The show enjoyed phenomenal popularity and was an American family ritual, with young and old gathering around the television to watch Ed Sullivan. He was regarded as a kingmaker, and performers considered an appearance on his program as a guarantee of stardom.

We were chuffed to bits as up to that point Tom had always appeared solo on the Sullivan Show. We were packing away our instruments and suits backstage at the 'Flamingo' when Vince Silvestri turned up to say 'goodbye'. The band had clubbed together and bought him a music themed oil painting. It was a small token of our gratitude for all his kindness toward us. Vince was touched and thanked us. Then he asked us to accompany him to his office near the casino floor. Vince sequenced some numbers into the wall safe and when it swung open he produced four small cellophane bags. He tossed the bags, one to each of us in turn and said, 'Here, take these silver dollars. The only hands to ever touch them was mine, there's five coins apiece for each of you. Pass them onto your grandchildren and let them know it's from Vince.'

The coins were uncirculated silver dollars dated 1922. It was a very special moment for us all. What a wonderful gift and what a wonderful man. The Vegas Mafia was very much alive and kicking in 1968, and we had heard a fair amount of stories from croupiers and waitresses about Vince's affiliations, apparently he knew where all the bodies were buried in the big Nevada desert. But, what are you gonna do? To us he was a diamond of a man, a quietly spoken, unassuming gentleman, never to be forgotten.

The American tour had lasted a little over eight weeks, and during that period Tom and the band had given forty-eight performances. We hopped on a Boeing from Vegas to New York and booked back into the 'Goram Hotel' a day ahead of our appearance on the show. We were scheduled to fly back to the UK directly after. The show went by in a blur and we left the gig in our stage gear, making a dash for the airport and our connection back to London. The security guys tried to get us to sign out of the studio, but we were already in the taxi speeding away. Arriving at Kennedy Airport we boarded a Trident Airliner, and compared to the Boeing it was a dream of a flight. The journey across the Atlantic was the most comfortable I had ever experienced. I have never understood why the magnificent Trident was pulled out of service in favour of the Boeing, it was 'The King' of air travel in my opinion.

Time changes everything, and number 4 Tonbridge Road was very much changed upon my return. Tony Cartwright, flush with the success of Freddie Lennon's hit record in Germany, had found himself a girlfriend, Pauline, and left Tonbridge to move in with her. When I returned and paid Mu my back rent she decided to take the family on a holiday to Southsea. 'The thing is Vern, I'm going to have to ask you for your keys while we're away.' I was shocked and asked her if she wanted me out, it was not the homecoming I had been expecting.

'Only for the fortnight Vernon, what with Noel Redding, Freddie Lennon and that lot treating the place like Piccadilly Circus, well I'm not here to keep an eye on things,' I was a bit crestfallen and wondering where I was going to find digs at such short notice. Mu was obviously ahead of me on that score and had arranged accommodation at The Magpie Hotel in Lower Sunbury-on-Thames. All I could do was thank her and wish them all a happy holiday. 'I knew you'd understand Vernon. What do you bleedin' fancy for dinner, what about a nice steak with all the trimmings? Mum, get yourself down the butcher's will ya, we're 'aving steak.'

The Magpie Hotel stood on the main 'bottleneck' road running through the village. Sunbury was an affluent and picturesque place. The Magpie was a popular pub and its white-pillared entrance led into a spacious bar and lounge. The pub backed onto the River Thames and customers could take a seat on the patio and watch cabin cruisers, barges and row boats glide up and down the river. Every once in a while you'd catch sight of a sea-going cruiser drifting by. The crafts had rich owners and guests sunbathing on the decks, knocking back champagne.

The Magpie was run by Harry Pern and his Lithuanian wife, Elsa. They had two teenage twin daughters, and were a lovely warm family. Harry was a heavy set fellow in his late fifties, and wore big horn-rimmed spectacles. He offered me the cheapest room in the pub, a second floor box-bedsit with a lovely view of the Thames. It would become my home for the rest of my time with The Squires and for some time after.

Mia was still living with her aunt and uncle in North London. I could have probably stayed there for my two week exile from Tonbridge. They had a large house but I didn't want to impose on them, especially as they had two young children and a very busy schedule. They were both school teachers, and her uncle Viv had the added responsibility of being headmaster.

After two weeks at the Magpie, I was adopted by the customers and the staff. It felt as if I'd lived there all my life, I'd become part of the furniture in no time at all. It was pretty special to just wander downstairs and prop up the bar at your 'local'. Harry and Elsa very kindly said they'd got used to having me around, why not stay? I decided to make it my new home. I had been very lucky to have been staying with Mu, I'd really landed on my feet there, and I had some wonderful memories, but it felt like the right decision at the time. Mu gave me her blessing and wished me all the best, we promised to keep in contact. I bought myself a small portable stove and lived off tinned food and fry-ups in 'Le Chez Vernon', my box-bedsit restaurant! I obviously missed Mu's cooking, but there was a decent curry house in the village and that was my blow-out venue, when I wasn't on the road with Tom.

Ironically both Tom and Gordon decided to move at the same time I did. The American tour had been an astounding success and they were both drowning in cash, it was decided to sink some of the profit into new properties. Tom, Linda and Mark moved into Tor Point, a new mansion in St George's

Hill, Weybridge. Robin Eggar, the author of 'Tom Jones: The Biography', described Tor Point as, 'a serious address, an indication of how far Tom had come from the basement rooms in Cliff Terrace. To a snobbish Englishman, living in St George's Hill was a sign not of breeding but of new money'. John Lennon and Cliff Richard lived nearby. Gordon and Jo Mills moved into a sprawling Tudor mansion just down the road a little. Englebert and Pat were also nearby in Glenbank.

Tor Point was by far the largest property, a seventeen-room sprawling turn of the century pile. It never could make up its mind whether it wanted to be grand or comfortable. The front porch was surrounded by white Doric columns. It was secure from rabid fans behind electronic gates and set in five acres of woods and carefully sculpted lawns overlooking St George's Hill Golf Club, one of the most exclusive courses in southern England. Despite Tom's proximity to the first tee and unlike many of his friends, (Jimmy Tarbuck was a fanatical golfer and both Gordon and Englebert became very keen,) Tom never showed any interest in picking up a putter. Instead he invested thousands of pounds in building a state-of-the-art fitness centre, which contained a double tennis court, a squash court, fitness room, a sauna bath and an indoor L-shaped 25 metre swimming pool. The pool had a kiddie slide and a Welsh dragon in red mosaic tiles on the bottom of the pool.

No expense was spared in doing up the house. The interior decoration was closely supervised by Linda who showed sophisticated taste for a Valleys girl. She eschewed modern furniture for classic, antiques and tropical hardware panelling. There was an enormous drawing room with three chintz sofas and matching armchairs, a chandelier and a marble fireplace. The dining room contained a mahogany dining table that could seat sixteen, a crystal chandelier, silver candelabra and gilt mirrors. The kitchen was all mod cons, an electric hob in a melamine-covered central island and an old-fashioned Aga topped with a beaten copper lintel.

Downstairs at Tor Point there was masses of stuff, each piece sitting dust-free and proud in its appointed place. Linda still did most of the cleaning herself. Copper ornaments, antique bellows, carriage clocks, bowls piled high with porcelain fruit, antique firearms on the wall, the mantelpieces crowded with ornaments, each tasteful in its time and place but indicative of mass purchase. Tom's wood-panelled study was packed full of little knick-knacks and a phone with a gold leaf receiver. There were very few books. Instead, the glass cabinets were full of framed gold and silver discs, his Grammy Award and other assorted medals and presentation scrolls. The grate in the white marble fireplace was replaced by an electric fire and surrounded by copper kettles and antique bed warmers, while the coffee table featured a green onyx lighter, with a matching ashtray and cigarette box. There were always vases full of flowers and fresh fruit on display.

The first floor contained four bedroom suites and a separate wing with two further bedrooms, a bathroom, Mark's playroom and a kitchenette for the live-in staff, who never came. The top floor was Tom's playground with its full-sized billiards room, a bar with proper bitter in the barrel and a sixteen-seat cinema, plus an upstairs toilet so guests did not have to fall downstairs to recycle the beer.

Tom had become eye-popping rich, it was hard to believe that just a few years previously we had all been sharing squalid digs together in the 'Calcutta', Ladbroke Grove. The rest of us hadn't been allowed to share in the enormous wealth. The band were pretty disgruntled as we were all working together touring and releasing new records, yet Gordon and Tom were pocketing all the profits and we didn't get a look in, not even a small increase in our forty pounds a week. It was a bitter pill to swallow.

Gordon and Jo's pile was equally as impressive as Tom's. Gordon had christened his sprawling Tudor manse, 'Little Rhondda' and it was set in three acres of landscaped gardens. It also had an indoor swimming pool, with an underground viewing gallery. There was a glass wall beneath the pool's waterline that allowed visitors to sit and watch the antics of those in the pool. Almost immediately after settling in, Gordon installed a state-of-the-art high tech recording studio. Later he built a mini-zoo, with tigers, orangutans, chimpanzees and Ollie, a one-eyed silverback gorilla. Ollie absolutely hated men, but loved women, he had a particular soft spot for Jo.

Tom and Gordon were always trying to outdo each other in the luxury spending stakes. As soon as Tom caught sight of Gordon's zoo he rushed out and bought a couple of racehorses and a yacht. Both of them were drowning in luxury cars with garages full of Rolls Royces, Bentleys and Mercedes Benz sports cars. During that summer, Englebert also decided to join in the hysterical spending contest. To say it was uncomfortable for the band to witness would be an understatement. The band just got on with it; our entreaties to Gordon about a more equitable split were met with a stony face and outright contempt. Tom refused to even discuss the matter, and always fell back on, 'Take it up with Gordon, it's got nothing to do with me.' I pointed out that he was a board member of MAM, Gordon's company, and therefore it had everything to do with him. Tom always insisted he knew nothing about the business end of things, which was all left to Gordon.

My new life at the 'Magpie' sometimes threw up some unsavoury contacts; some of the pubs clientele were of the roguish variety. Don Henderson was a one-eyed old school villain. He always carried a gun with him and was never reticent about showing it off. Don practically oozed 'intimidation' from every pore of his body. He was around forty years of age, thick set, dark and brooding. His lifeless glass eye gave him a particularly cold and menacing stare. I wouldn't see him for a few days, and then he would turn up laden with jewellery, stolen from some grand house or other. Don always told me Tom's house was on his hit list, but I think that was just bravado as he'd always give a little wink. I tried to keep out of his way as much as possible, he was bad news. He would sometimes be seated in a dark corner of the bar, in animated conversation with other rogues, no doubt planning his next 'job'. A number of travellers were also regulars there, usually during the daytime, and they used to 'take orders' to knock off whatever you desired. Harry Pern wasn't fussy about who his customers were, or what they got up to in their lives, as long as they settled their bar bills on time.

At closing time, Harry would lock the pub's doors and all the regulars would take their drinks downstairs to a little basement bar. From outside the 'Magpie' would look completely dead to the world, completely innocent. But below ground the party used to get into full swing. Being an adopted fixture, I became a regular of the basement bar, when I wasn't on the road with Tom. Derek the barman, who wrote a couple of crime novels for Hank Jansen, the master crime novelist, would always see me okay for drinks until I got my wages from Chris Ellis on Fridays.

Chris Ellis was still lodging with Mu's sister in Thames Ditton at the time. But he eventually moved into the 'Magpie' as well. Our drummer, Chris Slade and his new bride, Lynne, were struggling with a new mortgage. They'd found themselves a little semi-detached in Upper Sunbury-on-Thames. Lynne had secretarial work and their combined wages just about made the house purchase possible. Vic Cooper, our former keyboard player, was having a rare old time of it in Hollywood. Vic was on the set of the film, 'Toomorrow', with Olivia Newton John. When we spoke on the phone he would tell me all about his exploits in L.A. Vic was living it up, good and proper, he told me it was the best thing he ever did, leaving the band. Vic couldn't understand how the rest of us could bare to put up with it a moment longer. Harry Saltzman, the film's producer, had recently sent Vic and Olivia on an all-expenses paid holiday to Acapulco. He wanted them both fit and tanned for the movie. I remember mentioning this to Gordon at one of our rehearsals and he practically turned puce. He told me never to mention Vic's name in his presence ever again.

Bill Parkinson, our rhythm guitarist, and his wife Jenny were still renting a flat in Muswell Hill, just around the corner from

Mia's aunt and uncle. At that time, Bill and I began writing songs together. We would cut the demos at Regent Sound, Tin Pan Alley, where we'd cut the original demo for 'Not Unusual' back in '64. One afternoon, a few weeks after returning from America, we went into the studio to lay down a new track. The song we had written was called 'The Gardener' and it was all about a labourer falling in love with the grand lady of a country house. We had booked a keyboard player, but he didn't turn up. Denmark Street was awash with musicians, so we rushed out and found ourselves a pianist. He was a chubby young fellow who used to run errands for one of the sheet music publishers based in Soho. I remember him sitting at the piano and cleaning the lenses of his spectacles. I explained what we were after and we laid down the track. He gave 'The Gardener' a period-type almost classical feel, which much later, when he was famous, became very much his signature. Job done satisfactorily, I paid him a fiver as agreed. I'll never forget him sauntering out of the studio with a grin from ear to ear, 'Just ask for Reg Dwight, next time you're stuck for a keyboard player' he said. Of course Reg Dwight later became our national treasure, Elton John.

Not long after Bill left The Squires, he struck pay dirt with a song he had written about his mother, 'Mother Of Mine'. The song was recorded by the child star Neil Reid, who had won 'Opportunity Knocks'. It went racing up the charts making Bill a very happy man in the process. 'Wee Neil Reid' was eleven years old at the time and the record sold over 250,000 copies in the UK and over 2.5 million globally.

At the beginning of May, Tom and the band were booked for another month at the 'London Palladium'. The band joined up with our old friends the 'Ted Heath Orchestra' to help fill out the sound. We were delighted that Johnny 'The Boot' Harris was also drafted in to conduct the orchestra. He had lost none of his zip and went at it like a man possessed. The Palladium audience used to only ever have eyes for Johnny. He was so theatrical swirling around, chopping the air with his baton, and shaking his mop of fair hair. Gordon thought he was a distraction and was taking the shine away from Tom. He took Johnny aside and told him to cool it, 'you've got ants in your pants, it's distracting to the audience, they've come to see Tom not you!'

Johnny tried to calm down a little, but he loved his music and pretty soon he was like a 'wild man' yet again, throwing himself into it with gusto and stamping his boot. Gordon lost patience and fired him. Johnny 'The Boot' Harris got the boot and never worked with Tom ever again. Johnny took it all in his stride and just shrugged his shoulders. He went onto to create a fabulous album of music, 'Movements'. One of the tracks, 'Footprints on the Moon', was used by news channels worldwide to introduce the Apollo space programme news alerts. Johnny also had a regular feature on Lulu's BBC show 'A Happening For Lulu'. The show used to feature different Eurovision hopefuls each week along with one of Johnny's instrumentals. Shirley Bassey became a great friend and loved his unique arrangement of 'Light My Fire' so much she recorded it on her next album.

Another familiar face started showing up on a regular basis at the Palladium, Mary Wilson of the Supremes. Since they had first met at the 'Bambi Awards' in Munich they had kept in contact. She even visited him in Vegas before Linda arrived for the opening night. Tom was seriously smitten by the gorgeous Supreme, more so than any of his other conquests. I'd never witnessed him fall for anyone like he fell for Mary, he was besotted. Tom confided that he had never felt this way about another woman, other than Linda. He seemed totally at odds with himself, it was a real emotional ride and he was uncertain how it was all going to end.

There was another problem causing him sleepless nights at that time. Tom was very unhappy about how much tax he had to pay the Inland Revenue. Although he was now a multimillionaire he just couldn't get his head around the amount of money he was losing to the exchequer, he told me his taxes were 'shocking'. Tom took it up with Gordon and demanded he do something about the current state of affairs. Gordon duly phoned Bill Smith, Tom's accountant, and gave him a rocket, he told him in no uncertain terms 'sort it out or you're fired'.

It was typical Gordon to turn Tom's sleepless nights into restless nights for poor Bill Smith. Bill came up with the idea of putting all of Tom's affairs under the auspices of Gordon's company, MAM, short for Management, Agency and Music. Tom was able to claim expenses on running his fleet of gas guzzling Rolls and Bentleys, employing staff, and all the other expenses involved in touring the world. The tax rate on company dividends was far lower and it practically halved his tax bill in one fell swoop. Gordon introduced Bill to Tom at the next MAM board meeting and Tom embraced him, grinning ear to ear. When Tom told me all about it later, I remember asking 'If you and Gordon can reclaim such huge amounts on allowances, why is the band stuck on such a meagre wage?' Tom was peeved that I'd punctured his euphoria and looked at me darkly, he was about to say something, but I cut him off. 'I know, take it up with Gordon.' He wasn't happy with that and I guess looking back it was the beginning of the end for me. I've had a lot of time to dwell on it all and I've asked myself countless times 'was it all down to a sadistic streak in both of them?' I guess I'll never really know, they both certainly had no respect for us, it was a wonder to me that we were all still a band at all.

Our time at the Palladium came to an end and before we could draw breath we were off to Bournemouth's Winter Gardens for another month of shows. It was the usual arrangement with two shows a night and three on a Saturday. Roy Castle was also on the bill, he was a very modest and extremely likeable character. Roy was a multi-instrumentalist, singer, tap-dancer, actor and he was full of boundless energy. This made it all the more poignant when he was struck down with lung cancer caused, he firmly believed, by the intake of tobacco smoke from performing in clubs and theatres throughout the UK. Roy's main instrument was the trumpet, and being compelled to draw in huge gulps of air to play it, he was breathing in room's full of tobacco-stale air at the same time. Although Roy is no longer with us, he left a legacy, and a charity bearing his name lobbied successive governments about the dangers of passive smoking, leading to the ban on smoking in public places today.

Bournemouth was truly exhausting, as there was no downtime. Gordon had booked us into countless television slots around our stage time. Being just an hour away from London, it was a case of straight off the stage and into a studio, then back to Bournemouth for the next scheduled show. I remember recording the 'David Nixon Show' one Sunday, and another around it, and so it went on. By the end of the month we were all exhausted and Tom phoned Gordon to let him know just that, in no uncertain terms. Also Tom was being a bit distant with me since our altercation about money, and this rancour started to enter our stage set, much to my mortification. Tom used to introduce us individually on stage, 'This is Vernon, my bass player, this is Chris on drums', and we would all get a great round of applause and cheers from the audience. But this all now changed and Tom took to introducing us at every show with, 'An 'ow about a round of applause for those bunch of 'ooligans at the back then, don't clap too loud or they'll want a bloody rise in their wages!' Talk about kicking you when you're down, the band was gobsmacked. It was a real low blow. We had been humiliated in so many callous ways over the years by both Tom and Gordon, but this was a new low altogether. Our loyalty and respect toward them both was now all but spent.

Tom had rented a luxurious house in a secluded area of Bournemouth for the duration of the tour, and pretty soon Mary Wilson flew in from the States to join him. Chris Ellis was staying at the house, along with his new Swedish girlfriend, Eva, an au pair. Linda, Tom's wife, was still up at Tor Point, doing a pretty good impression of Howard Hughes. She was completely isolated in St. George's Hill, popping champagne corks ten to the dozen, surrounded by acres of woodland and not a soul to talk too. She had refused to employ any staff and her only company was a flute of champagne. Blocked in, blocked out, it was bizarre, especially with Tom increasingly flaunting his fling with Mary. Chris was at Tom's beck and call, running errands, keeping the fridge well stocked and driving him to the Winter Gardens and wherever he chose to hang out afterwards.

One evening Chris turned up and recounted a particularly hairy episode. Mary Wilson had offered to make dinner for Tom, Chris and Eva. Chris was sent out to buy a chicken and Mary cooked a delicious meal from a recipe her grandmother had given her. They all ate good and proper, congratulating Mary on a fine meal and quite a lot of champagne was consumed. But there was quite a bit left over, so Mary popped it back in the oven for later. Everyone was feeling particularly amorous after the meal and drifted off to their respective bedrooms. By all accounts it was quite an evening and everyone slept in the following morning.

That same morning Linda was reading the morning newspapers. Splashed across the front pages were Tom and Mary meeting illicitly in Bournemouth. The phone rang in Tom's bedroom and the stunning Supreme nudged him awake, passing over the receiver. Tom later told us all about it:

'Hallo, 'said Tom.

'Get that cow out of there now,' screamed Linda

Tom tried to bluff it out, 'What are you talking about? Calm down!'

'I know that bloody Mary Wilson is in bed with you. Get her out now, or I'll kill the both of you. I'm driving down now and I'll be there in five minutes. Get her out!'

Tom was confused as it was over an hour from Tor Point by

car. 'What do you mean, where are you?'

'I'm in the bloody phone box just down the road, you bastard!' and Linda slammed down the phone.

Tom, in a panic, sprang from the king-size bed like a cat with its tail on fire, screaming for Chris. Mary sat bolt upright wondering what the hell was going on. Tom leapt down the stairs in his dressing gown and practically dragged Chris out of bed, 'Wake up Chris, she's on to us, we're in big trouble, come on mun!' Chris was still half asleep so Tom ran back upstairs and ordered Mary to get dressed and pack her bags. She was obviously dumbfounded, but he explained that his wife Linda was on her way to kill the both of them. That got her started packing and Chris helped throw her suitcases into the Rolls Royce parked outside. Tom hysterically ran down the drive-way waving Chris and Mary away, and Chris drove like a bat out of hell back to the Mayfair Hotel in London. Chris reported that Mary cried her eyes out the entire journey, whilst listening to Tom singing 'The Green, Green Grass Of Home' on a small portable tape recorder, over and over again.

After delivering Mary to the Mayfair Hotel, Chris made a U-turn and drove straight back to Bournemouth. He pulled into the driveway of Tom and Mary's love-nest to be confronted by a lone figure staggering around in a daze. Tom had walked down the road to the nearest phone box to confront Linda, but there was no sign of her, he carried on checking every phone box within a mile radius, but with no result. Finally, giving up, he'd knocked on a neighbouring house and been welcomed inside for tea. Chris said he was in a complete state of shock!

Linda eventually turned up later that afternoon, chauffeur

driven and accompanied by her black labrador, imaginatively named Blackie. She was in a rage, and stormed around the house looking for evidence of Mary. Her suspicions were confirmed by the long strands of dark hair she found in the en-suite bathroom. Confronting Tom, she pointed an accusing finger at the hairs in the bath. Tom pointed to Blackie and accused the dog of having jumped into the bath. Linda was fuming and headed for the kitchen, where she found the remains of the previous evening's chicken dinner.

'That looks nice Tom, did you cook it?' Tom stared awkwardly at the floor, avoiding her gaze.

'I don't know why I bother to ask. The only thing you ever cook up is a pack of lies.'

'Chris cooked it, honest,' said Tom, 'he's been reading up about cooking and everything. He's even gone and bought himself a bloody cookbook.'

'Don't talk bloody rubbish. Chris Ellis doesn't know how to boil an egg. That bitch cooked it.'

Chris was to witness many a row between Tom and Linda, enough to fill a book, or so he tells me. Chris always said that Linda had a fantastic aim, especially when it came to throwing crockery at her promiscuous husband. She could certainly get physical, lashing out at Tom until she had exhausted herself. Tom used to just stand there and take it, unflinching; he certainly knew he deserved it. You would have thought that after the beating from Linda, he would have cooled things down a bit with Mary. But he didn't, he was smitten, hook, line and sinker, and the liaison never let up. In fact if anything it got even more passionate. I remember Tom telling me, 'Mary is so easy going, cool, calm and collected. The first time she undressed, it all seemed so natural and unaffected, like we were as one. You know Vern, its love, not lust.'

Gordon was having kittens about their affair. He had bitten what was left of his fingernails to the quick. It was 1968 and things were certainly not as enlightened as they are now. A relationship between a married white man and a stunningly beautiful black woman, let alone two superstars, was heavily frowned upon, especially in America, where they were still in the dark ages regarding race and colour. Gordon pleaded with both Tom and Mary, urging them to end their high-powered relationship. 'Can't you just be good friends? The public will settle for that.' Gordon's pleading fell on stony ground, neither one of them wanted to end it, and the affair continued.

16

FOUR SUITS

Tom and the Squires were glad to see the back of the Winter Gardens. Tom was still jittery after Linda confronting him about Mary, and the band was not best pleased with the acoustics of the large venue. The house PA was under considerable strain and the audience would sometimes complain that the Ted Heath Orchestra was overpowering Tom's voice. We were all glad of a few days break before embarking on another gruelling schedule of shows.

Mia was working a summer season in Jersey at the time. The island was a relatively short distance from Bournemouth so I took the boat and went to visit. Mia was on the same bill as the comedian Lenny Bennett and the impressionist Paul Melba, both unknown at the time. Lenny went onto to become famous, presenting the show 'Punchlines' during the 1980s, and was a regular star on the popular quiz shows 'Blankety Blank' and 'Celebrity Squares'. Paul went onto to appear on the television series 'Who Do You Do', 'The Val Doonican Series,' and 'The Comedians'. He was a regular performer at the Palladium and Talk of the Town. We all became great friends, and they persuaded me to take up snorkelling and water skiing during my stay in Jersey.

Pretty soon it was time to head back to the Magpie, and we were back on the road again playing venues up and down the country. Due to all of our television appearances it became increasingly difficult to exit the pub. All the regulars would corner me as soon as I headed for the front door, 'Derek, pull Vernon a pint please.' Some of the customers thought I was loaded, what with being on television, and would tap me for money. I soon put them right on that score and took a leaf out of Tom's book, 'Take it up with Gordon!'

We were booked to appear at Caesar's Palace, a huge nightclub in Luton, twenty miles up the M1 from London. We had appeared there a number of times before. Cliff Richard, Shirley Bassey and the cream of UK and American talent regularly graced the stage. The manager, George Savva, was one of the most recognizable figures on the cabaret scene. He was nicknamed 'Mr. Show-business' and ran three of the most successful clubs in Britain, Caesar's, Blazers of Windsor and his own Savvas in Usk. George was responsible for bringing Johnny Mathis, Judy Garland, Jack Jones, Frankie Laine and a host of trans-Atlantic stars to his venues.

Whenever we appeared, George would be the perfect host. He of course made sure Tom was being looked after, but also went out of his way to treat us all equally well. George was the kind of true gentleman that believes in equality. Whether the artiste had the star dressing room or the one next to the communal toilet, everyone was treated with equal respect. Shirley Bassey had appeared the week before us and George was not best pleased with the diva's behaviour. Although he did say that once Bassey set foot on stage she transformed into a goddess, an absolute sensation, and his dislike for her melted away.

George told me that Shirley Bassey had summoned him to

her dressing room, during a break in rehearsals 'Are you the manager of this shit house', she asked him. George nodded and Bassey told him to sort out the dressing room. She wanted it re-decorated and a chaise longue found or she simply wouldn't perform. George rushed out and found a contractor to decorate the walls with gold embossed wallpaper. He bribed a local furniture store owner with some free show tickets and managed to borrow a chaise longue. When Bassey arrived that evening ahead of the performance she gave George a right ear bashing. The chauffer driven Rolls Royce sent to collect her was black and not white, as stipulated in her contract. There were no further complaints about the dressing room, but no thanks either.

The supporting act that evening was a ventriloquist and as part of the act he would chain smoke cigarettes whilst the dummy entertained the audience. George had ordered a stage hand to sweep up the dog-ends before Bassey made her spectacular entrance. But for some reason this had not been done that particular evening. Shirley sang her opening number and then paused; her eyes fell on the cigarette butts littering the stage. George was mortified; she had a face like thunder.

'Look at all this muck, ladies and gentlemen, George can't the management afford a cleaner?'

There was laughter from the audience and one of the stage hands threw a broom onstage. George told me he died a thousand deaths. Shirley picked up the broom and swept up the dog-ends. The audience loved it and there were howls of laughter. But as soon as she came off stage there was absolute mayhem and she tore the place apart looking for George. He hid himself in the cleaner's closet near the reception cloakroom, and refused to come out until she had left the venue!

George's favourite superstar was Iris Williams, the Welsh songbird, who had a number one hit with 'He Was So Beautiful', which was later used as the theme for the movie 'The Deer Hunter'. Iris was the complete opposite of Bassey, George used to describe her as 'pure class'. The Ponty-born jazz legend went on to have her own successful BBC television show, The Iris Williams Songbook. My path would cross with Iris later in my career and I always found her to be a wonderful person.

The Caesar's Palace shows went really well and on the last evening I was helping Chris Ellis load our equipment into the van. Suddenly Tom pulled over in his new Silver Spirit Roller, the electric windows slid down and he poked his head out. He was puffing away on an enormous cigar and casually flicked ash over one of the amps, 'Vernon, I've got three or four suits I'm chucking. You can 'ave 'em if you want.'

I exchanged glances with Chris, who looked startled; it was very unusual for Tom to give anything away. I nodded and said, 'Thanks Tom, I'd love to have them.' Tom smiled and said, 'Okay, come up to Tor Point on Monday, around two o'clock, and I'll have them ready for you.' Up slid the electric windows and the Rolls sped off. Chris piped up, 'He can't be feeling well. I've never known Tom to give the skin of his shit away, let alone a suit.' I must admit I was a bit bemused also, but I appreciated the gesture. The only suit in my possession was the one I wore on stage. How wonderful it would be to wear a West End tailored suit. My luck was definitely on the up. When I arrived back at the Magpie in the early hours of the morning, Harry's wife Elsa had left a television set in my room as a surprise. They had installed a new set in the bar. I remember watching the first Moon landing on that TV, as if it was only yesterday.

I remember watching Elvis's comeback TV special on the set. It was his first public concert in ten years. It was amazing to think I'd been chatting with him in the Flamingo just two months previously. He looked cool and collected dressed in a black leather outfit, the magic was still there. Elvis was performing in an intimate setting. James Burton, the guitarist, and the rest of his musicians were all huddled together on stage. I really enjoyed watching them go through all the old rock n roll classics. Suddenly I recognized a familiar face in the bottom left hand corner of the screen. It was our old friend from L.A, Lance Legault, the bit part actor who had pumped us for information on Tom. There he was at the side of the stage playing tambourine. I remembered meeting him beside our hotel pool when he told us he was on a 'covert operation'. In that moment it all became clear. Elvis had sent him along to find out all about Tom in advance of him turning up at our show in Vegas. No wonder Elvis seemed to know everything about Tom and the band before we met; Lance had reported everything back to him.

My appointment with Tom was at 2pm. Tor Point commanded St George's Hill, the mansion stood at its highest point, overlooking Weybridge. I drove there in my old green Triumph 2000, looking a bit out of place amongst all the luxury vehicles. The road rose steeply and there was no mistaking who lived behind the wrought iron gates to my right, the name emblazoned across the gates, 'Little Rhondda'. I gave Gordon's Tudor mansion a toot on the horn as I passed on by. It was a glorious summer's day and I pulled into the private estate full of the joys of life. I introduced myself over the intercom and the gates, emblazoned with the Welsh dragon, swung open.

I knocked on the studded oak door, admiring the Greek pillars either side, and waited. After an eternity the door finally opened. Tom stood there, bleary eyed, wearing a white-towelling dressing gown. Letting out a large yawn he shrugged himself awake and said:

'Ow's it going Vern, alright?'

'Yeah, sorry to get you out of bed Tom,' Tom didn't bother to invite me in.

'Come for the suits 'ave you?' and with that he shuffled off inside leaving me standing on the doorstep like the milkman. 'Wait there, I'll go and fetch them.' Tom shuffled down the vast hallway in his slippers and disappeared through a side door. I was quite stunned by the opulence on display in the hallway, it was crammed full of antiques and fine oil paintings. Eventually Tom returned, puffing away on a Monte Christo, with four neatly folded suits clutched to his chest.

Tom handed me the suits. 'Right there's four suits there. Dougie Millings the West End tailor made them for me. He's measured me for some new ones, and there's bugger all wrong with these.'

'Thanks Tom I really appreciate it,' Arnold 'Dougie' Millings was known as 'the Beatles' tailor' and was famous for designing their collarless suits. He had even appeared in a small cameo role in the Beatles movie 'A Hard Day's Night.' I was chuffed to bits and couldn't wait to wear them. I could see that Tom wasn't going to bother inviting me in for a cup of tea so I smiled and said, 'Well thanks once again, I'll be on my way.'

'Old on a minute, where do you think you're going?'

Finally, I thought, he's going to offer me a cup of tea. But it wasn't that. 'You 'aven't paid me yet,' he said. I was absolutely stunned and just stood there with my mouth gaping. 'Well you don't think I'm going to give them away for nothing, do you? I want six quid each for 'em.' I was incredibly humiliated and Tom seemed to be taking pleasure in my discomfort. I told him I only had the rent for my room at the Magpie, and passed him back the suits. He held up his hand, refusing to take them back. 'Don't worry about it. Chris Ellis can take six quid out of your wages every week, 'til you've paid them off.' Tom closed the door in my face, leaving me standing there. I was angry and upset; we had certainly come a long way from our days together in Ponty. I'll never know why he treated me with such contempt. In retrospect it might have been his way of getting me back for the Fender bass guitar, still gathering dust in Soho, and the court fine for the Corsair incident all those years before. Tom could certainly hold a grudge. Whatever the reason, it was petty and mean. Our friendship was all but now over. I paid off the suits in four weekly instalments, but I should have asked for a discount, the sleeves were too short and the pockets too long to get money out of them.

At that time Tom's parents Freda and Tom Senior came to Tor Point, not to visit but to stay. Tom also persuaded his sister Sheila and her husband Ken Davies to move in. Tom's parents had lived in Laura Street since the Second World War and it had taken Tom a great deal of coaxing to persuade them to leave their friends and neighbours. Tom's father was still a working miner and his camaraderie with his workmates was very strong, he was also used to the slow pace of Valleys life. But Tom wouldn't take no for an answer and kept on at them until they finally relented. It was agreed that his parents would move into Tom's old home, nearby in Manygate Lane. Tom moved his sister, Shelia, and her husband Ken into the gatehouse at Tor Point. Tom employed Ken as gardener and odd job man. He was kept pretty busy, having five acres of landscape garden to look after.

Ken Davies was a great guy, affable and easy going. Sheila was a lovely girl too, it was very sad that they couldn't have children, they would have made great parents. Ken was a sensitive soul and he wasn't really cut out for being involved in Tom's high-powered grand lifestyle. I used to regularly bump into him around Weybridge and we would catch up on all the gossip from back home. He confided in me that Tom wasn't the same brother-in-law he remembered from back in Ponty. Ken really missed the friendliness of the Valleys, and being able to meet his old pals down the local pub. Ken and Shelia liked the simpler life and didn't really take to all the show business lifestyle of flash mansions and endless parties. Chris Ellis told me that Ken would cry quite openly to him about the emptiness he felt inside. He thought the whole of show business was a two-faced rat-race of money-motivated greed. He continued going through the motions but just wanted away from it, and this caused quite a bit of friction with Tom.

Sheila wasn't very happy at Tor Point because she hardly

ever saw Linda. When they had all lived in Ponty, just around the corner from each other, they were inseparable. Now, at Tor Point, they went weeks and weeks without seeing each other, despite living just yards apart. When Tom was away on tour, Linda would wander around the eighteen room mansion, flower arranging, moving ornaments, a feather duster in one hand and glass of bubbly in the other, playing Tom's hit records over and over again. Even when I bumped into Freda and Tom senior in Weybridge they complained that they never saw Linda, she was locked up behind electronic gates, hiding away.

Tom had wanted his father out of the mines, and quite rightly so. Any son would want the same. But it was a different proposition uprooting him from everything that was familiar to him back home in Wales. The only person who thought this was a good idea was Tom. Family members and friends were of a different opinion and tried to dissuade him, but he took no notice. Tom even tried to get his mother-in-law, Vi Trenchard, to leave the Valleys and move to be near them. But Vi was having none of it. Her feet were firmly planted in home soil, and that was where she was staying.

Vi's younger daughter, Rosalind, had recently married Tony Thorne, the owner of the infamous Ford Corsair that Tom had taken without permission all those years before. Despite all the trouble he had got into at the time, Tom bought the newlyweds a nice detached property in rural Church Village, on the outskirts of Ponty. Tom senior grumbled to Chris Ellis that that would have done him and Freda quite comfortably. Rather than uproot them away from home, they hardly saw him and Linda anyway. Tom was always away gallivanting around the world, and Linda was a recluse, he reckoned they saw more of them both when they were back in Ponty and Tom and Linda would occasionally visit. Ken Davies didn't last at Tor Point very long. By 1974 he had had a gut full of it all. Ken and Sheila were increasingly arguing about everything. Ken fell for another woman and he ran off with her. Tom was incensed, furious; he even threatened to pay someone to have poor old Ken 'worked over'.

Quite by accident, the house that Tom had bought Rosalind and Tony Thorne, I had helped build. Back when we were starting out in Ponty and I was working at the local newspaper, The Observer, I used to supplement my income with some labouring work. My fellow printer, Colin Donnallan, married the daughter of Fred H. Frey, the owner of Ponty's only record shop. Tom and I used to spend hours in there every Saturday afternoon. Colin, with the help of his father-in-law, bought the land in Church Village and decided to build a house there as an investment. Colin employed me to help him build it, the project lasted two years. During the late 90s, I happened to be passing Church Village and made a detour to see how the house was getting along; it was now part of an extended residential estate. Imagine my surprise when Tony Thorne emerged and called out to me, 'Hey Vern, how's it going?' I had no idea they were still living there all these years later. Rosalind followed him to see who he was talking too and they ushered me inside for a cup of tea. Tom could do no wrong in their eyes, having bought them such a lovely house, they pumped me for questions about Tom and the Squires and our rancorous parting. I was quite truthful about his behaviour, and Tony confided in me that he was forever getting into scrapes defending Jones's honor. Ponty was still a small place and it didn't go unnoticed that he was forever cheating on Linda.

I very soon became Harry Pern's favourite lodger at the Magpie. Chris Ellis had now moved into the room next to mine and pretty soon Tom and Englebert were regular visitors along with the rest of the band. The pub was starting to become a bit of a celebrity hang out, and Harry was over the moon with the bar takings. He started to slip me the odd free pint with a nod and a wink, as a thank you. Then my old mates Mick Avery, the drummer with the Kinks, and Tony Cartwright, Freddie Lennon's manager started calling in regularly with all their mates. Harry took me aside and told me he thought he'd, 'died and gone to heaven'. Musicians are renowned for liking a drink or two and pretty soon his bar take had doubled. I must admit to feeling a bit dreamy at the time, sitting there at the bar with Tom, it reminded me of the old days back at the White Hart in Ponty, when we were still dreaming about stardom and trying to get that first break. There had been a lot of water under the bridge since then, and things certainly hadn't flowed in my favour. But Tom was all smiles and mucking in with the rest of us, so I just went along with the flow.

I remember that when the bell used to ring for last orders, Tom would be in a bit of a panic. He was still tight-fisted and thrifty even then. He'd pipe up that it was so and so's round, and to get them in quick as he'd bought an earlier round. He hated being out of pocket. It became a bit of a running joke amongst the band and we'd always programme the jukebox, around closing time, to play one of Tom's songs, 'Help

Yourself', which was released in the autumn of 68. The irony was completely wasted, as he would just sing along, but we would all be laughing into our pints.

Gordon had decided to expand, with two successful acts on the books, Tom and Englebert, he wanted to branch out. At the beginning of 68 he latched onto an American singer, the larger-than-life Solomon King. Gordon brought him to the UK and he had a massive hit with, 'She Wears My Ring'. Unfortunately the partnership didn't last very long. Solomon had a quality tenor voice, but lacked a certain amount of sex appeal, and Gordon was disappointed with his next release, 'When We Were Young.' The song flopped and Gordon dropped him like a pancake, pretty soon he was on the first plane back to the States, cursing Gordon for all he was worth. Gordon, undeterred, latched onto Lee Graham, better known as the singer 'Leapy Lee'. Lee had a worldwide hit with 'Little Arrows', it sold over three million copies and was awarded a gold disc.

Gordon, at that time, had seen Tom transplant his family from South Wales and decided he would do something similar. Gordon confided in me that he wanted someone from back home who was honest and reliable, but who would take orders without question. I remember thinking, 'charming', at the time, but it was all to end tragically. Gordon settled on his old school friend, Gordon Jones. It was Gordon who had originally tipped him off about a new band called 'Tommy Scott and The Senators'. That was the first time I met Gordon Mills, when he was introduced to us to by Gordon Jones at the Lewis Merthyr Club and later at 'The Top Hat'. Gordon Jones was a laid back, unassuming guy with horn-rimmed glasses, he always struck me as looking a lot like Roy Orbison. It was a considerable leap for Jones to uproot his wife and children and make the leap from the Valleys to Shepperton. Naturally he was very reticent about taking the kids out of school and leaving their home in Tonypandy. But Gordon, as usual, won the day; he had a knack for wearing you down.

Gordon installed the Jones family in the property he had retained after moving to St George's Hill, a detached three bedroom bungalow. He let them live there rent free, but there was always a catch with Gordon. He paid Jones a mere pittance, telling him he was taxing him at source for rent on the house. Things got so bad that Jones's wife had to take on a part time job, whilst the kids were in school, to make ends meet. Jones having burned his bridges, by making the move to London under pressure from Gordon, was now at the mercy of his ruthless fellow Welshman. Things did not go well for him, especially after he accidently dented the wing of one of Gordon's sports cars. Gordon went ballistic and demanded he pay for all the costs of the repair bill. The family could hardly afford to eat, let alone settle a garage bill for a luxury car.

In 1972 I married Mia, after a four year engagement. I happened to be in 'The Riverview', a little nightclub in Shepperton, celebrating with a few friends who had been unable to make the wedding due to prior tour commitments. It had been almost three years since the Squires had disbanded at that point. I had been playing in a trio with 'Leapy Lee' and touring Australia whilst Mia continued pursuing her singing career in the UK. Suddenly Gordon Jones made an appearance and came over to chat. He was in high spirits telling me that

Mills had an unreleased album on his hands that he was raving about. The album was called 'Band On The Run', by Wings, Sir Paul McCartney's band. We caught up on old times and he toasted my recent wedding. Sadly it was to be the last time I ever saw him.

Gordon Mills sacked Jones rather unceremoniously a short time later. He was good at that, sacking people, Gordon had a pretty long track record. Although it was an all time low, the way he treated Jones and his family. Jones had been at Gordon's beck and call travelling the world, watching him lose millions and thousands of dollars gambling in Vegas, and wherever there was a roulette wheel or card game. Gordon had always been addicted to gambling. Jones had become accustomed to being treated with contempt by Gordon, but he had also become used to the thrill and glamour of a first division showbiz life. Suddenly that all came crashing down around his ears. It was a very abrupt and harsh end. Jones tried to struggle on to makes ends meet, but he had been left beggared by his former employer, especially after the family was turfed out of their home. He took up a position with Dyno-Rod, clearing blocked drains, but he was in debt and could barely make ends meet. Tragically, deeply depressed, he attached a hose to the exhaust on his vehicle and ended his life, leaving a distraught wife and children to cope on their own. Gordon Mills didn't even bother to send a wreath to the funeral. It was all a very long way away from the band I had formed in Ponty all those years ago.

Tom was booked to appear for the second time on the Royal Variety Performance. The band had supported him on the previous occasion, but he felt confident enough to go it alone. But Gordon still booked us to appear to augment the orchestra. It was quite a different scenario from our previous appearance. The Squires had to crawl through a tunnel beneath the stage, to change places with the rhythm section of the Jack Parnell Orchestra, before Tom's performance. The show went well and Tom took his bow before the Queen, we scurried back through the underground tunnel back to the dressing room. Gordon stopped off afterward to tell us we were all off to Germany.

Gordon had organized a tour of Germany with the Ted Heath Orchestra, under the musical direction of Ralph Dollimore, a brilliant pianist. Ralph had a real liking for his food and was rather rotund, he was a true gentleman, sadly no longer with us. The band had worked with the Ted Heath Orchestra long enough to know what to expect. The only difference between Ireland and Germany was that they were now knocking back one litre Steins of lager as opposed to Guinness. The tour covered the cities of Weizbaden, Cologne, Hamburg, Berlin and Munich. The entire tour was dogged by gremlins. Tom's vocal chords were going haywire and many shows had to be cancelled and the money refunded. At one 12,000 seat venue there was a riot by disappointed fans.

Things didn't get any better. One evening I was heading back to the hotel with Bill Parkinson, our lead guitarist. It was around 2am in the morning, suddenly there was the most almighty crash between two speeding cars, it created a huge pile-up, we went over to try and help the survivors but by then a crowd had gathered and it was bedlam. When we got to Berlin, the wall was still up, and the iron curtain was still very much in force. We all decided to take the opportunity to visit East Berlin. Arriving at Checkpoint Charlie, I was carrying a Little Richard album I'd bought that very morning in a small record shop in Berlin. The American guards cheerily waved us through, and about halfway across the checkpoint we were collared by a miserable bunch of Russian guards. We were ushered at gunpoint into a drab little room, forced to hand over our passports, and then searched from head to toe. Little Richard's was immediately confiscated and tossed into a large bin, never to be seen again.

The Eastern side of the wall was laced with fierce looking barbed-wire fencing. It looked almost impossible for anyone to escape, but desperation works wonders and thousands of souls managed to do just that, although many suffered a terrible fate, with a bullet through the heart. We ventured about a mile from the Checkpoint into East Berlin. It was truly miserable. The city had suffered massive devastation by both Russian and Allied Forces during the War. The West had all piled in and ensured that West Germany had recovered; it was a gleaming metropolis in comparison to its drab twin. The Russians seemed to have no intention of reconstructing East Berlin, it was quite bizarre. Office workers were in three or four story buildings, where the top floor was missing, having been demolished under bomb attack during the war. All the buildings were scarred by machine gun bullets and shrapnel. Wherever you looked, family homes were now down to using the upside bedrooms as the roof, it was a real eye opener. It was hard to believe that, just a couple of blocks away, the 'swinging sixties' were in full swing. Everything lacked colour and just looked incredibly drab, every food store we passed looked practically empty and uninviting. There was an eerie stillness everywhere, we would try to catch people's eyes, but they would hurry away. We couldn't wait to get back to the west, and made our way back to the Checkpoint.

Unfortunately the Russian Guards pulled Bill Parkinson out of the line and frog marched him off. They tried to wave us on through but naturally we refused to leave our band mate behind. We were all escorted to join him in a drab little room with peeling paint falling off the walls. Bill's passport photograph had been taken many years earlier, and it showed him with neat, short cropped hair. The guards sent for a barber, and he duly arrived and went to work on Bill, until he looked more like his passport photograph. We crossed back over to the west with Bill looking like Yul Brynner. We knew we shouldn't have laughed, but we couldn't help ourselves, we were in hysterics, Bill was mortified.

On one of the last shows of the fateful tour we performed to an audience of 10,000 screaming fans. The audience noise was deafening. It's hard to believe today but back then we had no stage monitors feeding back. We couldn't hear Tom's voice or our vocals. We couldn't even hear the instruments, it was an absolute nightmare. We tried our best to belt out the set and at one stage I accidently trod on my guitar lead. The fact that the Fender bass had stopped playing fazed nobody, with all those kids screaming, no-one could hear a damn thing anyway. I remember shoving the jack plug back in and just got a loud crackling, the lead was broken.

I replaced the lead with a spare and carried on playing.

Suddenly that gave out too. Back in the Sixties most leads were very badly designed. These days the jack plugs are molded around the wiring, making them far more durable and virtually unbreakable. Tom left the stage, sweating absolute buckets, the stage lights were blinding and no doubt the heat thrown off by 10,000 screaming fans had taken its toll. Back in the Squires' dressing room, after the show, I fixed the broken lead and then changed out of my stage gear. Suddenly, Colin Berlin charged into the room looking for me. Colin was an agent from the Acuff-Rose Agency in London, he had represented Tom and the band from just before 'It's Not Unusual' and continued to do so. He was a bald headed, tubby little man, normally very friendly and easy-going. I saw a completely different side to him that evening, he pointed his chubby little finger at me and waved it under my nose, 'Tom wants to see you in his dressing room now,' he screamed,' he's furious about that lead crackling!'

I thought he was pulling my leg, and looked to the rest of the band, everyone shook their heads, the noise had been so deafening on stage, no one had heard any crackling lead. I remember saying, 'You're kidding me, right?' But Colin turned puce and said, 'You're in big trouble young man.'

I decided to go and visit Tom and see what all the fuss was about. I followed Colin to Tom's dressing room. Colin's nephew was there and opened the door to us, there were three other characters there I'd never met before. Tom was seated on a plush Regency style, gold backed chair. He was in his customary white towelling dressing gown, a fat cigar in one hand and a flute of vintage champagne in the other. Something wasn't right, the whole atmosphere was incredibly cold and unnatural, even though there was a very pretty young woman draping herself around Tom he looked waxen faced. Tom, posing on his throne, looked right through me, he didn't even acknowledge my presence. Suddenly the chorus of agents all piped up, hitting me verbally from all sides. They threw the book at me, going on and on about the crackling lead and how unprofessional it was, apparently I'd let down Tom and the band, it was a travesty and would harm the brand. The ridiculous rant continued ad nauseum and all the while I stared at Tom, just letting it wash over me. He had a look of utter disdain on his face, and just kept staring through me as his latest conquest kept pawing at him.

Finally the chorus of agents exhausted themselves and fell mute. Throughout it all, I had said nothing, not a word. They waited for my response, there was a pregnant pause, and I smiled wryly at Tom, gave him a little wink, and turned on my heels and left the room. As I was leaving, Tom finally piped up, 'You want to get that fuckin' lead fixed before the next show, Vern.'

Back home in Wales I loved and admired Tom. I believe we had a high level of respect for each other. We were both proud young men, with shared views regarding the world around us. Both bred in the Valleys, we were the closest of all the band members. We both came from tough backgrounds and strove to better ourselves. But what suddenly crystallized for me, in that German dressing room, was that the Tom I had known and struggled with on the road to stardom no longer existed. He had now metamorphosed into someone I no longer knew, or even cared to know. Tom had become a mollycoddled, arrogant prick. He didn't even look like the Tom from back home, what with all the facial reconstruction and mouthful of pearly-white crowns. Perched on his Regency chair like some sun king from eons ago, fawned on by acolytes, he had completely lost the plot. It was all very sad indeed.

17

MYRON AND BYRON

Christmas 1968 was now upon us. Chris Ellis and I travelled back to Wales to spend time with our friends and families. Mia was also visiting her family in the Swansea Valley and I spent some time with her. Mia, her seven siblings, parents and friends all took me to the local pub, The Ancient Briton. I found myself sat at the old honky-tonk piano, belting out carols and sing-alongs, vamping out the chords and having a fine old time. Whenever I paused to take a break, the lid of the piano would be lined with free pints of Welsh bitter, 'Don't stop playing Vern!'

After the miserable German tour and my run in with Tom and the Agents, it felt good to let my hair down and put the pathetic incident behind me. The icy way Tom and Gordon were behaving towards me and the band spoke volumes. None of us felt particularly confident that that there would be a band to go back to in the New Year. Gordon would normally brief us about our tour schedule and commitments before leaving London. But he had been reticent about meeting and there were no dates marked in the calendar. But I put it all out of my mind and thoroughly enjoyed my stay back in Wales. Spending time with family and friends helped restore my faith in human nature.

The reason for Tom and Gordon's icy demeanour soon became quickly apparent. A cold front from the past had settled in and was causing them many sleepless nights. Myron and Byron, our former managers, had started legal action against them both. Myron and Byron had been biding their time, observing with keen interest the rise of Tom to superstardom and more importantly the huge rise in his earnings. They had dusted down the old contract with Tom and the band and were intent on redress. They wanted their promised cut of profits from Gordon. Gordon had casually told both managers, 'Your contract's not worth a light,' but we all remembered him promising them five percent of Tom's future earnings, when and if he ever became famous. Well, famous he now was and they wanted to collect. Gordon never had any intention of honouring the contract, but Myron and Byron had called on Legal Aid and the case had reached the High Court.

Back in London in the New Year, I was seated in the bar of the Magpie, gazing into my pint, feeling a bit sorry for myself. There had been no news from Gordon about any future tour dates. The icy weather had kept many of the regulars away from the pub, and that suited my present mood just fine. I was in no mood for conversation. Upstairs, my room had zigzag patterns of ice forming on the inside of the window. I loaded the bed with old blankets and even my overcoat to try and keep warm. I'd managed to find an old hot water bottle and was also putting that to good use. At precisely 10:30pm, Derek rang the final bell and placed tea-towels over the beer pumps, to call time. Almost simultaneously the phone started ringing off the hook. Derek answered and passed the receiver across the bar to me, it was a clearly agitated Chris Ellis on the other end, 'Vernon, I'm up at Tor Point, Tom needs you to do a favour for him. Tom and Gordon want you to testify for them at the Old Bailey tomorrow.' I remember being a bit taken aback. 'What do you mean Chris? They want me to take the stand? Testify to what exactly?'

'Well you were at the Thorn Hotel when you all originally signed with Myron and Byron. I'm not sure what you're meant to say, I'm just the messenger, I'm sure Gordon and Tom will let you know in the morning. Tom's told me to pick you up first thing in the Rolls, is that okay?'

'I guess I'll see you in the morning, 'I said and the phone went dead. I spent the night, shivering under the blankets, barely able to sleep a wink. I was worried about what Gordon and Tom wanted me to say. It was the bloody Old Bailey and not some local magistrates' court. I obviously didn't want to be put in a position where I wasn't telling the truth, perjury is a serious crime in the UK and the penalties are pretty draconian. Chris picked me up in the Rolls around 7am and then we collected Tom from Tor Point. I was expecting him to fill me in on what was expected of me, but deprived of his usual morning slumber; Tom stretched out in the back of the Rolls and slept the entire journey, all the way to the front door of the Law Courts. I was having kittens, if called to the stand I had no idea what I was going to say.

The Old Bailey is an awesome and intimidating building, located 200 yards from St Paul's Cathedral. It's named after the street on which it is located, which follows the line of the original fortified wall, or 'bailey', of the City of London. The initial location of the courthouse close to the infamous Newgate Prison allowed prisoners to be conveniently brought to the courtroom for trial. On the dome above the court stands a bronze statue of Lady Justice, executed by the British sculptor F.W. Pomeroy. She holds a sword in her right hand and the scales of justice in her left. I found myself standing in the vast hall inside, feeling pretty surreal about the whole experience; I was wearing one of Tom's old suits for the occasion, which seemed apt somehow. There were so many familiar faces there from Tom's past and present it was like an episode of 'This Is Your Life', I fully expected Eamon Andrews to jump out at any second clutching his famous red book.

Myron and Byron were standing in a huddle with their lawyer and were surrounded by a whole bunch of recognizable faces from the Pontypridd area of South Wales. Byron caught my eye and came on over, grinning from ear to ear, 'Vernon, how are you, long time no see,' he stuck out his hand and I shook it, 'I hope you're keeping well. Sorry about all this, but it's all down to Gordon. No hard feelings.' I was reeling a bit and the back of my neck felt hot. Tom and Gordon were staring daggers at me from across the hall, Gordon looked as if he was about to explode at any moment. I managed to find my tongue and said, 'Yea no problems Byron, I hope you take them for all their worth.' That drew an even bigger smile and he clapped me on the shoulder before rejoining his lawyer.

I spotted another familiar face making his way toward me; it was Bryn 'The Fish' Phillips. Bryn told me he was there to speak on behalf of Tom, and talk about all the early shows with the Senators up and down the Valleys. Gordon wanted him to spell out that Tom and the band were getting nowhere fast, until Gordon had shown up and led us to stardom. I was sorry to puncture the bubble, but I told Bryn in no uncertain terms that Tom might have achieved stardom under Gordon's tutelage, but it was a far different story in relation to the rest of the band. He looked a bit confused and asked me if I was appearing on behalf of Myron and Byron. I had to be completely honest and told him I had no bloody idea who I was meant to be appearing on behalf of; nobody had bothered to tell me anything.

Gordon was huddled in conversation with Tom and the agent, Colin Berlin, and then their wigged lawyer and his legal team swept in and joined them in conversation. The air was electric; you could have cut it with a knife. It all turned into a bit of a spaghetti western, with both camps facing off and staring daggers at each other. I was stuck in the middle between both camps, which increased the surreal feeling I had. What with all the other cases waiting to be heard, the hall soon became an echo of manic conversation, white wigs and black gowns flittering every which way carrying reams of documents. Gordon kept checking with Tom, the law team and witnesses they had called to testify, he checked with everyone except me. I managed to intercept him and asked, 'Gordon, hold on a minute. Am I taking the stand today?' Gordon gave me one of his best put down sneers and said, 'Probably, why, is that a problem?' I had just about reached the end of my rope with Gordon Mills and said, 'Well what exactly am I expected to say, not guilty your honour?' I swear I saw steam coming out of his ears. 'Piss off Vernon, I haven't got time for your jokes, just answer their fucking questions, and remember which side your bread's buttered.' Off Gordon scampered back to Tom and that was that. I was none the wiser on what to expect.

A few moments later Tom, Gordon, Myron and Byron filed into courtroom number one following their respective legal teams. I remember thinking at the time it was like two international rugby teams walking onto the pitch at Cardiff Arms Park, ready to do battle. I stood with Bryn 'The Fish' outside the courtroom, along with all the other witnesses, waiting to be called in to testify. It was a nerve-wracking experience. Bryn, like Gordon, had a habit of biting his nails and I swear you could see the pile of spent nails gathering around his feet. After about two hours of watching him make a meal of his nails, Bryn launched into all the latest material from his comedy act, pretty soon he had drawn a crowd of witnesses and everyone was in hysterics. Suddenly the court doors swung open and it was announced that both parties had agreed to settle the case. I drew a great sigh of relief; I wouldn't be called to testify after all.

I found out later that Tom's lawyers were so concerned that the case was not going their way, they decided to fold and agree a settlement. Gordon had pressed the lawyers to ensure that there was a news blackout on the amount of the payout. Gordon was adamant about their spurious contribution to Tom Jones's rise to fame. Gordon insisted they had seen Tom and the band at the 'Green Fly' and realised the potential for making a lot of money, quite how that differed from him doing the same at the 'Top Hat' is anyone's guess. Gordon insisted to the court that Byron and Myron had been given over a year to prove themselves and had failed. On the other hand he had the experience, financial backing, power and influence to take Tom and the band into orbit, as was proven by the success to date. The judge listened and then awarded Myron and Byron £100,000. This was a massive amount in 1969 and they were both over the moon. Tom and Gordon were furious, but what could they do? Not a lot, they just had to accept the verdict.

Byron stopped on the way out, with a tear in his eye, and shook my hand; he was too choked to say anything. I'd always had a lot of time for Byron, he was a real likeable guy and I was happy for him. Myron on the other hand was as slimy as a wet fish; no-one I knew had a good word to say about him, he just strode out of court without saying a word to a soul. After the case, despite Gordon's proposed news blackout, it was widely reported that Mr. Michael Eastham, QC for Tom Jones, claimed the singer had agreed to the five percent payment, but only until he had paid off what might be due under the earlier agreement. But Myron and Byron had insisted that the original agreement stated that it was five percent in perpetuity. Mr. Justice Megarry was clearly taken aback. 'Are you saying you want five percent of this man until the end of time?' Myron answered, 'Yes'. You can hardly blame him for trying, but he got nowhere with that particular avenue. Still, a £100,000 payout can't be sneezed at.

They even subpoenaed our old guitarist, Mickey Gee, to testify that they owned five percent of Tom for all time. Mickey said at the time, 'They wanted me to come and speak up for them because of a conversation I was supposed to have heard. I didn't want to go but the court forced me too. But eventually it was all settled and I didn't have to appear. They got £50,000 each, which is a bit rich, as they did nothing for the band. They never got us a hit record. They just booked us into pubs and clubs in the Valleys. I wish every one of the Squires got

£50,000. If anyone deserved it, we all did, but we got nothing apart from lots of heartache.'

Exiting the Old Bailey into the chill winter air I remember thinking, I haven't got a pot to piss in and I've been working my nut off with Tom all these years, as had the rest of the band. Myron and Byron had been a minor bump on the road to success and they had just coolly pocketed £50,000 each for booking us into a couple of clubs, it was madness. After the initial shock Gordon and Tom realised they had got off quite lightly, £100,000 was nothing in respect of what was flowing through the MAM Empire, and it was a mere drop in the ocean in comparison to what they were raking in. Gordon perked up and organized an impromptu party to celebrate the end of the case. Colin Berlin suggested the 'Wig and Pen' in the Strand, they had a magnificent selection of quality champagne. Nobody invited me, so I walked off for the nearest tube station. Suddenly a familiar voice piped up, 'Vern, where do you think you're going? Come on 'mun', Tom motioned for me to join them.

The bar in the 'Wig and Pen' certainly lived up to its name, it was crammed full of QCs and barristers enjoying their lunchtime in a very liquid form. Tom stood in the corner with a customary cigar and flute of champagne, chatting away with his lawyer. A waitress was doing the rounds topping up everybody's champagne glasses. I've never had a taste for champagne, so declined, and bought myself a pint of bitter from the bar. Tom excused himself and came over to join me at the bar, 'Ow's it going Vern, you alright?' I told him I was fine and pretty glad the case was all over and I hadn't been called to testify.

'Yeah, too right the bastards. Myron and Byron? More like Pinky and fuckin' Perky. Look, Chris is going to drive me to the West End for a meal and a piss up. I won't be back 'ome till God knows when. Gordon is going to drive you back to the Magpie, he wants to have a word like. That okay?'

'Okay Tom, no problem, see you later,' I said. It would be much later before I saw him again, years in fact. 'Nice suit,' was his final comment as he rejoined his lawyer, obviously recognizing one of his cast offs.

Gordon fired up his sports car and we exited the underground car park in central London. It put me in mind of our journey together, all those years before, travelling through the South of France. Heading west out of the City, we were passing through Knightsbridge. Gordon lit a cigarette and said, 'Before I drop you off, do you mind stopping off at St George's Hill? I've got a song I want to play you.' I was a bit taken aback as it had been quite a while since he'd asked my opinion on anything. 'Sure Gordon, I'd love to listen.' Gordon scowled and said, 'I want the Squires to record it and bring it out as a single. I'm sure it's going to be a massive hit.' I remember being confused. 'What do you mean, record it without Tom?' Gordon nodded, 'Yeah, the only thing Tom will be recording over the next few months is his new TV series. Lew Grade has finally given him a spot at Elstree Studios. I can't have you boys twiddling your thumbs, we'll cut a disc in the meantime.'

It was all news to me, and I asked him if the Squires were to be involved in the new TV series. Gordon hummed and hawed a bit and I should have seen the writing on the wall right then. 'Well Vern, they've booked in a load of musicians who can sight read, it's that kind of show, I went to bat for you boys, but the decision's been made.' Gordon quickly changed the subject and went on to talk up the new song, 'This new song is by Joe South, he's a great American singer, the song's called 'The Games People Play', it's already a hit in the US, if we cut it here quick it'll be top of the charts in no time at all.' I smelt a rat but kept my counsel. We arrived at 'Little Rhonda' and Gordon played me the song in his state of the art recording studio. Joe South wasn't a particularly good singer, but the song seemed great. The opening bars positively zinged to the strains of an Indian stringed instrument, called a sitar. It was the first time I had ever heard one played on a pop record, this was before the Beatles famously used it in their recordings, and the whole sound really blew me away. It was certainly a unique song and I could understand why Gordon would want to release it, but not without Tom on vocal.

Gordon passed me the demo and told me to get busy rehearsing it with the rest of the band. Gordon had booked us studio space, and told me the clock was ticking, so we needed to move pretty quickly. I thanked him and turned to leave but he wanted my opinion on another track. Gordon played me a song by a fella called Ray O'Sullivan. I listened to the track and to be perfectly honest, the tune was okay but I thought the singer sounded like George Formby. Gordon scowled and said, 'He's from Ireland not the North, and the kid's got a future.' Of course Gordon was right and I was wrong, Gordon launched him as 'Gilbert O'Sullivan' and went onto make millions of pounds with his compositions. Gordon dressed him up like the kid from the memorable 'Hovis' advert, the one where he pushes a bike up a hill, and he went down a storm with the UK audience.

The band agreed that Bill Parkinson should sing the lead on 'Games People Play'; we all believed that his voice had a certain edginess that complemented the metallic sound of the sitar. The rest of us piped up as backing vocal on the catchy sounding chorus. Gordon had arranged for us to record the song in Barnes, South London. It was a pretty mediocre studio compared to what we were used to in Soho and Gordon had booked us in after the midnight curfew, to ensure it was nice and cheap. We were all pretty pleased that Gordon had turned up to oversee the recording. However, he seemed totally disinterested in events, and didn't contribute at all. At one stage he pulled a pornographic magazine out of the sound engineer's briefcase and, feet up on the console, leafed through it for the duration of the recording. He seemed oblivious to what was going on in the studio and didn't offer any kind of input. It was all pretty bizarre. Normally he was incredibly hands on for all our recordings. He just seemed to be going through the motions. As soon as the session was over, he picked up the tapes and made a hasty exit.

A few days later I nipped out of the Magpie to pick up the morning newspaper. I was leafing through the paper on my way back when suddenly my attention was caught by a glaring headline: 'TOM JONES AND THE SQUIRES IN AMICABLE SPLIT'. My legs turned to jelly, I was in utter shock. It was the first I had heard of any split, amicable or not. The report contained a release from Tom's management that went onto explain, 'The Squires have been with Tom right from the start but there are reasons they now have to amicably split. Tom will be spending most of the year making his new television series, any future tours will be with the Ted Heath Orchestra. The Squires have, for some time, wanted to branch out on their own, and will soon be releasing a new single.'

'Melody Maker' and 'New Musical Express' ran the same story. It was a huge shock; the band was stunned, especially as Gordon and Tom hadn't even had the courtesy to even inform us beforehand. The penny now dropped and everything made perfect sense. Gordon and Tom had obviously discussed getting rid of the band prior to the court case to limit any further liabilities. Gordon's proposed new recording had all been a sham, so he could point to it as being the Squires breaking out alone and splitting with Tom. It was all very cunning and just what you'd expect from Gordon Mills. I don't know why I was surprised, the writing had been on the wall for quite some time. Still, it's a shock when you're hit with a juggernaut like that. We didn't know at the time, but later I was informed that a new employment law had just been introduced stopping an employee sacking his staff unfairly, it put a stop to the unfair practice of sacking a worker summarily. Gordon had circumnavigated that by getting shot of us before the law was fully introduced and he also had the Barnes recordings to point to us as deciding to leave Tom's employ. We should have taken a leaf out of Myron and Byron's book and started legal proceedings, but we were all just so tired and demoralized after our years of ill treatment at the hands of Gordon and Tom, in some ways it was a mercy to be shot of them both.

Lucy Ellis and Bryony Sutherland described the split in their biography, 'Tom Jones, Close Up', as 'Gordon creating the perfect scenario for dismissing the Squires. In offering them the opportunity of fame in their own right, he effectively separated them from Tom, while at the same time he determined to half-heartedly promote their record thus ensuring failure. Lack of sales could then be used as a legitimate excuse to let the Squires go. As Gordon had insisted that the group did not have written contracts he was able to sack them without so much as a week's wages, confident they had no legal grounds on which to sue for compensation. 'Chris Slade just about summed it all up when he said, 'Gordon was a crafty sod, it was all oh, sorry fellas, you've failed, so you're out, bye bye. It was that sort of scenario.'

I never knew what happened to our version of 'The Games People Play'. I'm not sure it was even released, as there was zero promotion. To add to our disappointment Joe South later released the song in the UK and it shot straight to number 10 in the charts. The band insisted on trying to get hold of Tom for a meeting but I told them to forget it, this was all down to him as much as it was Gordon. They persisted but got nowhere; he had gone to ground and refused to return phone calls. The final insult was when our band van was reclaimed by the MAM Empire; it was battered beyond belief after touring the UK incessantly for years and being regularly attacked by adoring Tom Jones fans. In all likelihood it probably wasn't worth its weight in scrap. But Gordon, being Gordon insisted it be confiscated, how incredibly petty.

The band called an emergency meeting and we discussed where we went from here. We decided to go on but our hearts weren't really in it. We enlisted a new singer, Mike Stephens. The Cardiff born soul singer had recently moved to London. But it never really worked out. Mike was never on time, we'd call for him at his flat and he'd be in the bath, or shaving, or stuffing his face, it always made us late for gigs, which didn't go down too well. We took him aside and had a talk with him, but no change, it was like dealing with a tortoise. One night we caught a gig at Ronnie Scott's Jazz Club, but by the time we had coaxed Mike into the van and raced across town it was too late, needless to say we weren't booked again. Disenchanted we all decided to call it a day and went our separate ways.

I was really in the dumps; I didn't know what to do with myself. Robin Eggar, the author of 'Tom Jones, The Biography', with the benefit of hindsight, describes that time better than I ever could: 'Some months later, Vernon received another bill from the tax man for £4,000 (a considerable amount back in 1969). The Inland Revenue wanted to be paid for all the TV appearances Vernon had done. Every time the Squires had done a radio show each member had been paid a set fee that had been pocketed by the management. Nor did they receive any royalties or recording fees for the live EP, 'Tom Jones Live with the Squires', 'Live At Talk Of The Town', or the opening theme music for the TV series 'Pop The Question'. The math is relatively simple. In four years Vernon, a backing musician, actually earned Gordon an astronomical amount and got paid peanuts. The tax bill was sent to MAM and nothing more was heard about it.'

I have to be completely honest, I'm still hurting from the shabby treatment we received, who wouldn't be? It was premeditated, vindictive and downright unnecessary. How difficult would it have been for Tom and Gordon to sit down with us and just say, 'Look guys we're moving in a different direction and your face doesn't fit, no hard feelings, huh?' We all could have lived with that and at least parted on amicable terms. After all we still felt that old Valleys bond, that's where we were all bred, and we lived by that code, or so I thought. Now Tom had renounced all that history, and didn't even have the Welsh grit to face us man to man, he had delegated all the unpleasantness and run away to hide. Even to this very day I feel an unbridled shame for Tom Jones, I feel even more shame for Tommy Woodward. What a pathetic and sordid end to an enduring friendship, from the Valleys to the pinnacle of superstardom. Without the Senators there would be no Tom Jones, Tommy Woodward would still be plying his trade in the pubs and clubs of the Valleys for pocket change, wondering what might have been. Hats off to Myron and Byron, they got £100,000 for doing absolutely nothing, we got absolutely nothing for doing everything.

I was in a very dark corner, and didn't know which way to turn. Luckily the pianist Ralph Dollimore threw me a lifeline. Ralph was still contracted to run the Ted Heath Orchestra, and approached me, Chris Slade and Bill Parkinson about becoming their rhythm section. We had fitted in well with them over the years, when they'd been hired to support Tom, so it was an easy decision to make. The orchestra offered us £100 a week, which was a great deal more than we had ever got from Gordon and Tom. Pretty soon we were boarding a plane for Germany. The orchestra had been booked for a month long tour. It was a great opportunity and we were very grateful to Ralph, it certainly kept the wolf from the door for a little while.

Back in the UK after the tour, the orchestra didn't have any further commitments. I stood in for a few local musicians, gigging in and around London. I also found some work driving a lorry, delivering parcels, furniture and bric-a-brac throughout the Home Counties. But it was spasmodic and insecure work. Then Arthur Regis approached me about putting together a band. Arthur was a Londoner and a great keyboard man, we soon found a drummer and a guitarist and re-launched as the Squires. Arthur knew the theatrical agent Joe Collins, the father of the actress Joan Collins and novelist Jackie Collins. Joe had begun his show business career as office boy with Moss Empires theatres in London and later became a theatrical agent. The first artist he signed was the dancer Lew Grade, who later became the television producer Lord Grade. Lew was Joe's partner in the theatrical agency for some time then left to set up on his own. Joe took the new Squires under his wing and started to get us regular bookings. It put a smile back on my face.

Unfortunately Bill Parkinson and Chris Slade had prior commitments. Undeterred I called Arthur Regis and we quickly decided on a new set for the occasion. We pretty quickly put a set together and the day of the investiture was upon us in no time at all. The historic ceremony was directed by the Constable of the Castle, Lord Snowdon. The Queen invested The Prince with the Insignia of his Principality and Earldom of Chester: a sword, coronet, mantle, gold ring and gold rod. The Prince's formal response was, 'I, Charles, Prince of Wales, do become your liege man of life and limb and of earthly worship and faith and truth I will bear unto you to live and die against all manner of folks.' A loyal address from the people of Wales was read in Welsh and English by Sir Ben Bowen Thomas, President of the University College of Wales, Aberystwyth, where The Prince had studied Welsh language and history in the months before the ceremony.

After the ceremony the Prince, along with The Queen and the rest of the Royal Family, travelled through the crowded streets to loud cheers from the people of Wales and the many international visitors. There was a great deal of security around the town: soldiers, police and plain-clothed officers. Suddenly there was a huge explosion. Welsh Nationalist extremists had detonated a bomb. They were protesting the crowning of an Englishman as Prince of Wales. It caused a bit of a stir, but thankfully the explosion was a good half a mile away, and no one was injured. I don't think the extremists ever had any intention of harming anyone; it was purely an act of defiance against the Establishment.

After the ceremony we were given directions to the stately manor, and set off to unload the equipment and sound check. We were met by a butler who directed us to the back of the premises where a gigantic marquee had been erected specially for the occasion. It was so large it made Billy Smart's Circus Top look like a scout tent. I started to get butterflies when I noticed the huge stage set up inside. It needed to be big, the Ray MacVay Orchestra were going through their sound check and they were a very big band. They had left a spot for us on the right wing of the stage and we quickly set up our equipment. Looking out from the stage you couldn't help but be impressed. There was row upon row of tables resplendent with silver dinner services, bone-china crockery, cut glass crystal, champagne buckets and amazing floral decorations. They had left a space in front of the stage for dancing. We were all glad we had worn our suits; I had on one of Tom's for the occasion.

Pretty soon the dignitaries started to arrive and the Ray MacVay Orchestra performed their set admirably. The audience was a mass of penguin-suited gentry and elite, accompanied by ball-gowned companions, dripping with jewellery. There must have been about fifteen courses of food, and nobody had any inclination or stamina to get up and dance when the orchestra went through their set. Toward the end they clocked on to the mood and laid off the foxtrots for something a bit slower and one or two couples duly obliged with a circuit of the dance floor. I remember thinking at the time it was going to be a tough old audience, and I was certainly proved right.

We kicked off with the 'Resurrection Shuffle' but got nowhere fast, nobody took to the stage and we drew a lot of open mouthed stares. The band continued to up the tempo but seemed to be on a hiding to nothing. Changing tack we tried a few ballads, but everyone remained rooted to their plush seats. There was simply no response from the audience at all, it was very discouraging indeed. We changed tack again and tried a soul number, 'Dancing In The Street'. Miraculously it seemed to work. Suddenly the entire audience was on their feet and clapping like hell. This was followed by loud cheering. At last, I thought, we've cracked it!

But I was to be disappointed. It suddenly dawned on me that the loud cheers weren't being directed at us at all. A bunch of latecomers had just sauntered into the marquee. It was the entire front bench of the Conservative Party, led by the then Prime Minister, Edward Heath. I had to crack a smile because as Ted Heath led his cabinet and their wives across the deserted dance floor he broke into dance and started performing 'The Twist', showing the audience the appropriate response to 'Dancing In The Street'. Hats off to Ted, within a matter of seconds the marquee had erupted and the dance floor was packed with gyrating bodies. Pretty soon some other latecomers arrived and joined in the dancing: Princess Margaret and her husband Lord Snowdon, Princess Anne and her brother Prince Andrew. Perched up on the stage watching everyone let their hair down was pretty bizarre.

I remember phoning Colin Berlin at MAM after the event to report on the gig. Colin told me that Tom had originally been booked to appear, but due to other work commitments he couldn't make it. Rather than lose the booking fee he had suggested the Squires fill the spot. Gordon had been reticent at first, but relented when he saw the size of the booking fee. Just like a blast from the past, and almost entirely to form, it took us a few weeks to finally be paid for the event. Colin called and told me to pop into MAM's accounts department in Bond Street to pick up the £400 in petty cash. I had quite a shock when I saw the accountants' ledger. As she was counting out the money, I noticed that MAM had pocketed a cool £4000 for the gig and as usual paid us peanuts. Some things never changed!

It had been a great final gig for the Squires, a real high. The manor house put us up for the evening and I remember waking the next morning thinking it was a fitting end. As I drove back to London, I decided to take the scenic route, travelling through the magnificent mountains of North Wales via Mount Snowdon, and down through the Black Mountains. That's when it all finally hit home, the rollercoaster of the previous years, the highs and the lows, the constant battles with Gordon and Tom. I found my peace, it was the closing of a chapter in my life, and I finally put the Squires to bed, and decided on a new direction. I was going to have to explain my intentions of calling it a day to Arthur and the new band members, but we could always branch out as a new band. The Squires were dead to me now, it was time to lay the past to rest, it was time for a complete change.

I arrived back at the Magpie just as Derek was ringing last orders. Derek greeted me in his usual jovial manner and asked me about the investiture. I told him it had gone really well and with his cut-glass Cambridge accent he piped up, 'That's a knighthood for you then.' I smiled and asked him if there had been any messages and Derek told me that Arthur Regis had been phoning constantly, apparently it was quite urgent. I called Arthur, feeling a bit apprehensive about telling him my decision on the Squires, but was dumbfounded by the latest news. Arthur had received a call from Joe Collins and was relaying the news, he was spitting feathers. Joe had received a call from Gordon Mills warning him to quit representing the Squires or face the consequences. Gordon told Joe in no uncertain terms that he would ban him from booking Tom Jones and any of the other acts on the MAM books, including the new singer-songwriter Lynsey de Paul who was a massive sensation at that time. I was shocked and the blood drained out of my face, Derek must have noticed because he drew a double whiskey from the optic and thrust it into my hand, 'Get that down you,' he urged.

The whole demise of the Squires had been taken out my hands by Gordon Mills. I have no idea, even to this very day, why he was so cruel and vindictive about the band trying to make its own way in the world post-Tom and Gordon. It was almost as if he wanted to completely rub us out of history.

18

SALAD DAYS

I sat on the edge of my bed in the Magpie, staring out across the Thames and toward the distant St George's Hill. With no band, no money and nothing on the horizon I was pondering my next move. Tom had just embarked on a six month world tour. I had been surprised to receive a phone call from our old drummer, Chris Slade. Gordon had approached him to join Tom on the tour. Naturally, after all the unpleasantness of the Squires demise, he was a bit reticent. Chris had phoned around the ex-band members to get our opinions, we all gave him our blessing and wished him the best. Although with the natural proviso, watch your back! Chris took up the offer and joined Tom's new band for the duration of the tour.

'Big' Jim Sullivan had replaced Bill Parkinson as guitarist and the ex-Shadows bassist, John Rostill had replaced me. Big Jim was one of the most sought after guitarists throughout the 1960s and 1970s and, together with Richie Blackmore and Pete Townshend, persuaded Jim Marshall to make his now famous amplifiers. Big Jim remained touring with Tom for five years and eventually left to set up his own label, Retreat Records. Both Chris and John Rostill left Tom and Gordon's employ a good deal sooner than expected and in very different circumstances, one tragically. John Rostill was found dead in 1973, electrocuted by a guitar that was believed to be improperly grounded. It was a tragic loss, John was way ahead of his time and used to include double-stopping in his technique, he also played bass finger-style rather than use a plectrum and this was very unusual back then.

Chris Slade soon found out Gordon was up to his usual tricks. Chris was shocked when Derek Watkins, Tom's leading trumpeter, inadvertently let slip that Gordon was paying him £1000 a week for the duration of the tour. Chris was getting paid a fraction of that amount, but what really made his blood boil was the fact that this was more than four times the combined weekly wages the Squires had been receiving up until very recently. Chris confronted Tom about the unfairness of it all, he pointed out that all these new musicians had been with him less than eight weeks, whilst he had been with Tom for eight years, through thick and thin. Tom rolled out his stock response, 'Go and see Gordon, it's got nothing to do with me, Chris.' He did just that and was told to take it or leave it. Chris left it, after telling Gordon, in no uncertain terms, exactly what he thought of him. Chris Slade wasn't out of work for very long, he joined Manfred Mann's Earthband and used that as a platform for even greater things. Chris went onto join a host of super groups: Led Zeppelin, Uriah Heep, Asia and ACDC. He now lives in L.A but we keep in regular contact.

With the summer now drawing to a close, the other Chris, Chris Ellis, returned to the Magpie after working on Tom's world tour. Chris had been kept on, after we were unceremoniously dumped, to work as Tom's road manager and fixer. We caught up and Chris told me he was moving out of the Magpie. Chris and his Swedish girlfriend, Eva, had decided to move in together. They rented a top-floor flat nearby in Ashford. Around the same time Mia moved out of her relative's house in North London and we decided to move in together also. The owner of the Magpie, Harry Pern, also owned a listed Georgian mansion nearby, 'Orchard House'. Harry had converted the property into five flats. We rented the top floor flat of the impressive three-story building. It was a handsome property with a massive walled garden.

Mia had been disgusted with our treatment at the hands of Gordon's MAM Empire, and now that the Acuff-Rose Agency had been bought out and subsumed by MAM she wanted out. She instructed Colin Berlin to terminate her contract and inform MAM she would find representation elsewhere. About the only furniture we owned when we moved in together was a bed, a table and two chairs. But we were both deliriously happy. When we had visitors, they had to make do and sit themselves on empty beer crates, courtesy of Harry Pern from the Magpie. Our situation gradually improved with me picking up local gigs playing bass and Mia securing regular gigs in workingmen's clubs throughout the area. We took each day as it came, and had no-one to be responsible for other than ourselves. We were young and carefree and just got on with life.

The first winter in the flat wasn't so carefree. Tony Cartwright came a calling and couldn't get over just how cold the flat was. Tony had come a long way since Tonbridge Road and his days of managing Freddie Lennon. He was now a recognized and reasonably successful manager of some fine up-and-coming talent. When he called we were huddled around the ancient gas fire trying to keep warm. Having once been a large grand house the lounge and two bedrooms were incredibly spacious and difficult to keep warm without central heating. In honour of our guest we lit the three gas rings on the stove and kept the oven door open to create a little more heat. Tony thought it was hysterical and with typical Liverpool humour put the word around that poor Vernon and Mia were sitting around a 'polo mint' to keep warm.

Tony was a great friend and contacted me a few weeks later. The singer Leapy Lee was enjoying huge popularity on the back of the success of 'Little Arrows', and was now looking for a new bass player to join his band. Tony told me he was offering £50 a week, which was £10 more than I'd ever got with the Squires. What was even better was that all the scheduled gigs were around London and the Home Counties, which meant being able to get back to Mia after each gig. I leapt at the offer. The job was a godsend and Leapy was an incredibly generous person, it was a real pleasure to work with him. My new band mates were a cracking bunch of lads and I really took to them all. Pete Kirshner was on drums, he had formerly been with the band 'Honeybus' and they had enjoyed a hit single, 'I Can't Let Maggie Go'. They were the comedian Kenny Everett's favourite band of all time and he was devastated when they eventually split. Mick McNeil was our guitarist and had previously played with the Irish balladeer Val Doonican. It was just the tonic I needed after the debacle with Mills and Jones.

It was at around that time, in 1972, I decided to 'tie the knot' with Mia. Leapy and his wife, Mary, were appointed as witnesses at Ashford Registry Office. All our guests piled back to the flat afterwards for a lavish buffet and pretty soon we all staggered across the road to the Magpie for a knees up. Not long after the wedding Mia became part of an established cabaret act working in and around London, they were very popular and were offered a season playing in the Bahamas. Things were looking up for Leapy and the band as well. We were offered a summer tour of Australia and jumped at the opportunity. Returning to London after a successful tour I hopped onto the next available plane and joined Mia in the Bahamas. Whilst I was away Leapy was involved in a serious incident that eventually resulted in him receiving a three year prison sentence.

The afternoon Leapy arrived home from the Australian tour, absolutely jet-lagged after the forty-eight hour flight, he went straight back to his spectacular house in Sunningdale to get some much needed rest. The manor was a grand residence set in two acres of landscaped gardens. It was painted bright pink, typical of Leapy's colourful character. The actress Diana Dors lived nearby and Leapy had become very friendly with the whole family. Diana Dors was the English equivalent of the 'blonde bombshells' of Hollywood, and was forever described as a home grown Marilyn Monroe. Her movie career was on the wane at the time, but she was still hugely successful through her cabaret work and regular 'celebrity expose' tabloid headlines, which mostly featured in Rupert Murdoch's News of the World. Dors was renowned for throwing adult group parties and the Archbishop of Canterbury once famously denounced her as a 'wayward hussy.' Diana Dors's parties were notorious at the time, being so heavily publicized in the press, and she always ensured that a number of celebrities and young starlets were brought into close contact, with ample supplies of alcohol and drugs, against a background of soft and hard core porn films. Her former lover and party attendee, Bob Monkhouse, famously commented, 'The awkward part about an orgy is that afterwards you're not sure who to thank.'

Diana Dors's husband, Alan Lake, was there to meet Leapy at Sunningdale that fateful afternoon. Alan persuaded Leapy to join him for a drink down at the local pub and refused to take no for an answer. Lake also had his baby son with him, so Leapy assumed it would be a quick drink and relented. They travelled to Sunningdale's The Red Lion, the local pub, and Leapy told him all about the recent Australian tour. They arranged to meet in the same venue the following evening. Alan and Leapy kept the appointment and were ordering their first drinks from the bar when the landlord demanded payment for a Babycham that had been ordered for Alan Lake's baby son the previous day. Both Alan and Leapy denied any knowledge of ordering the Babycham and pointed out it must have been one of the customers, having a laugh.

Events quickly became heated and tempers boiled. The landlord got physical and it all degenerated into a punch up, with some of the customers joining the fray. Leapy was fairly short and quite slight of build, in no time at all he found himself on the floor. The landlord had armed himself with a golf club in the melee and now stood above Leapy, raining down blows on the diminutive singer. Alan Lake thrust a pen-knife into Leapy's hand and the Landlord received a two-inch cut to his forearm. It was bedlam and the police were called.

When I finally returned from the Bahamas the case had just got to court. Leapy Lee was sentenced to three years for stabbing and Alan Lake was sentenced to eighteen months.

Tragically, upon his release Diana Dors presented Alan with a mare named Sapphire, he was a keen horseman, and he was unseated when the horse ran into a bough which resulted in him breaking his back. Alan did eventually make a recovery but he had begun drinking heavily and never quite recovered his spirit. Leapy's career was in tatters, the Judge had wanted to set an example and he had certainly accomplished that. Leapy's marriage broke down when he was in prison and his reputation was shot, there were no further tour bookings for the band.

Leapy worked in the prison hospital wing and with good behaviour was eventually transferred to La Verne Open Prison, on England's South Coast. With exemplary behaviour he served half his sentence and was finally released. Leapy found it impossible to get any work afterward and eventually emigrated to Majorca in Spain. Leapy eventually remarried and is the proud father of twin boys. He is now in his seventies and still wowing holiday audiences with his mix of comedy and music throughout Spain, he tours regularly. If you ever get the chance go and see him, I do whenever I'm in Spain. He is a lovely fella and a real gem, what a trouper!

Tragically, Alan Lake eventually committed suicide with a shotgun after the death of Diana Dors. She had succumbed to cancer; grief stricken, he couldn't face life without her. Lake burnt all of Dors's clothes, took their son to the railway station and put him on a train to stay with relatives, then returned to their Sunningdale home and killed himself in their son's bedroom.

I talked over our options with Mia and we decided to form our own duo act, 'Two's Company'. We played a few local gigs and got a warm reception. Pretty soon we were approached by the Wally Dent Agency and agreed to representation. It was a good fit and before very long we were appearing on the television programs, 'Rising Stars' and 'New Faces'. It certainly helped with our bookings and everything was going really well. We then started to pick up slots supporting a wealth of household names: Jim Davidson, Frankie Vaughan, Tom O'Connor, Freddie Starr and a host of other familiar faces. Then Mia became pregnant and we took a break until our lovely daughter Tara was born.

Tony Cartwright phoned and congratulated me on the news of Tara's impending birth. Tony asked me what I was up to and I truthfully told him I was examining my options. He told me he might have just the thing to keep me occupied. Tony was managing the handsome and fair-haired singer, Malcolm Roberts. Malcolm had arrived in the music industry through a previous career as an actor; he had appeared briefly in the ITV soap, Coronation Street. It was while appearing in 'West Side Story' in London that he got his first big break. Lionel Bart spotted him and cast him in a number of West End productions, the most notable of which was 'Maggie May' at the Adelphi. Malcolm had gone on to enjoy a number of hit singles: 'Time Alone Will Tell', 'May I Have the Next Dream With You' and the Les Reed and Barry Mason penned number 'Love is All'. At that time Malcolm had broken big in South America and was in demand. They absolutely idolized him out there. Tony was quick to capitalize and was putting together a band to tour South America, we quickly agreed terms and I was on board.

The very next thing I knew I had been summoned to

Malcolm's magnificent house near Guilford for rehearsals with the rest of the band, prior to embarking on the South American tour. I was working with the legendary guitarist, Mick Green, who had been a founding member of 'Johnny Kidd and the Pirates'. They had enjoyed numerous hit songs, probably the most notable being 'Shakin All Over' and 'Please Don't Touch', but their influence on future musicians was profound. Their stage act was very theatrical which anticipated and influenced all the rockers of the 1970s, like Alice Cooper and Marc Bolan, and helped usher in the whole glam rock phenomenon. Led Zeppelin, in the early days, covered all of their songs. It was great to meet Mick, it felt like we were old friends, as our mutual friend Vic Cooper had been the keyboard player for both the Squires and Johnny Kidd. The other musician was the drummer, Pete Wolfe, who had just completed work on the famous West End Musical 'Jesus Christ, Superstar.'

We set off for Buenos Aires in the spring of 1974 for the first leg of the tour. Tony Cartwright accompanied us and we landed just as winter was approaching. We were picked up by two black limousines from the airport and whisked into the centre of the city. It was Malcolm's fifth tour and he turned to me quite puzzled, there were no billboards or posters announcing the tour, apparently this was very unusual. The whole city seemed to be wall-papered with posters of Juan Domingo Peron, President of the Republic.

Peron had recently returned from his eighteen year exile in Spain. On the day of his return, a crowd of left-wing Peronists had gathered at the Airport to welcome him. Camouflaged snipers opened fire on the crowd killing at least thirteen people and injuring over three-hundred and sixty. It became known as the Ezeiza massacre. It precipitated an armed conflict between left and right wing factions and pretty soon there were death squads targeting all opposition parties. The 'dirty war' was in full swing and we had landed right in the middle of it all.

We arrived at the American owned Hilton Hotel and I was unpacking my suitcase when suddenly there was an enormous explosion that rattled all the windows. I quickly went out onto the balcony and the stench of acrid smoke stung my nostrils. Below, near the entrance to the hotel, were the charred and twisted remains of a flat-bed truck. A bomb had been detonated maiming a crowd of pedestrians. The hotel staff informed us anti-Peron terrorists were to blame. They went onto inform us that the bomb was probably to mark the anniversary of the blowing up of the Hilton's thirteenth floor just a year earlier, which was still empty. We didn't sleep easy as the tour party was all booked into the fourteenth floor just above. Apparently Peron had the full backing of the United States and any American interests were prime targets, the Hilton was a favoured target and we all just wanted to get this leg of the tour out of the way as quickly as we could.

Tony Cartwright arranged for two armed bodyguards to follow us everywhere. They became part of the family the whole six weeks we were in Argentina, accompanying us to every gig, TV show, radio show and all interviews with the press. On one memorable occasion we passed Peron in our limousine, being driven the other way in his armoured limousine flanked by a cavalcade of police motorcycle riders. We were advised never to venture too far from the hotel and absolutely never get into a taxi with a red and black ribbon tied to its aerial. We may have been mistaken for Americans and never seen again. We made sure we only ever flagged down a taxi with a blue and yellow ribbon from then on.

One afternoon, taking a rare break from the hectic tour schedule, we were in a bar close to the Hilton. Suddenly there was the unmistakable sound of heavy gun fire outside. We tentatively stuck our heads out of the bar and witnessed five masked terrorists dragging drivers out of their vehicles and shooting up their cars. It had happened at the height of rush hour traffic, and had been replicated throughout the city causing major traffic grid lock. By the time we headed for the airport we were a bunch of quivering wrecks. I arrived back in London in perfect timing for the birth of my daughter, Tara, and was so glad to be back in one piece!

1975 saw me and Mia performing as a duo once again. We made our act a mixture of mainstream, country, soul and rock n roll and pretty soon we were booked solid for the year. The Wally Dent Agency was over the moon as they were turning down bookings because we were jam packed. I have to admit it was incredibly liberating not having to rely on any other artiste for our income; it was a very happy time. Since being sacked by Gordon and Tom my finances had blossomed, it was a world away from living hand to mouth. I was incredibly thankful and my faith in human nature was all but restored.

Pretty soon a local venue asked us if we would become the resident band around our touring commitments. It was regular money and close to home, so how could we refuse. The 'John O'Gaunt' in Walton-on-Thames sits between Sunbury and

Weybridge, and became our regular residency. It became very much a family affair and we built up a fanatical following with our friends from show business regularly dropping by and joining in with the odd spot. I don't think I've ever been happier, it was a great period in our lives. One particular Thursday during mid-summer we had returned from another tour and were due to play our regular gig at the 'John O'Gaunt'. I pulled into the pub to park in our reserved spot and was pretty shocked to see a white Rolls Royce hogging our parking space. I remember commenting to Mia, 'Maybe it's a record producer?' The Wally Dent Agency had recently sent out our latest demo with a view to releasing it. We were both pleasantly surprised and intent on performing a great gig.

We set up on stage and went through a quick sound check. Imagine my surprise when Tom Jones waved at me from the back of the room. Tom was accompanied by two stunning blondes draped on each arm and his PR, Chris Hutchins, hovering a little behind them all. My jaw practically hit the floor, I was in shock. Mia noticed and nudged me to ask what was wrong. I pointed out Tom cheerily waving and smiling from the back of the room and she told me to ignore him. The last time I had seen him was in the 'Wig and Pen' all those years before, leaving Gordon to deal with the axing of the Squires, and now here he was as bold as brass. I should have listened to Mia but natural curiosity got the better of me and I found myself wandering through the packed room toward him.

'Ow's it going Vern, wanna a pint?'

I was speechless and he turned to the barman and ordered a pint of bitter. I regained my composure and asked him what brought him to this neck of the woods, 'I'm taking these birds up the West End to make a night of it. I'd ask you to join us like, but you've obviously got a gig on.' It was all turning a little weird, we'd not seen each other since the court case and the sacking. I must admit I was a bit flummoxed by the whole scenario.

'Ow are things, are you doing alright?'

I managed to find my tongue, 'I'm doing okay Tom, and you?' Tom looked at his two blonde companions and smiled. I was a bit emotionally disturbed by his presence and told him how let down I felt by the whole manner of my exit from the band. Tom lit a cigar and looked me in the eye, 'Well Vern, you know that was all down to Gordon'. What a bleedin' brazen cheek I thought, 'Well Tom, after all we've been through together don't you think it would have been a bit more dignified if you and Gordon had sat down with the band to let us know it was over?' Tom looked uncomfortable and asked Chris Hutchins what time their reservations were arranged up West. I couldn't just leave it there. 'For God's sake Tom, we all had to read about it in the papers.' He was about to say something, but I cut in, 'I know, take it up with Gordon.' I turned on my heel and made my way back to the stage.

Picking up my guitar, I announced the opening number of our set. Normally it would have been a blaster to set the pace for the evening. Instead I chose a song that Tom had originally introduced me too, way back in the days when we would spend our Saturday afternoons together in his mother-in-law's front room. I could almost picture Tom dropping the stylus on his Dansette record player. The song was called 'Wolverton

Mountain'. It was the hit record that launched Claude King's career and was based on a real character, Clifton Clowers, who lived in Arkansas.

'This song should strike a chord with someone tonight,' I announced over the microphone, 'I remember a very long night a long time ago, and an even longer walk home the next morning, covered in pigeon shit, this song kept our spirits up.' Halfway through the song, Tom and his companions passed within feet of the stage, without so much as an upward glance and slipped out of the pub. It would be another twelve years before our paths would cross again. Shortly afterwards he emigrated to the United States to avoid paying tax in the United Kingdom.

Most people remember exactly where they were when someone famous dies in tragic circumstances. It often leaves an indelible imprint in the mind: President Kennedy, Princess Diana, John Lennon, and Elvis. On August 16th 1977 I had nipped out of the flat for a pint in the Phoenix Pub, in Lower Sunbury. At approximately 10pm the radio behind the bar announced the sudden death of Elvis, at his home in Graceland. It came as a complete shock to everyone in the pub. The pub's jukebox had been playing away non-stop most of the evening and as a tribute to 'The King' a customer chose an Elvis song. The jukebox packed in, and we couldn't get it started again. The next morning, Mia and I travelled up to the West End for a publicity photo-shoot, organized by the Wally Dent Agency. During the shoot, at the Roger Crump Studio, Elvis was on everyone's lips and all the radio stations were playing his records non-stop, everyone was in shock at his sudden death.

The following year things were going really well and we moved from the flat to a semi-detached house in nearby Shepperton. Then in 1982 we moved upmarket again and bought a lovely property nearby on Old Charlton Road. The day we moved in there was no running water, but thanks to our kindly neighbour we were supplied with bowl upon bowl of fresh water until I managed to get the problem fixed. Our kindly neighbour became a great friend, his name was J.G. Ballard.

Jim Ballard was an unassuming gentleman in his early fifties. Jim told me he had been born in Shanghai in the 1930's and was interned by the Japanese during the war. After his release he came to England and studied medicine at Kings College, Cambridge. He was also a qualified pilot in the Canadian Air force. It wasn't until sometime later that he told me he was a novelist. Typical modest Jim, I got my hands on some of his books and found out he was a great novelist. Probably his best-known books are 'Crash', adapted into a film by David Cronenberg, and the semi-autobiographical 'Empire of the Sun', made into a film by Steven Spielberg. I'll never forget the premiere of the movie in 1986, in Leicester Square, attended by The Queen and Prince Phillip. Jim gave us a wave as he was chauffeured away in a black limousine and we watched him on television, lining up with the rest of the stars to shake hands with the Queen. He told me later he was over the moon, but it didn't stop him from publicly refusing the CBE he was offered sometime later. Jim described it as, 'a Ruritanian charade that helps prop up our top-heavy monarchy'. He was a real character.

Over the twenty-three years we were neighbours we spent

an awful lot of time in each other's company. You have Jim to blame for the reason you are reading this memoir right now. Jim told me to write a novel, he was kind enough to point out I had more than one sitting in my head and just waiting to be released. Jim set me on the path to writing this memoir and helped mentor me with my next novel (my publisher informs me he's hard at work editing that and it will be released directly after this book!). I'll never forget Jim telling me, 'Take ideas from all your adventures in show-business, the lows as well as the highs, and create a novel, you can distil the characters from all the many entertainers you have bumped up against.' Even after I eventually moved home to Wales, we kept in regular contact by letter and phone. I was shocked to receive a letter from Jim in 2007, revealing he had been diagnosed with prostate cancer and given just two years to live. Jim was typically philosophical about it all and reckoned that aged seventy-seven, these things were to be expected. Jim insisted that I go for a PSA blood test as a precaution, something that hadn't occurred to him and was now obviously too late. I was upset by the letter and immediately phoned him, we had a long conversation and it was evident that Jim was calm and philosophical about being struck down in his prime, but there was also a raging fire about the situation, an incredible frustration. Sadly Jim passed away from prostate cancer in 2008. It was a tragic loss, but his influence on popular culture is undiminished and enduring.

A few months after Jim's death I was driving to a gig and happened to catch 'The Archive Hour' on BBC Radio 4: the author Will Self was narrating the life and times of J.G. Ballard. I was struck by just how well the programme had been put together; it was a fitting tribute to the great man and his novels. The accuracy and poignancy of Will Self's personal narrative was incredibly moving. The following day I was inspired to put pen to paper and wrote a letter to Will Self explaining just how incredibly moved I had been by the programme. I shared some of my wonderful memories of Jim Ballard, his generosity, kindness, wisdom and advice. It was a heartfelt letter and quite unexpectedly I received a reply from Will, thanking me and requesting permission to read the letter at a Memorial Service being held for Jim at Tate Modern in London. I was deeply honoured and humbled to have my tribute read aloud to Jim's family and friends. Jim was a great friend and mentor and is sadly missed.

Mia and I took a break from touring in 1986. Mia wanted to spend more time with our wonderful daughter, Tara. I decided to take up the offer of a six month summer residency at the Potters Holiday Complex in Great Yarmouth. I shared the bill with an up and coming young comedian, Shane Ritchie, who went onto to become a stalwart of British television, appearing in the soap Eastenders. At the end of July, a fellow entertainer stopped me and asked if I had heard the news? Gordon Mills had died aged fifty-one. Naturally the news took me aback. I had wished Gordon his comeuppance for many years, but I never wished him dead. Johnny Laff, the comedian, reported that the article said he had been ill for some time. I guessed that it was stomach cancer. Johnny asked me how I knew and I explained that Gordon had always lived on his nerves, and that in turn exacerbated his stomach ulcers. I had seen him throw up on more than one occasion when he was suffering a severe bout of stress. Stress and stomach ulcers are a clear pathway to stomach cancer. I needed some time alone to gather my thoughts and made my excuses to Johnny and left.

Gordon had always thrived on stress, especially when the rewards from enduring it were so high. Ever since he had begun managing Tom, Englebert and then Gilbert O'Sullivan, he kept on gambling everything; it was inherent to his make-up as a human being. It hadn't entirely escaped my notice that over the preceding few years things had begun to unravel for Gordon. He was not the kind of person to take that lying down and, no doubt, would have been raising the stakes to ever greater heights. I guess events had finally taken their toll.

Just prior to his death, Gilbert O'Sullivan had taken Gordon to the high court. Gordon must have experienced a sense of déjà vu after his last visit to the Old Bailey with Myron and Byron. Gilbert was demanding millions of pounds in back pay. The crux of the case was that Gordon had fraudulently 'fleeced' Gilbert of all his earnings. Gilbert's lawyers argued that the singer had been living on just £10 a week pocket money the whole time he was topping the charts. I remember thinking at the time, no change there then. The lawyers went on to point out that even when Gilbert had become an international singing sensation, Gordon had only started to pay him £150 a month. When the shy and diminutive singer eventually took the stand in court, he reported that whenever he queried his royalty statements, Gordon would scold him for it. The revelations dumbfounded the judge, and he said that Gilbert was, 'an honest and sincere young man, the same can't be said of his manager.'

The court ordered all Gordon's accounts to be seized and

when they were thoroughly looked into it was found that millions and millions of pounds had just disappeared into thin air. It was widely reported in the press that from 1970 until 1978 Gilbert's singer/songwriter royalties had grossed £14.5 million and he had received just £500,000. The Judge awarded Gilbert O'Sullivan £7 million and also ordered Gordon to pay all of O'Sullivan's costs. Chris Ellis had been in court at the time and reported back that Gordon had been tied in knots by Gilbert's lawyers, something he had been doing to others for many years. Gordon left the courtroom, tail between his legs, he hated losing. His gambling addiction had really taken hold at the time and losing the court case had effectively bankrupted him. The judgment blew the finances of the MAM Empire apart and it never recovered. Within weeks the offices in Bond Street were closed and MAM was no more.

Gordon was back to square one and only had Tom on the books. Englebert had jumped ship and retained Tony Cartwright as his new manager. Colin Berlin and the rest of the old Acuff-Rose Agency had seen which way the wind was blowing and deserted MAM sometime previously. It was a very unceremonious end to the whole shooting match, much like the way of the Squires abrupt demise in retrospect. Chris Ellis wasn't to last much longer either.

Chris Ellis had kept in contact over the previous years, and we continued to meet up whenever he was back in London. Chris was Tom's road manager and fixer and did just about everything required to keep Tom happy when touring. Chris was very bitter about being unceremoniously dumped not long after the court case. He confided in me exactly how it all came about. Chris, Tom and his son, Mark, were staying in a rented farmhouse on the outskirts of Paris. Tom wasn't allowed to enter the UK, due to tax reasons. They had recently flown in from L.A for rehearsals in Paris prior to a European tour. Tom had asked Chris to carry onto London to pick up a white Mercedes for his use on the tour. The evening before Chris was due to leave they went on a bit of a pub crawl. Chris said that by the early hours of the morning, Tom was thoroughly depressed; he'd had quite a bit to drink and was very maudlin. Tom was not happy about the direction of his career and the fact that he wasn't selling any records. Chris told him things were cyclical and although it might not be his time now, things would come around and he would have his time again. Chris left a weepy Tom and flew on to London.

Back in London, Chris was kept pretty busy; he had been tasked by Gordon with getting all the necessary permits and documentation together for all the musicians who were participating on the European tour. In his downtime he drove Linda, Tom's wife, around to various shopping engagements. Then the day before the tour was to start he received a phone call from one of Tom's agents, telling him he wouldn't be needed on the tour after all. Tom's son, Mark, would be filling in for him, due to 'cutbacks'. Chris was gobsmacked and immediately phoned Gordon, they had a massive row, screaming down the phone at each other. Chris asked Gordon why Tom hadn't just told him at the farmhouse in France that his services were no longer required. Gordon told him to get over it and hung up. Chris immediately phoned Linda at Tor Point. Linda told him it was all news to her; she admitted that Tom had been talking for some time about taking Mark on, but she never imagined it would be at the expense of Chris. Linda asked him if there was anything she could do, then she offered to phone Tom in France and demand an explanation. Chris asked Linda, 'Talk to him and tell him to call me, I want to know what's going on. If I'm out I want to hear it from him, not one of his bloody agents. I've been with him too damn long for it to end this way.' Linda promised to call, and Chris waited patiently, but he would have some wait, Tom never ever contacted him again.

19

TOM JONES

Mark Woodward now cared for all his father's needs, he had learnt all about the tricks of the trade from Gordon Mills. Tom widely reported that after Gordon's demise he, 'felt lost, completely lost'. Mark settled into Gordon's shoes and took over his father's management. He had a tough job on his hands; Tom's career was at rock bottom. Mark has done an admirable job since then and Tom has gone onto become an icon, a living legend. But I would run into Tom again long before he had regained his place in the firmament, long before his capable son's expert management returned him to superstar status.

One Friday evening in February, I was getting myself spruced up, ahead of a solo gig in Kingston-upon-Thames. The phone rang and I was pleasantly surprised to hear a wise-cracking Liverpool accent, it was my old friend Tony Cartwright. 'Bespopo, its Tony,' for some reason Tony had christened me 'Bespopo' ever since the time we shared digs together, 'I've got a message from Tom. He wants to see you. He's pining for you.' Tony was always a joker. 'Yea, pull the other one it's got bells on,' I laughed.

'Seriously, I'm going for a curry with Tom tonight in Weybridge. He wants you to come along.' Naturally I was pretty shocked and a little curious, but I'd committed to a gig and told Tony that. Tony tried his best to get me to cancel the gig and join Tom and him, but I stuck to my guns, 'I just can't,

I'm already getting into my coat to head over to the gig, maybe next time.' Tony could see he wouldn't be able to change my mind and we said our goodbyes and arranged to catch up soon. I was a bit baffled by this turn of events; twelve years had passed since Tom had suddenly turned up at my gig in the 'John O'Gaunt'. What on earth was he up to, wanting to meet up after all this time? I put it out of my mind and headed for the gig.

The following Monday, Tony called once again, 'Hey Bespopo, Tom was really disappointed you couldn't make it. Look, he's playing over at Lakeside tomorrow night and wants you to come along.' I was taken aback and Tony went on to say, 'Look it's only twenty minutes from Shepperton, Tom's expecting you, he's left instructions at the box office, what have you got to lose? I can't make it, but I'll tell Tom you'll be there, okay?' The line went dead and I had some thinking to do. Part of me didn't want to bother; the whole demise of the band was still pretty raw, even after all these years. But then again I was curious as to what he had to say. I also thought it might provide the perfect opportunity to find out whatever happened to my song, 'With a Little Luck.'

In 1972 the miners went on strike, resulting in soup kitchens up and down the country and families living hand to mouth. The conditions inspired me to write a song, 'With a Little Luck', about riding out the storm. It was a country song that focused on a family getting by during the bad times. My publisher, Teedes Music, recorded the demo with Mia and me performing the vocals, and sent it out to potential artistes. Gordon Mills had received a copy whilst in LA and Chris Ellis was with him when he listened to the demo, Chris told me at the time that Gordon was interested in recording it. But I had subsequently never heard anything back about a potential recording. Sometime later after Chris had been sacked he'd popped around for a catch up over a beer or two, and the song came up in conversation. Chris asked if I'd ever made any money out of it and I was a bit confused and asked him what he meant. Chris told me, 'Well Gordon played the track to Tom and asked him if he knew who was singing it, Tom shrugged his shoulders and Gordon told him it was you. They thought it might be a hit so recorded it in LA.' It was the first I'd heard about any recording and contacted my publisher, but they confirmed they'd never heard back from Gordon Mills. It was all very mysterious. I remember pumping Chris for information on the recording and he told me Gordon had hired in some top LA session musicians and Tom had laid down the track. The only thing missing, apparently, was the strings section and female backing vocals, which he assumed Gordon would have added later. I was interested to find out what had become of the recording and with Gordon now dead the only person to ask was Tom.

It was raining heavily when I arrived at the plush nightclub in Lakeside. My name was on the door and they had been expecting me, so ushered me past the waiting queue. I settled myself near the bar, a fair distance away from the stage; I don't mind admitting I was pretty nervous seeing Tom after all this time. The place wasn't as packed as I'd been expecting, Tom was in a bit of a trough at the time, but would soon bounce back. Mark was just about finding his feet as manager and pretty soon he would have Tom back at the top of his game. The houselights went down and Tom's band appeared, I didn't recognise a soul. Big Jim Sullivan and Derek Watkins had long ago left the stage. The band kicked off and Tom made his entrance. It was the first time I had seen him in the flesh for almost twelve years. I remember thinking at the time, I was more used to seeing him from behind, belting out the set on my trusty bass guitar. Tom's voice as always was superb and showing no signs of wear and tear, but his once lithe stage movements were now a bit restricted. Time stands still for no-one and Tom was looking his age.

I felt a pang of sadness and I don't mind admitting my eyes got a little moist. I watched the hour-long set and my mind wandered back to our time together in Ponty, starting out, and then roughing it in London, the tough times at the 'Calcutta' in Ladbroke Grove and all the experiences we had shared, right up until success came a knocking. I remember thinking that nothing can ever take that away from me. Certainly it had been an emotional rollercoaster but there were plenty of good times to remember, as many as there were bad. It was just too sad for words, the way it had all ended as it did. Tom took his final bow on stage. I was still undecided as to whether to join him backstage in his dressing room. I wasn't sure I could handle it as I was feeling pretty emotional. Then I caught sight of the comedian Jimmy Tarbuck and a whole entourage of people filing backstage to meet Tom. That made my mind up for me and I slipped out, heading for the foyer and then home. As I was collecting my coat the clubs PA system crackled into life. 'Can Vernon Hopkins please make his way backstage. Tom Jones is waiting for him.'

A few seconds more and I would have been able to quietly slip away. Now I found myself heading backstage and knocking on Tom's dressing room door. The door was opened by a bodyguard, who invited me inside. Tom was standing at the mirror, in his dressing gown and towelling his hair, fresh from a shower. There were about a dozen people milling around, the only person I recognized was Jimmy Tarbuck. Tom tossed the towel aside and we shook hands. Then completely unexpectedly he embraced me, 'How's it going, alright?' Tom's face gave nothing away and I noticed his diction had become far more refined, no doubt from all the interviews he had given over the years. After getting over my initial shock I told him, 'I'm good. I caught the show, you were really good. It felt a little strange watching you perform though, I'm so used to standing behind you on stage.'

Tom smiled, 'Yeah I was thinking that too as it happens.' Tom took me by the shoulder, 'Let's go over to a quiet corner for a chat, do you want a drink?'

'I'll have vodka if you have it?'

'Vern this isn't a pub, its champagne or nothing. I suppose you heard about Gordon?' I nodded. 'I went to see him at the hospital in LA. He was on his death bed. He looked awful. There were tubes running from his nose and mouth and his eyes were rolling around. He asked me what his chances were and I told him the doctors had given him a 50/50 chance. You know how Gordon liked to gamble; even though he was full of pain killers he told me the odds weren't good enough. I told him not to worry, if it came to the worst I'd be there for his family. The next day he was gone.'

Tom looked visibly shaken; he was obviously taking Gordon's death very hard. He was still clearly in mourning and wanted to talk about Gordon and we reminisced for quite some time. The rest of the entourage in the room were looking a bit restless, so Jimmy Tarbuck wandered over to try and get Tom to meet and greet everyone. Tom seemed a bit disjointed and lost in thought; he clearly just wanted to carry on talking and remembering Gordon. Jimmy made a crack about me and Tom having a love affair and it backfired. Tom gave him a rotten look and I really thought he was going to knock him out. Jimmy picked up on the vibe and quickly scampered away. The entourage left a little later and Tom barely acknowledged them.

We had both sadly lost our fathers and our conversation soon turned to commiserating with each other about that. Tom Woodward Senior had passed away in October 1981, aged seventy-one. With a lifetime working underground behind him, his lungs had finally succumbed to all the coal dust he had inhaled over the years. My father, Evan, passed away in 1983, aged eighty-one, after suffering a massive heart attack. What with being so close back in Ponty, we obviously both knew each other's fathers very well and we keenly felt the loss. We both got a little misty. As he was changing into his suit I told him it had been good to catch up and I'd better head on home. I asked him about my song, 'With A Little Luck' and he remembered recording it in L.A. 'Gordon wanted me to do something with it, but it got shelved after he became ill.' I nodded and told him I'd like to hear the track. 'Okay I'll try and dig it up when I get back to LA.' I turned to leave and he stopped me, 'I'm playing the Albert Hall tomorrow, why don't you come along?'

The following evening I parked my car near the Albert Hall and made my way to the foyer. I looked around, hoping to see a familiar face, maybe one of Tom's agents or PR guys, and then ran into Barry Clayman, his agent and Mark Woodward, his son and manager. We had not seen each other since 1968 and quickly caught up on all the latest news. Barry told me Tom was in his dressing room getting ready for the show, he told me to grab a seat in the public bar and he'd let him know I'd arrived. I hung around in the bar for ages; Tom had asked me to come along before the show started. Finally, about five minutes before curtain call, Steve Montgomery, Tom's bodyguard, materialized and led me up to Tom's dressing room. It was an entirely different scenario to the previous evening. I got the distinct impression that Tom wished I wasn't there, and, in my uneasiness, so did I. Tom was a bit stilted and uncomfortable. I think it was a relief to both of us when he said, 'Oh well time to go on, see you around Vern.' The dressing room door opened on cue and the bodyguard led me to my seat in the auditorium. I only watched half the show, having seen it the night before, and slipped out to head on home, wondering what on earth it had been all about.

Driving back to Shepperton I had time to think and the only reason I could imagine for the sudden olive branch was that Tom wanted someone to reminisce with, someone who knew Gordon as well as him. I had listened patiently to Tom as he rambled about Gordon, and had been happy to share my memories. But I had told Tom that in my view Gordon was a vindictive and callous man, of course I was sorry for his death, but there was no escaping the way he had treated the band over the previous years. I'm not sure Tom saw things in the same light; Gordon could do no wrong in his eyes. I had expected some thread of atonement from Tom regarding the way we had been treated. But none was forthcoming, he couldn't even bring himself to enquire about the rest of the band, and when I had tried to let him know what everyone else was up to, he had seemed disinterested and quickly changed the subject of conversation.

About a month later a parcel was delivered with 'Tom Jones Enterprises' embossed in gold lettering above my address. Inside was a cassette tape with a song, 'Matador', printed on the A-side and 'With A Little Luck' on the B-side. I believe the A-side was a song from a prospective Broadway musical, but it had never got off the ground. I don't believe the song was ever released, but it was a real kick to hear Tom singing 'With A Little Luck'.

Sometime later I was getting on with life when I received another unexpected visitor. I was playing a gig in Wimbledon when I recognized a familiar face in the audience. It was my old band mate Vic Cooper. He had been booked to appear at the same venue the following week. It had been over twenty years since I'd last seen him. Vic had quit the Squires for a Hollywood film career, making the jump to appear with Olivia Newton John in the film, 'Toomorrow'. It was a pleasure to catch up and he filled me in on all the preceding years. Vic had lived the LA high life. Unfortunately the movie had bombed at the box office. It had been released in 1970 and the plot centred on a group of musicians who encountered aliens from outer space.

A sound track had been released to accompany the movie, but that didn't do a lot better. Vic had naturally been disappointed but he had still accrued a tidy little nest egg. He even showed me a parting gift from the legendary movie producer Harry Saltzman; it was a three thousand pound gold watch with the inscription 'Fine Cockney Role' engraved on the back.

Vic told me he and his girlfriend had decided to move back to the UK, but were increasingly spending most of their time in Spain. Vic had steady bookings along the Costa del Sol and the upmarket resort, Puerto Banus, which was frequented by all the stars. Vic mentioned that there was lucrative work in the Swiss Alps and would I be interested in performing with him as a duo? In 1990 we found ourselves practicing yodelling and skiing the slopes of a village called Chateau D'Ay. We were booked into a sumptuous hotel as the resident band, with free a la carte, free drinks and a black London taxi, with dodgy brakes, ferrying us around to our free skiing lessons.

'Vic and Vernon', as we were billed, belted out a steady stream of Rock n Roll to the affluent skiing fraternity throughout the winter season. Vic always was and still is a Jerry Lee fanatic, so that formed the bedrock of the set along with Elvis, Little Richard, Chuck Berry and the Everly Brothers. Vic had been correct about it being a lucrative gig; we each got £600 a week and didn't have to spend a penny as everything was complimentary. After the season was over I returned with Vic to Spain and we were soon booked solid in Puerto Banus, along the 'Golden Mile'. It was a regular celebrity hang out at that time and we kept running into a lot of old and new celebrity acquaintances: Rod Stewart, Englebert Humperdink, Peter

Stringfellow, Frank Bruno, Des O'Connor, the list was endless. You never knew who you were going to bump into in 'Joy's Bar'.

Things were going so well that Vic and I discussed reviving the Squires, there seemed to be a lot of interest. We contacted Chris Slade to enquire if he would be up for re-forming the band. Chris's career had soared since his parting with Tom. His CV was amazing and looked like a who's who of top rock bands: Manfred Mann, Uriah Heep, Led Zeppelin, Pink Floyd, AC/DC. Sadly all the years of touring with those bands had had an adverse effect on his marriage. Chris and Lynne divorced, but luckily remained the best of friends. Chris still lives in L.A to this very day and plays with the successful rock band, 'Asia'. His two children, Callum and Cerys are both based in L.A and Callum has followed his father's 'foot pedal', becoming a great drummer. Cerys works for a record company. At the end of the 90's Vic and I teamed up with Chris and the Squires were re-born. It gave us all the opportunity to get together for old times' sake and wallow in the realms of nostalgia. It was fun while it lasted, but pretty soon Chris had been summoned back to L.A to begin another tour with the super group Asia.

With the dawn of the New Millennium, 12th August 2000 was a very special occasion for me. I proudly walked my darling daughter, Tara, down the aisle of St Mary's Church in Shepperton. I had a tear in my eye as I watched her husband-to-be, Richard Smith, nervously slip the wedding band onto her trembling finger. The Church was a stone's throw away from The Anchor, the pub which I had staggered out of all those years before, on the way to take my driving test in Tom's car. It was a magical day, and later in 2002 Mia and I were overjoyed to become grandparents to Bradley Lewis Smith. Then in 2004 along came our second grandchild, Liberty Beatrice Smith. After a great deal of consideration the family decided to relocate back home to Wales. We settled on a charming village, Pontardulais, on the edge of Gower, near Swansea.

The name Liberty, for our second grandchild, was no accident. Although my daughter, Tara, had always adored that name I had recently composed a battle hymn, 'The Liberation Hymn (Let Truth Be My Guide)'. The hymn was recorded by the legendary Treorchy Male Voice Choir. The hymn was inspired by the First Gulf War, which was thankfully over in two weeks. But it didn't see the light of day until Saddam Hussein was defeated in 2003. The Treorchy Male Voice Choir recorded the hymn at the Pop Factory in Rhondda and all proceeds went to charity, in support of our Armed Forces, the wounded and their families. The hymn was picked up by the BBC and aired regularly on radio, it became very popular with listeners and people wanted to know where they could purchase it. Unfortunately we had been unable to persuade a major record company to release it. Then the comedian Jim Davidson rang me one morning. I had worked with Jim for many years supporting him on shows throughout the UK, he had heard the 'Liberation Hymn' and wanted Katherine Jenkins to record it in aid of The Falklands Veterans Foundation. I of course gave my blessing and the plan was to release it for the 25th Anniversary. As the date got closer it was announced that Mark Knopler of Dire Straits was releasing 'Brothers In Arms' in support of the Foundation and it seemed crazy to release both at the same time so plans to release 'Liberation Hymn' were put on hold.

In 2008 I took some time out and flew to Chicago with fellow musician and friend, Roger Simmonds. The plan was to take in a bit of America without all the rigours of a touring schedule crowding it all out. It was a great trip and we moved onto LA and then Vegas. Tom was playing at the MGM Casino at the time. I wrote him a personal note. It was by no means a berating letter, just a note clarifying some of the unresolved issues raised in this memoir. I never expected to hear anything back and I wasn't disappointed, Tom had never been a letter writer, I remember he used to get the band to write letters back to Linda when we were starting out in London. It had been almost forty years to the day since I had first seen Elvis and his entourage sweep into the Flamingo to watch Tom and the Squires. It was now a very different hotel and had been dramatically extended. I stood in the foyer in exactly the same spot and Roger took a photograph of me re-enacting the moment. We both goofed around and had a fantastic time in Vegas, re-visiting all the old haunts from years before.

I returned to the UK re-invigorated and determined to get 'Liberation Hymn' released in aid of our Armed Forces. I contacted Kevin King, the owner of Optimum Records. Kevin set about helping me and on 22nd June 2009 'Liberation Hymn' was finally released. The CD contained two further tracks, 'The Brave Bar None' and 'The Bridge Of Sails', which Jim Davidson had persuaded me to compose for Katherine Jenkins. The CD was released in support of 'Help For Heroes'. Thanks to Kevin King's resolve and hard work the CD flew up the charts with proceeds going to the charity. I received many letters of support for the project, the most notable being from HRH Prince Charles and the Prime Minister Gordon Brown. The hymn soon got adopted by our Armed Forces and is regularly played at military events throughout the UK and abroad. I was surprised and incredibly proud when Cardiff City Football Club adopted the hymn for the opening of their new stadium and it's now played before every home match for both football and rugby.

Kevin King is a complete workaholic, with interests in music publishing, his record company and artiste representation, there never seems to be enough hours in the day to cram in all the business he seems to get through. Kevin contacted me in 2010 about a new album he was putting together in support of the three Welsh Regiments. It was to be an entirely Welsh affair. The album 'The Brave Bar None' is a compilation of songs by Welsh artists, including Ponty-born Iris Williams OBE and Rob Allen and many others. Iris performed one of my compositions, 'Travelling Through The Valleys' and made me a very happy man. It was a real honour and privilege to see her perform the song supported by the Treorchy Male Voice Choir on her successful 2011 tour. Iris, born in Pontypridd, is a legend; she had a massive hit with 'He Was So Beautiful' and has appeared a staggering fourteen times in the Royal Variety Performance, a record unequalled by any other performer.

Things had been going so well it was a real shock when I received some tragic news in 2009. On a bitterly cold day in January I attended the funeral of my dear old friend and fellow band mate, Mickey Gee. Mickey had passed away aged just sixty-four. After acrimoniously leaving the Squires, Mickey had gone on to record with Dave Edmunds, Shaking Stevens, Bruce Springsteen and a host of other show business luminaries. We had kept in touch over the years and the Squires' demise would inevitably always crop up in our conversations. Micky had taken the way he had been treated by Tom and Gordon very badly. We were all bitter about our treatment, but Mickey more than any of us, he had always had a sensitive nature and he never really got over it. Micky would curse Tom and Gordon and really work himself into a rant. He would always end with, 'Why Vern, can you explain it?' Well obviously I couldn't, none of us could.

Micky had suffered more than his fair share of tragedy. His brother had committed suicide and his long-term girlfriend had died in a car crash. The poor man was carrying a lot of emotional scars. When his father passed away he cared for his sick mother, until his own death from emphysema. It was heartbreaking to see him toward the end; he was choking for breath and could barely hold his beloved 1965 Fender Telecaster. He knew he was on the way out and his last words to me were, 'I'll never get to ask Tom why he did it, Vern.' It was all very sad.

The funeral service was held at the crematorium in Cardiff. It was very well attended by over three hundred mourners, Mickey had touched a lot of people, and nobody had a bad word to say about him. A lot of fellow musicians came from far and wide to pay their respects to a great guitar picker. After the service I walked away lost in my own thoughts and saw Mickey's aged wheelchair-bound mother about to be lifted into the limousine and went over to help. I offered my condolences and she turned to me and weakly said, 'Thank you Vernon.

He's an evil man.' I was very taken aback, I thought she was referring to her son. Then she looked at me and said, 'Mickey never got over the way Tom treated him, he thought he was a friend.' I watched the limousine pull away. It was a very sad day.

Over the years there have been many biographies published about Tom Jones. I've been asked and willingly agreed to contribute to a great many of them. Biographers have so much information to squeeze into the pages that there has to be a certain conciseness regarding the interviews with all those connected with Tom Jones. The biographer has to limit the depths of the material he uses, otherwise the book would run to a mammoth length. A biography is a report, in many respects it is a clinical, logical, unemotional observation. In January 2010, I set about writing these memoirs, unlike a biography these pages hold deep, emotional and heartfelt accounts of exactly what went on back then and I hope they help set the record straight. My story is now almost at an end and the journey has been a rollercoaster of emotions. Much of it I wish I didn't have to write, but it had to be said. Shakespeare was on the right track when he wrote, 'but at the length truth will out.' (The Merchant of Venice, 1596)

The rest of the band had been on at me for some time to put our side of the story across, why these things should always fall to me I'll never know. But after Mickey's death it hit home that none of us are getting any younger. My intentions to put the record straight were, funnily enough, hurried along by the BBC. Twenty-Five years after the release of 'The Green, Green Grass of Home' I was contacted by a producer at BBC Wales asking me to be involved in a documentary about the 25th anniversary of the number one hit. The show's director, Suzanne Phillips, a charming young lady asked to interview me in Ponty's YMCA, where it had all began. I agreed on condition I could speak my mind about all that had gone on behind the scenes. I'll never forget the shocked look on Suzanne's face when I enlightened her on what to expect. She assured me she would do her best to see it all included in the final programme. I put my faith in her, but was understandably a little sceptical that the hierarchy at the BBC would include it all.

The day of filming came around and the camera rolled. I duly answered all the relative questions right up until the point about smuggling the light ales on stage for Tom's first appearance with the Senators. Then the question I had been waiting to hear for such a very long time, 'Vernon, when Tom parted company with the Squires, the newspapers reported that it was an amicable conclusion, is that correct?' I went on to explain the truth about just how far from amicable it had all been. It was heartfelt and emotional and afterward Suzanne told me she was interviewing Tom next. When the programme aired a few weeks later, my segment had been cut back considerably, for obvious reasons. I remember the closing statement was, 'Tom didn't care for the rest of the boys after the success of Not Unusual. He betrayed us through and through, and when it all fell apart he left us stranded. It was a pathetic end and it didn't have to end that way.' Immediately after, Tom's segment appeared, and Suzanne challenged him about the band. Tom coughed nervously into his hand, something he always did when he was nervous or in a tight spot.

'Well no, it was like this, I had to get rid of the band because they couldn't read music. But they understood.'

Understood? Well hardly. The Squires had performed on almost every major stage around the world, thousands of TV appearances, Royal Command performances, the London Palladium. We were good enough to perform in front of Elvis; he even tried to coax our drummer away. Then quite suddenly four years after 'Not Unusual' we were unceremoniously dumped without even the common courtesy of a face to face meeting with Tom and Gordon.

'They understood,' Tom shrugged into the camera lens.

Okay we couldn't read music, but that had never held us back any. If our faces didn't fit why not sit down with us and agree to split in a proper manner? Nothing lasts forever, but what a brutal way for the band to end. The documentary was later released in Sweden and Chris Ellis was glued to the screen, he phoned me after the programme in a right old temper and told me he had thrown his shoe at the screen, we had a laugh about that.

A few months after the documentary a gentleman by the name of Robin Eggar phoned me. He had seen the documentary and was intrigued by the comments. Robin wanted to interview me regarding a biography he was writing about Tom. Robin is a prolific author and I was familiar with his work so readily agreed. Over a long three hour interview I gave him my insights about the band's years on the road and our dismissal. A little time later he contacted me again and asked if I would accompany him to Sweden to interview Chris Ellis. Chris wanted me to be there for support. It was great to see my old friend and his lovely wife,

Eva. Robin ended up interviewing Chris for three days, as he is a wealth of information; he continued working with Tom long after the band was dismissed. Robin Eggar's biography, 'Tom Jones', was released in 2000 and was the definitive version of his life, it became the focus for an ITV documentary and I was included in that and given the opportunity to clarify things.

Then a few years later I received another call from the BBC asking if I would appear in another documentary, 'Tom Jones at 70'. It was planned as a celebration of his birthday on 7th June. After the previous programme I thought it was a wind up, and insisted on phoning them back to ensure it really was the BBC. It was and I did appear, the producer was aware of the acrimonious split but nevertheless though it would be disappointing if I didn't make a contribution. I've always regarded Tom as head and shoulders above any entertainer in popular music, and I've always expressed that opinion so was happy to go along with it. I nearly burst a blood vessel when at the end of the interview I was asked to turn to camera and wish Tom a happy 70th birthday. My phone was ringing hot after that, I didn't half cop some flak from the band. Sadly the broadcast of the programme was delayed because the drummer Stuart Cable, of the Stereophonics, was tragically found dead the morning of the scheduled broadcast. Out of respect the transmission was delayed a week.

The documentaries and the Robin Eggar interviews had certainly helped me remember all the early days with Tom and were a real help in completing this book. The final push that I needed came from the BBC Drama department. They contacted me about a proposed drama about the formation of the

Senators, Tom joining the band and all the events leading up to the success of 'It's Not Unusual'. They asked for permission for one of their researchers to pay me a visit and record my voice and mannerisms, apparently this would be very helpful for the actors they were lining up to play Tom and the band. Naturally I was flattered, who wouldn't like to see themselves immortalized in a film? I remember asking, tongue firmly in cheek, if they could get Clint Eastwood to play me. I'd met him once, long ago and thought he would be perfect. The Drama Department tried to get in touch with the rest of the band and I obviously helped as much as I could. But Dai Cooper had long ago disappeared to South Africa, Mickey was sadly passed away, and Chris Slade had permanently moved back to LA and was always touring with the band Asia. The whole project seemed to fizzle out and it never saw the light of day. So I thought why not, and here it is, the story warts and all. It has been a pleasure and a privilege to work the stage with Tom Jones, from the moment he first joined the Senators at the Ponty YMCA to the Flamingo in Las Vegas and meeting Elvis. Tom drove the band and the band drove Tom, and the audiences responded and bless them all for their support. It all worked beautifully, it was a beautiful time and a beautiful bunch of boys from the Valleys in South Wales followed their dreams and against all the odds got noticed. Now who could argue with that?

J. G. BALLARD

36, OLD CHARLTON ROAD
SHEPPERTON
MIDDLESEX
TW17 8AT

TEL: WALTON-ON-THAMES
225692

Dear Sir,

My neighbour Vernon Hopkins has suggested that I write
to you, and I'm very happy to do so, and strongly recommend
to you his first novel ONE OF THE BOYS, which is partly based
on his years as a professional musician with Tom Jones and
the Squires. I must say how impressed I am by the sheer power
of the novel, and its very candid view of the music world and
the ruthless people, like the late Gordon Mills, who operate
within it.

Vernon brilliantly conveys the strange world of the rock
musician, with its groupies, double-dealing managers and
exotic foreign cities. He brings in real figures like Elvis
Presley whom he met in Las Vegas. As Vernon makes clear
in his introduction, his hero Johnny Raven is _not_ based on
Tom Jones, but is an imaginary composite based on all the
singers he came across in his career.

I hope you will read the novel and be impressed by both
its narrative power and its remarkable insider's view of the
music industry, the real world behind the one we see on Top of
the Pops.

Yours sincerely,

J G Ballard

ONE OF THE BOYS

I was privileged to have lived next door to J.G. Ballard for almost 25 years, before settling down in West Wales in 2003. It was Jim who initially suggested that I write this novel, based on my experiences in show-business. His advice and encouraging mentorship led me to the final draught, which Jim then edited. We remained firm friends until the end.

Vernon Hopkins

The teenage singer Johnny Raven yearns to break free of the mining valleys of Wales. Johnny buys his first guitar and joins one of the many local bands. He has a powerful voice and startling animal magnetism. But success comes slowly until he is spotted by a ruthless manager. Johnny and the band are catapulted into the London music scene, and become embroiled in a world of Fleet Street gossip columns, groupies, sex and drugs.

Although the group have always played together, it is clear that Johnny Raven is the star, driven by a streak of callousness that leads him to neglect the other members of the band, his young wife, and everyone who stands in the way of his success.

Johnny tours the world in a hectic whirl of celebrity, and returns to England to find he is now an international star. But he has paid a huge price, losing his wife and child, his friends and the band. He becomes caught up in a spiral of alcohol and drugs, and his mental state deteriorates leading to a severe breakdown.

Eventually he becomes a voluntary patient at a private nursing home, but finds no relief from his demons. At last he breaks out and returns to the abandoned home of his dead parents in Wales. There he confronts the weaknesses that have been responsible for his downfall. He resolves to give up drugs and alcohol, win back his wife and remake his shattered career…Will he succeed?

PROLOGUE

As Curly Smithers delivered volley after volley of quick-fire jokes, the audience at the London Palladium were doubled up in their seats with uncontrollable laughter. The black American's body writhed and convulsed as though an African witchdoctor was stabbing at an effigy of the comedian behind the curtain backdrop, enraged with his 'brother' for spewing out self-wounding racist jokes.

Curly didn't give a damn about offending anyone tonight, black or white. As long as his audience continued laughing like a pack of hyenas, he was determined not to waste a second of the five minutes allocated to him at the prestigious venue.

Behind the curtain was a silent mayhem of stage-hands moving scenery, technicians setting up microphone stands, and entertainers taking up positions marked for them at rehearsals. They smiled their confident, easy smiles, but their stomachs churned with very different emotions. Household names paced the boards, muttering over-rehearsed lines to themselves. Some had travelled from the far side of the world, but no fee would be paid tonight. This was the Royal Command Performance, the ultimate high-tension breeding ground for passports to an early grave. And for what, many asked themselves? A seal of royal approval stamped on their headstones.

Curly's five precious minutes were at an end. He bowed again and again to his applauding, watery-eyed audience; their cheers and whistles the sound of his agent's telephone ringing non-stop for months to come, rather than the pleasurable emotion of being liked. He didn't even like himself. Curly Smithers was an empty soul.

The applause only subsided when the ageing comedian side-stepped into the wings, his smile side-stepping his face at the same moment. A stage-hand offered him a towel, before flying off in another direction with another vital chore to complete. Curly dabbed the sweat from his face as he made his way back to his dressing room. Escaping the back-stage mayhem, he accidently collided with an aluminium stepladder. Unruffled, he sniggered, 'Hey, baby. What's a pretty little thing like you doing in a bum place like this?'

He gave it a vicious kick, sending it raking across the floor, screeching its protest. 'Get this fuckin' hooker outta here!' he yelled at his startled onlookers, before marching purposefully towards the fire-door leading to his dressing room.

The reason for his foul-tempered haste was waiting for him in the pocket of his flamboyant dressing gown. Without so much as a glance at the much younger man seated and applying make-up at the illuminated mirror, Curly dipped his hand into the pocket and produced a wrap of cocaine. Sprinkling some of its contents on the glossy surface of the wall-to-wall dressing table, he addressed the handsome singer at his side.

'Johnny Raven. You look as nervous as shit, man,' he said, coarsely. 'They'll smell it from the Royal Box, as soon as you walk on that stage. 'You need something to calm you down, son.' Gathering the white powder and trimming it into a neat line was second nature to the comedian, having been under its influence for the biggest part of his long and tempestuous career, and he operated with the enthusiasm of a bio-chemist about to unravel the ever elusive secret of the Fountain of Youth.

Wiping the sweat from his forehead with the back of his hand, Curly hurriedly removed the blond wig that was his trademark, tossing it onto the table. 'It was hell out there, man' he moaned, 'having your Queen looking down on me, without so much as a smile. I couldn't have cared less,' he nodded at the line of cocaine, 'until this stuff lost its edge.' He gazed at his reflection in the mirror. 'Huh, the things I do for charity.'

Johnny Raven turned in his seat and looked up at the tall, bone-thin comedian. 'Why complain?' he offered. 'You had that audience in the palm of your hand, and that's all that counts. Royals are always reserved. You've got your act, she's got hers. You couldn't go wrong.'

The singer's voice was tight, nervous; his striking blue eyes failing to conceal the discomfort of not knowing which way his career would spin when he presented himself on that famous stage. Curly responded with a chuckle, but his eyes never smiled. 'I would have gone wrong, if it wasn't for this stuff,' he grunted.

Pressing his finger to the side of his nose, the tip sliding along the surface of the dressing-table, he snorted the drug into canals of inflamed membrane. The addict raised his head, sniffing, eyebrows raised as he stared into the mirror. He was the star of the show again. Curly Smithers, wig or no wig.

Johnny turned his head away, disgusted at the sight of this wreckage of an entertainer, like a sagging glove puppet with a grimace of a smile painted on its face.

Smithers picked up what was left of the wrap of cocaine. But before returning it to the pocket of his dressing gown, he glanced at the singer beside him. For the first time, the comedian was aware of the tension that had stiffened the younger man's face. He smirked, knowingly, aware that Raven despised him, but no longer caring.

In time, he thought, even this handsome and cocky performer would need a little help, the kind of courage that came from a wrap of powder or a plastic syringe. Besides, there was something evasive behind that aquiline nose and square jaw, a hint of insecurity.

Curly slid the wrap towards the singer. 'Wanna try some, kid?' he offered. 'You'll slay 'em...'

Read the complete book – available from www.iponymous.com